ON THE OTHER SIDE OF LIFE

Exploring the
Phenomenon of the
Near-Death Experience

ON THE OTHER SIDE OF LIFE

Exploring the Phenomenon of the Near-Death Experience

EVELYN ELSAESSER VALARINO

Translated by
Michelle Herzig Escobar

INSIGHT BOOKS
PLENUM PRESS • NEW YORK AND LONDON

Library of Congress Cataloging-in-Publication Data

Elsaesser Valarino, Evelyn.
  On the other side of life : exploring the phenomenon of the near
-death experience / Evelyn Elsaesser Valarino ; translated by
Michelle Herzig Escobar.
     p.   cm.
  Includes bibliographical references and index.
  ISBN 0-306-45561-7
  1. Near-death experiences.   I. Title.
BF1045.N4E57   1997
133.9'01'3--dc21   96-49353
                                                    CIP

Excerpts from *Heading Toward Omega*, © 1984 by Kenneth Ring, reprinted by permission of William Morrow and Company, Inc., New York, and Sobel Weber Associates, Inc., New York.

Excerpts from *Life after Life*, © 1975 by Raymond A. Moody, Jr., reprinted by permission of Mockingbird Books, St. Simons Island, Georgia.

Excerpts from *Transformed by the Light*, © 1992 by Melvin Morse, M.D., and Paul Perry, reprinted by permission of Piatkus Publishers Ltd., London, Sobel Weber Associates, Inc., New York, and Random House, Inc. / Alfred A. Knopf, Inc.

Excerpts from *The Little Prince*, © 1943 and 1971 by Antoine de Saint Exupéry, reprinted by permission of Harcourt Brace & Company, Orlando, and Reed Books, London.

German edition: *Erfahrungen an der Schwelle des Todes: Wissenschaftler äussern sich zur Nahtodeserfahrung*

1st edition Ariston Verlag, Geneva/Munich 1995
2nd edition Ariston Verlag, Kreuzlingen/Munich 1996
3rd edition Ariston Verlag, Kreuzlingen/Munich 1997
Book club edition Bertelsmann Club Gütersloh, and
  Buchgemeinschaft Donauland Kremayr & Scheriau, Vienna 1995

ISBN 0-306-45561-7

© 1997 Plenum Press, New York
Insight Books is a Division of Plenum Publishing Corporation
233 Spring Street, New York, N.Y. 10013-1578
http://www.plenum.com

An Insight Book

10 9 8 7 6 5 4 3 2 1

Printed in the United States of America

To my daughter Isabel

Foreword

Evelyn Elsaesser Valarino's book, *On the Other Side of Life:
Exploring the Phenomenon of the Near-Death Experience,* is to
my knowledge both unique and a uniquely valuable contribution to the rapidly expanding literature dealing with
near-death experiences (NDEs). In the last twenty years,
for example, there have been more than two score books,
published in various languages, which present the essential facts about these fascinating encounters with death
and are replete with many examples and case histories of
NDEs, and quite a few volumes that explore the phenomenon from a variety of points of view, ranging from the
narrowly and reductively scientific to the dogmatically
theological and even the unabashedly spiritual, depending on the particular predilections of their authors.

Entirely lacking among this literature until the appearance of Evelyn Elsaesser Valarino's book, however,
has been a thoughtful and penetrating theoretical and
philosophical examination of the NDE and its implications by persons who have achieved eminence in various

fields of science—biology, neurophysiology, physics—as well as philosophy and religious thought. Here, in *On the Other Side of Life*, Elsaesser Valarino has provided all those with a serious interest in the NDE with the opportunity to encounter and ponder the thinking of a very distinguished and diverse group of scholars and researchers as they themselves reflect on this phenomenon from the perspective of their own professional specialties. (I am honored to be included among them, by the way, but I do not mean to assign to myself the adjectives I have used to describe my coparticipants!) The result is an extremely stimulating cross-disciplinary approach to the theoretical understanding of the NDE, which affords a level of intellectual illumination to this experience unmatched by any previous work on the subject. In consequence, you now hold in your hands a book that for some years to come will surely be an indispensable reference for anyone who wishes to acquaint him- or herself with the most searching analysis of the nature and meaning of the NDE itself.

Although many of the concepts presented in this book about the nature of NDEs, brain functioning, and consciousness may be at times a bit abstruse, *On the Other Side of Life* is on the whole very accessible to the general reader because of the *form* in which this information is presented. Rather than each contributor writing a chapter on his specialty, for example, what Evelyn Elsaesser Valarino has done, and done superbly, is to have conducted interviews with each of her participants. The dialogues that result, then, have the sparkling immediacy of conversations between a thoughtful inquirer who knows where she wants to steer the discussion and the interviewee who is only too happy to oblige her lead and to engage her fully (and the reader eavesdrops) as he brings his own training and insight to bear on the phenomenon of the NDE.

In assembling this group of researchers and commentators on the NDE, Evelyn Elsaesser Valarino has performed a very great service to the field of near-death studies, and her book will certainly provide many professionals who read it with a further impetus not only to take seriously but also to study and explore the NDE itself. In consequence, the field of near-death studies will certainly be strengthened by its continuing to draw the attention of investigators and scholars in philosophy, science, medicine, psychology, and religious studies, as well as other fields that have something to contribute to our understanding of just what it is that is seen through this window of death that modern medical resuscitation technology has disclosed to us all.

The great American author, Herman Melville, in his most celebrated book, *Moby Dick*, observed, "And the drawing near of Death, which alike levels all, alike impresses all with a last revelation, which only an author from the dead could adequately tell." These "authors from the dead," whom Melville could only imagine in the nineteenth century, are the thousands of persons who in our own time have returned to speak of the revelatory nature of their NDEs. Their tales inspire us, amaze us, and puzzle us, but they can no longer be dismissed. Our task is now to understand them, how they may happen, and what they mean. Toward this end, the volume that Evelyn Elsaesser Valarino has given us is a giant step in our infinite journey in quest of discovering the ultimate secrets of death—and life.

Kenneth Ring, Ph.D.
Professor of Psychology
University of Connecticut
Storrs, Connecticut

Acknowledgments

Any attempt to write a book consisting mainly of dialogues takes one on a long and perilous adventure, whose path is strewn with both wonders and obstacles. Along this path, I have been privileged to meet some extraordinary characters, who are at once greatly inspired and greatly inspiring. I extend my wholehearted thanks to my traveling companions, who have made it possible to carry out this ambitious project: Professor Kenneth Ring, Professor Régis Dutheil* and his daughter Brigitte, Professor Louis-Marie Vincent, Professor Paul Chauchard, Monsignor Jean Vernette, Professor Michel Lefeuvre, Professor Jean-Pierre Girard† and Henry H. I am infinitely grateful to them for their kindness, their openness and the richness and abundance of their reflection.

I would especially like to thank Kenneth Ring, a man

---

*I am sad to note the passing of Régis Dutheil in 1995. He was not only an excellent physicist, but also a man of exceptional courtesy and graciousness.

†I am also sad to note the passing of Jean-Pierre Girard in 1996. I send Madame Girard my best wishes. He will be greatly missed by all who knew him.

who has attained worldwide recognition and is therefore very much in demand around the globe. For this reason, I was both surprised and delighted that he opened the door to his University of Connecticut office at the simple request of an unheard-of Swiss woman. He probably did not realize he would be giving one of the longest interviews of his career—in fact, we recorded throughout an entire day and our dialogue continues even now in a deep friendship that began one day in Storrs.

I would also like to thank Professor Louis-Marie Vincent, who has become a dear friend. His experience, valuable advice, and constant enthusiasm and support have accompanied me throughout this four-year journey.

Evelyn Elsaesser Valarino

Contents

"I shall look as if I were suffering. I shall look a little as if I were dying. It is like that. Do not come to see that. It is not worth the trouble ..."

"I shall not leave you."

....

And he took me by the hand. But he was still worrying.

"It was wrong of you to come. You will suffer. I shall look as if I were dead; and that will not be true ..."

I said nothing.

"You understand ... It is too far. I cannot carry this body with me. It is too heavy."

I said nothing.

"But it will be like an old abandoned shell. There is nothing sad about old shells ..."

The Little Prince, Antoine de Saint Exupéry

Chapter One

Introduction

DESCRIPTION OF THE NEAR-DEATH EXPERIENCE

The near-death experience (NDE) is a phenomenon that occurs, in some cases, at the farthest extremity of life, in a state close to that of death. It is an experience that assumes vital importance for those who emerge from it. The fact that it occurs in the interval between life and death places the NDE somewhere between the real and the transcendental.

In the vast majority of cases, NDEs occur in persons who are in a near-death state, and occasionally, in a comatose state. In very rare instances, however, they may also be experienced by perfectly healthy individuals who have been exposed to an intensely frightening or other highly traumatizing event.

I shall use the term *experiencer* to designate persons who have undergone a near-death experience. This immediately gives rise to the question of what is meant by "death," which is indeed a difficult concept to define. To oversimplify, we could say that all we know is that human beings exist, and that at a given point, separated from existence by a certain lapse of time, they cease to exist. Yet we know nothing, or almost nothing, about this interim period. This difficult issue will be discussed in the interviews with Professors Chauchard and Vincent. Consequently, I have avoided using the term *clinical death* and have kept to the more vague notion of "near-death state."

The NDE occurs in 30 percent of all near-death instances. Many questions concerning this percentage are discussed at length in the interview with Professor Kenneth Ring (e.g., Who undergoes an NDE? Why? Is there a typical experiencer profile? Do all persons in a near-death state have an NDE, but only 30 percent of them remember it?) The typical NDE may include the following stages:

1. *An out-of-body experience.* The subject leaves his or her body and views it from an external vantage point, at some distance above it. In a small percentage of cases, this stage is marked by a feeling of disorientation or a brief sensation of distress.
2. A passage through a *tunnel*, sometimes accompanied by a sound that is either harmonious and pleasant, or disturbing; an impression of weightlessness and dizzying speed.
3. The appearance of a *brilliant light* beckoning at the end of the tunnel.
4. An encounter with a *being of light*, personifying absolute love.
5. A feeling of *infinite happiness*, indescribable joy, and profound peace.
6. *An encounter with deceased loved ones or unknown guides.*
7. The vision of a *city of light*.

8. A *life review* (a timeless, three-dimensional vision of the significant events in the experiencer's life).
9. Access to *absolute knowledge*, which is partially or entirely lost upon returning to life.
10. The certainty of *being part of a harmonious universal whole*, of having a definite place in it, of belonging to a cosmic oneness, and of understanding its functioning and meaning.
11. Various representations symbolizing a limit or *boundary* which, if crossed, would make returning to life impossible.
12. A voluntary or imposed *return to life*.

It should be noted that one rarely finds all the above-mentioned features in a single near-death experience.

Experiencers all describe a nearly identical NDE progression and undergo very similar emotions. We can therefore start with the assumption that these are data that apply to human beings in general and inform us of their reactions when at the extreme edge of existence.

One of the essential components of the NDE, and certainly the most transformative one, concerns the encounter with the being of light. It is described as similar to being immersed in a sea of unconditional love, which engulfs, soothes, and releases; of being instilled with a feeling of absolute safety, like finding shelter from a storm, or returning to the womb. In fact, the picture painted by experiencers is one of all the archetypes; it is the quintessence of all symbols.

The life review, which brings back not only the most significant events—whether happy or traumatic—but also the ordinary episodes of a person's life, is primarily indicative of the immense power of the human memory, which, for the most part, lies buried in the unconscious.

Inaccessible during daily waking life, it is nevertheless present and able to be reactivated during the NDE. This life review—a distressing exercise if ever there was one—takes place in the presence of the being of light, who assists the experiencer in understanding his or her good and bad deeds. Interestingly, the subject experiences at this point whatever emotions, joy, or pain his or her words or acts may have produced in others. The experiencer's remorse and guilt feelings are eased by the kindness of the being of light, who points out mistakes in order to help him or her improve, not to punish. This stage of the NDE is once again highly symbolic, for it is linked to the notion of good and evil—one of the fundamental archetypes. In this context, and from the purely logical standpoint, it is difficult to see the usefulness of such an exercise, unless from the perspective of a future in which these lessons may be applied.

There are different ways of analyzing an NDE. Bruce Greyson, M.D., Professor of Psychiatry at the University of Virginia, proposes the following original classification, which consists of four categories:

1. A cognitive component, including time distortion, thought acceleration, life review, and sudden understanding.
2. An affective component, including feelings of peace, joy, and cosmic unity, and an experience of a brilliant light.
3. A paranormal component, including enhanced vision or hearing, apparent extrasensory perception, precognitive vision, and an out-of-body experience.
4. A transcendental component, including encounters with an apparently unearthly realm, a mystical being and visible spirits, and a barrier or

"point of no return" that, had the experiencer crossed it, would have precluded his or her return to life.[1]

NEAR-DEATH EXPERIENCE RESEARCH

History

Near-death experiences have no doubt been occurring since the beginning of humankind. Testimonies have been handed down through the centuries in written and artistic accounts. Descriptive fragments may be found in the Bible, as well as in the classic works of philosophy. However, active research into NDEs only began some twenty years ago, in 1975, to be precise, with the publication of the book *Life after Life*[2] by Raymond A. Moody. Although anecdotal and without academic pretension, this book may be credited with having motivated scientists from various fields to investigate this remarkable and intriguing phenomenon. After the appearance of Moody's book, publications began appearing at an increasing rate, creating a multiplier effect: As books on near-death experiences proliferated, the general public became more informed, which in turn allowed persons who had experienced an NDE to come forward and tell their stories. In 1980, Kenneth Ring, Bruce Greyson, and sociologist John Audette decided to create an association for the purpose of studying these phenomena. In February 1981, they founded the International Association for Near-Death Studies (IANDS USA) at the University of Connecticut. Its establishment allowed for the large-scale collection of research data and the launching of several research programs throughout the country. The numerous NDE testimonies gathered soon constituted a wealth of data to serve as a starting point for rigorous and diversified scientific investigation. A few years later, national IANDS centers were set up in Australia and in a number of European countries.

Incidence of Near-Death Experiences

In 1992, Kenneth Ring estimated the number of Americans who had undergone an NDE to be on the order of eight million. This figure was raised to thirteen million by Bruce Greyson, on the basis of a Gallup Poll taken in 1994. At this level of incidence, the figures are no longer very important in themselves, but are indeed proof that an impressive number of individuals have experienced this phenomenon, and that doubts concerning its authenticity are no longer justified. Since all of the studies conducted have unequivocally shown the NDE to be universal, not linked to a specific geographical area or culture, but rather to the general human condition, we can assume that an equivalent percentage of NDEs may be found in other countries around the world.

Nature of Near-Death Experience Research

Each near-death experience is unique in that it is linked to an individual, yet all NDEs share the same basic nature and produce the same effects.

Although the NDE itself remains unverifiable (despite the astounding similarity of the accounts of millions of experiencers), based as it is on testimonies replete with subjective feelings, the same cannot be said for the positive transformations observed in those who have undergone the experience. They emerge from it profoundly and lastingly transformed. Their values shift, and filled with a desire to help others, they often set out to give their lives new direction. Here again, these transformations are characterized by great similarity, despite the diversity of the experiencers. These radical changes in behavior lend themselves easily to thorough analysis.

The impressions and feelings of someone who has undergone a near-death experience are, by definition, subjective, intimate, and difficult to convey. NDE research is faced with a phenomenon that cannot be measured, quantified, or observed by the usual scientific means. With the exception of the out-of-body experience (OBE),[3] which is relatively easy to corroborate, NDE research necessarily entails a thoughtful inquiry into transcendence. There are two ways of looking at NDEs: The first consists of interpreting them as points of contact with the transcendent realm; the second is the Cartesian approach, which involves admitting only what is observable and "rational." Yet if we take this approach, the mystery will remain unsolved, for it seems to me that it is precisely the observable, the measurable, the material that obscures the truth—like a veil concealing what lies just beyond our vision.

Focus of Future Near-Death Experience Research

To date, NDE research has focused primarily on the psychological aspects of the experience. Numerous studies have analyzed the content and progression of the NDE, as well as the profound and lasting positive changes that typically occur in the lives of experiencers. Although the hypotheses and arguments put forth by researchers are far from having exhausted all aspects of this multifaceted phenomenon, current research now appears to be taking a more physiological approach. Such investigations, which are still in the embryonic stage, step outside the psychological realm to study the physiological changes observed in experiencers.

QUESTIONS RAISED BY THE NEAR-DEATH EXPERIENCE

Belief in the survival of consciousness has always been an act of faith and the very essence of all great religions. It seems to me that, thanks to the accounts of experiencers, there is now another, more empirical way— and one requiring less personal effort—to corroborate this ancestral idea.

Since the dawn of time, man has attempted to define reality, which is far more vast than what we perceive as real. The study of NDEs opens up new avenues of investigation, precisely because it provides access to a dimension that is no longer a purely theoretical concept, but may henceforth be studied on a more empirical level, given that it has been experienced and described by millions of experiencers. Philosophers have always studied reality from the space–time perspective. Yet, during an NDE, space and time no longer exist, or else it is an entirely different space–time, perhaps resembling the one advanced by quantum mechanics. I do not think it too bold to suggest that the study of NDEs might lead to major discoveries that would confirm quantum theory and perhaps invalidate classic philosophical notions.

Life, as we currently define it, is governed by time. Vital phenomena are distinguished from nonvital phenomena by the time factor, which is at the very source of their functioning. I believe the study of NDEs compels us to consider the possible existence of a reflective, emotional, hyperpowerful consciousness (thus possessing all the properties of a living being), that evolves in an atemporal dimension. Would this invalidate the laws that necessarily associate life with time? In addition, all philosophical thought is governed by the concept of life as within a body, never as without one. After hearing the numerous testimonies of experiencers, who clearly state that during their NDE they were conscious—even hyperconscious—but detached from their physical bodies, I wonder if we should not give some consideration to the notion of life as liberated from matter and space–time.

Research in the field of thermodynamics, conducted by Ilya Prigogine, in particular, has resulted in the concepts of entropy and of negentropy, which basically teach us that order arises out of disorder. Accordingly, we may state that the death of a human being results from the total disorganization of its vital functions, thus, from maximum disorder. When a vital system undergoes profound changes, this usually leads it to evolve toward a higher, more autonomous, and more efficient level of functioning. The disorder that occurs at the moment of human death could therefore be part of a predetermined process destined to lead human consciousness—the human essence—toward a change of state.

Since nature is constantly evolving toward higher complexity (an observation that may be verified at all levels), it would seem absurd from a logical, Cartesian point of view, for a being as sophisticated as man, with his highly evolved consciousness, to be destined to total annihilation upon death. Given the general functioning of living organisms, we could postulate that man evolves toward maturation by changing states. His matter, which is destined for disintegration, would be left behind, while his essence would meet with a completely different destiny.

THE EXPERIENCER

The NDE leads to a profound and lasting transformation in those who have experienced it. Such persons are rendered both more fragile and more strong by the event they have been privileged to witness. They are made more fragile by the fact that, having come so close to death, they have undergone a major trauma. After their NDE, experiencers often find themselves in a critical physical state, as a result of the illness or accident that led them to the brink of death. In many cases, they are unable to give a name to the event they have experienced, but are utterly convinced that it is of vital importance to them. Many experiencers have attempted to talk with their medical providers or families about their experience, only to run up against a lack of understanding or serious reservations about their mental state! In addition to their physical problems, they then find themselves alienated and left alone to assimilate an experience they feel is essential to their future. They are torn by their longing for the state of absolute serenity, happiness, and love they have just experienced, and the difficulty of rejoining a family and community whose preoccupations they no longer fully recognize, and whose values and aspirations they no longer truly share. This marks the beginning of a long journey, sometimes spanning several months or years, toward a new way of living. This personal transformation, which is common to all who have undergone a near-death experience, does not happen immediately following the NDE. It is the result of a long search, filled with questions, introspection, and vain attempts to regain their former selves. Experiencers sense that the course of their life has definitely shifted but are left wondering what direction it should now take. Often they resist and try to turn their backs on it, but the urgency and strength behind this need for change are stronger than the fear it engenders. If it is true that the NDE is a gift, and I am convinced that it is, it is also true that its assimilation is difficult and painful, yet at the same time necessary and unavoidable. Once they have found their way, experiencers are stronger and no doubt better people than we are—stronger because they have been released from the fear of death, and better because they are capable of finding true meaning in their lives. The somewhat theoretical values of religious teachings become obvious to them—they are seen as a natural course and a vital need. Although the directions chosen by experiencers may differ, all are based on a desire to be of service to others. Experiencers find peace only after they have understood and accepted this new path opening up before them.

Those who have had a near-death experience are also characterized by a tremendous thirst for knowledge and understanding. Their vision of the world changes radically; they have a sense of belonging to a whole whose contours they recognize, but whose mechanisms they feel a great need to understand.

Moreover, self-acceptance and self-esteem increase significantly following an NDE. Henry H., who has shared his near-death experience with me and whose account is reproduced later in this book, says very simply, "What's different now is that I can unconditionally love myself, because God accepts me just the way I am." The NDE is a powerful healing device—like an instant therapy that enables experiencers to accept themselves as they are. Self-acceptance is the key to opening up to others, since we cannot turn to our neighbor and help him unless we are at peace with ourselves. This inner peace is one of the gifts experiencers receive.

Although no experiencer seems to want to intentionally bring about a return to that wonderful state experienced during the NDE, all are unanimous in expressing a total absence of fear regarding death. They know they will find that state of grace once more when the time comes, and are therefore totally free from the fear of death, which is unquestionably the heaviest load that we, as humans, have to bear.

Experiencers are characterized by their great tolerance with regard to religions and beliefs. It does not seem to matter to them what name others give to their God, since it is a question of one and the same truth. Their position on religion may be summed up in one word: They do not *believe*, they *know*.

Profile of the Experiencer

Who are these individuals who have had the privilege of undergoing a near-death experience, of feeling this intense joy and indescribable happiness, of understanding what love is and of coming back to life with true values? Is it merely by chance that only a small percentage (30 percent) of those in the near-death state have an NDE, and not the others? Yet physics research seems to indicate that chance does not exist—not at any level. Are there then medical reasons—is the cause of the near-death state responsible? This is apparently not the case. Statistics show this figure of 30 percent to be consistent, regardless of whether the near-death state is induced by illness, accident, or attempted suicide. Should we look for the explanation in the personality of the experiencer, rather than in what led him to the threshold of death? No doubt we should. Scientists have undertaken extensive research in an effort to identify the common elements. Kenneth Ring has taken on this difficult task and seems to have found some clues in the childhood background of experiencers. Initial results seem to indicate that mental or physical suffering, associated with a traumatized childhood—one conditioned by abuse or illness—could be a determining factor. If this hypothesis is confirmed, it would seem as though the privilege of having an NDE were some sort of reward, or—to avoid any causal interpretation—simply due to the subjects' particular capacity to being open to the experience, perhaps because they are more sensitive, more receptive, or predisposed to gaining access to this altered state of consciousness. Indeed, understanding, and especially wisdom, often result from suffering. But what about the remaining 70 percent? Did they also have an NDE, only it lies buried in their unconscious, blocked by some defense mechanism? If so, then why have they not had the privilege of remembering the experience and of being able to benefit from it during the remainder of their lives? Is there some external reason, some selection process? Or is it due to an unconscious individual capacity or incapacity to be open to this experience and to be enriched by it? For the time being, no one knows, and the difficulty of understanding these complex mechanisms appears to be obvious.

Psychological Portrait of the Experiencer

The experiencer undergoes a wide range of emotions. The beginning of the experience, which coincides with the OBE, is sometimes described as slightly, or greatly, disorienting or anxiety-producing. As the experience progresses, the emotional impressions become increasingly positive, culminating in a state of indescribable joy and ecstasy, particularly during the encounter with the being of light. This is no doubt the most profoundly transformative stage of the experience. In the words of one of Moody's experiencers (*Life after Life*)[4]: "I *never* wanted to leave the presence of this being." Perhaps the feeling of strangeness or anxiety associated with the out-of-body experience at the beginning of the NDE is felt by all subjects, but simply vanishes as a feeling of absolute happiness overcomes the experiencer. I am also convinced that the negative or disturbing NDEs, which occur in a small percentage of cases, correspond to experiences that were interrupted prematurely. Whatever the case, it is clear that the subjects go through an accelerated and powerful emotional process. It is important to stress that experiencers feel they have full control over their fate. Many have said that, at a given point, it was they who made the decision to return to their bodies and to life. Apparently, they also have direct control over their physical bodies, confirming current medical opinion, which largely acknowledges the importance of the mind–body relation in the healing process. Let us hear what another of Moody's respondents (*Life after Life*)[5] has to say about this:

> It was wonderful over there on the other side, and I kind of wanted to stay. But knowing that I had something good to do on earth was just as wonderful in a way. So, I was thinking, "Yes, I must go back and live," and I got back into my physical body. I *almost feel as though I stopped the bleeding myself.* At any rate, I began to recover after that. [Emphasis added.]

IMPLICATIONS FOR THE RESEARCHER AND THE READER

Research into near-death experiences is fascinating on several accounts. To begin with, it is a subject that addresses each of us at the innermost level of our beings, for it concerns an experience that emerges from the very essence of human existence and summons forth our destiny. Furthermore, it touches upon all areas of human thought and leads us to inquire into such fascinating subjects as consciousness, memory and brain functioning, and the implications of discoveries in quantum physics, to mention only a few.

The NDE clearly does not fit into the same category as any other topic of research. The invention of the wheel or the discovery of the laws of gravity were undoubtedly of great importance to the evolution of mankind, but they did not lend meaning to man's existence. Exploration into NDEs is of a distinct nature, for it deals with humankind's essence, destiny, and progress beyond known limits. The near-death experience represents at once an immense hope and a formidable challenge. The fascination it holds for us derives from the fact that it will probably never be fully explained. Only a question that, by nature, must remain unanswered, has the magic power to push our thinking to the limit, thereby sublimating it. The NDE offers us fragments—priceless clues to understanding our sometimes happy, often difficult lives, which are always brimming with questions and uncertain hopes. Simply by listening to the near-death experiencers, the pieces of life's puzzle begin slowly but surely falling into place. Things take on their proper perspective, true values are revealed, and the meaning of life is implicitly understood. The magic of the NDE comes through in the testimonies of the experiencers. Their accounts are often simple, always marked by a sense of authenticity and conveyed in a spirit of sharing. I join Kenneth Ring in his belief that some phenomena are meant to be explained, whereas others are meant to be explored (see pg. 130). The process of exploring the NDE is one that enriches and transforms us. What matters is not the answer itself, but rather the path we follow in pursuing it. The solution is most likely inherent in the particular state of consciousness associated with the near-death state, and can only be assimilated in such conditions. The last piece of the puzzle will no doubt fall into place neatly and naturally at the crucial moment.

Chapter Two

Analysis of the NDE and Its Successive Stages, Illustrated by Experiencer Accounts

The purpose of this book is to provide an in-depth analysis of the near-death experience (NDE) in the light of the natural and social sciences. However, this chapter will be largely devoted to the accounts of experiencers. I have broken the NDE down into its various components, which are included in the following list and shown in bold. Those shown in italics correspond either to the aftereffects of the experience, or to the NDE in a much broader sense. It should be noted that this breakdown corresponds to my own personal analysis, which goes into more detail than the categories usually listed by NDE researchers. There is consequently a slight overlap between some of these subdivisions. Furthermore, I would like to stress the fact that, to my knowledge, no experiencer has ever undergone each and every one of these stages, although some have explored a good number of them. It is also conceivable that near-death experiencers have undergone the entire experience, but only part of it was recorded in their memory.

1. The out-of-body experience
2. The tunnel
3. The encounter with guides and guardian angels
4. The encounter with the being of light, or absolute love
5. The feeling of infinite understanding, happiness, and peace
6. Magnificent environments
7. The city of light
8. Access to universal knowledge
9. *The hunger for learning*
10. Heightened intellectual abilities
11. An enduring feeling of self-identity
12. The certainty of belonging to a universal whole
13. The altered perception of time
14. The altered perception of gravity
15. The impression of phenomenal speed
16. The sensation of no longer having a body, or of having a different kind of body
17. The encounter with deceased loved ones
18. The life review
19. The "last judgement"
20. The sense of sight
21. The sense of hearing:
Living persons
Deceased persons, or the being of light
22. The sense of touch
23. *The sense of smell and taste*

1. The **out-of-body experience** (OBE) is the first stage of the NDE. Subjects view their bodies from an external vantage point, at some distance above. It should be noted that OBEs can occur independently of the near-death state. Some gifted subjects can even bring them on at will. The OBE is among the most common of psychic manifestations. Approximately 16 percent of Americans have had at least one in their lives.[1] It is undoubtedly the most easily verifiable feature of the NDE, and the only one that is not derived exclusively from the subjective feelings of the experiencer. One anecdote, which has made the rounds of all NDE researchers and is a favorite in their speeches, concerns an American patient who had an NDE while undergoing surgery. During his out-of-body experience, he found himself on the roof of the hospital where he was being cared for. He had been brought to the hospital by ambulance in a coma, and had never before been to that particular hospital. During his OBE, he noticed that an old red shoe was stuck in a corner of the hospital roof. When he regained consciousness, he related this episode to the medical staff who found the story so preposterous

that they decided to have it checked out. It proved to be exactly as he had described it. This incident is difficult, if not impossible, to explain without allowing for the possibility that consciousness becomes detached from the physical body during an OBE, which, in this case, was linked to a near-death experience. Let us see what two experiencers from Raymond Moody's *Life after Life* have to say about this:

Someone said, "Let's swim across the lake." I had done that on numerous occasions, but that day for some reason, I went down, almost in the middle of the lake.... I kept bobbling up and down, and all of a sudden, it felt as though I were away from my body, away from everybody, in space by myself. Although I was stable, staying at the same level, I saw my body in the water about three or four feet away, bobbling up and down. I viewed my body from the back and slightly to the right side. I still felt as though I had an entire body form, even while I was outside my body. I had an airy feeling that's almost indescribable. I felt like a feather.[2]

About a year ago, I was admitted to the hospital with heart trouble, and the next morning, lying in the hospital bed, I began to have a very severe pain in my chest. I pushed the button beside the bed to call for the nurses, and they came in and started working on me. I was quite uncomfortable lying on my back so I turned over, and as I did, I quit breathing and my heart stopped beating. Just then, I heard the nurses shout, "Code pink! Code pink!" As they were saying this, I could feel myself moving out of my body and sliding down between the mattress and the rail on the side of the bed—actually it seemed as if I went *through* the rail—on down to the floor. Then, I started rising upward, slowly. On my way up, I saw more nurses come running into the room—there must have been a dozen of them. My doctor happened to be making his rounds in the hospital, so they called him, and I saw him come in, too. I thought, "I wonder what he's doing here." I drifted on up past the light fixture—I saw it from the side and very distinctly—and then I stopped, floating right below the ceiling, looking down. I felt almost as though I were a piece of paper that someone had blown up to the ceiling.

I watched them reviving me from up there! My body was lying down there stretched out on the bed, in plain view, and they were all standing around it. I heard one nurse say, "Oh, my God! She's gone!", while another one leaned down to give me mouth-to-mouth resuscitation. I was looking at the *back* of her head while she did this. I'll never forget the way her hair looked; it was cut kind of short. Just then, I saw them roll this machine in there, and they put the shocks on my chest. When they did, I saw my whole body just jump right up off the bed, and I heard every bone in my body crack and pop. It was the most awful thing!

As I saw them below beating on my chest and rubbing my arms and legs, I thought, "Why are they going to so much trouble? I'm just fine now."[3]

Experiencers sometimes find it difficult to recognize their bodies. This is probably because we are not used to seeing our bodies from the outside. Another of Moody's respondents in *Life after Life* put it like this:

Boy, I sure didn't realize that I looked like that! You know, I'm only used to seeing myself in pictures or from the front in a mirror, and both of those look *flat*. But all of a sudden there I—or my body—was, and I could see it. I could definitely see it, full view, from about five feet away. It took me a few moments to recognize myself.[4]

One man, whose account of a near-drowning incident was related to Melvin Morse and Paul Perry in *Transformed by the Light*, turns the question around by saying, "... I believe in God very much. I believe God took me out of my body and kept me in a very safe place when I almost drowned."[5]

2. Following the out-of-body experience, the experiencer has the sensation of entering a dark **tunnel** and moving at a very high speed toward a brilliant light beck-

oning at the end of the tunnel. This stage may be accompanied by a sound, often described as harmonious, sometimes as unpleasant. An experiencer interviewed by Raymond Moody in *Life after Life* explains:

> The first thing that happened—it was real quick—was that I went through this dark, black vacuum at super speed. You could compare it to a tunnel, I guess. I felt like I was riding on a roller-coaster train at an amusement park, going through this tunnel at a tremendous speed.[6]

Another experiencer, whose account appears in Kenneth Ring's *Heading Toward Omega*, describes it like this:

> I knew I was either dead or going to die. But then something happened. It was so immense, so powerful, that I gave up on my life to see what it was. I wanted to venture into this experience, which started as a drifting into what I could only describe as a long tunnel of light. But it wasn't just a light, it was a protective passage of energy with an intense brightness at the end, which I wanted to look into, to touch. There were no sounds of any earthly thing. Only the sounds of serenity, of a strange music like I had never heard. A soothing symphony of indescribable beauty blended with the light I was approaching.
>
> I gave up on life. I left it behind for this new wonderful thing. I did not want to go back to life. For what I knew was that what lay ahead was to be so wondrous and beautiful that nothing should stop me from reaching it.[7]

3. According to numerous experiencers, **guides** or **guardian angels** were waiting for them at this stage of the experience in order to comfort and accompany them. This is what one of Moody's experiencers recalls:

> While I was dead, in this void, I talked to people—and yet, I really couldn't say that I talked to any *bodily* people. Yet, I had the feeling that there were people around me, and I could feel their presence, and could feel them moving, though I could never see anyone. Every now and then, I would talk with one of them, but I couldn't see them. And whenever I wondered what was going on, I would always

get a thought back from one of them, that everything was all right, that I was dying but would be fine. So, my condition never worried me. I always got an answer back for every question that I asked. They didn't leave my mind void.[8]

I would also like to quote a boy whose experience was related to Morse and Perry in *Transformed by the Light*:

I looked up and suddenly I was falling, but it felt more like I was floating. I heard a voice tell me not to be scared, but to hold very still and to look up and not move my neck. It said that it would hurt but I would still be okay. I saw a little girl floating in the air next to me. She was all bright, but it didn't hurt my eyes to look at her. I did what I was told and landed hard and broke my collarbone. When I got to the doctor, I heard him tell my mother that if my head had been turned to the left or the right, I would have snapped my neck. I did just what the little girl told me to do and walked away okay.[9]

4. Next comes the encounter with the **being of light**, which is described as the vision of a dazzlingly beautiful light, personifying total love and absolute understanding, more intense than any earthly light, yet not blinding. The light seems to be infused with powerful symbolic meaning. Communication between the being of light and the experiencer happens instantaneously and without words. Below are the comments of four experiencers cited by Kenneth Ring in *Heading Toward Omega*:

It's something which becomes you and you become it. I could say, "I was peace, I was love." I was the brightness, it was part of me …[10]

An intensity of feeling rushed through me, as if the light that surrounded that Being was bathing me, penetrating every part of me. As I absorbed the energy, I sensed what I can only describe as bliss.[11]

As the light came toward me, it came to be a person— yet it wasn't a person. It was a being that radiated. And inside this radiant luminous light which had a silver tint to it—white, with a silver tint to it—[was] what looked to be a man.... Now, I didn't know exactly who this was, you know, but it was the first person that showed up and I had this feeling that the closer this light got to me, the more awesome and the more pure this love—this feeling that I would call love ...[12]

And this enormously bright light seemed almost to cradle me. I just seemed to exist in it and be part of it and be nurtured by it and the feeling just became more and more and more ecstatic and glorious and perfect. And everything about it was—if you took the one thousand best things that ever happened to you in your life and multiplied by a million, maybe you could get close to this feeling, I don't know. But you're just engulfed by it and you begin to know a lot of things.[13]

Let's also hear what one of Morse and Perry's experiencers in *Transformed by the Light* has to say:

I asked (the light) that my cancer would be removed. I prayed actually. And the light said that what we think of as prayers is more like complaining and we are frequently begging to be punished for something that we are simply going to do again in the future. He asked me to think of my own worst enemy and I did. Then he said to send all of my light to my worst enemy. I did and a sudden burst of light went out of me and returned as if it had been reflected back from a mirror. I became aware of every cell in my body. I could see every cell in my body. It was the sound and sight of light coming from my being. I was crying, laughing, shaking, trying to hold still and trying to catch my breath. When I finally recovered, the being of light said, "Now you have prayed for the first time in your life."[14]

5. The encounter with the being of light produces a feeling of **absolute happiness**, **total understanding**, and **profound peace**. It is surely one of the most symbolic and deeply transformative stages of the experience. Two accounts gathered by Kenneth Ring in *Heading Toward Omega* give a good description of this:

Even now when I try to describe something so beautiful I am mute with awe. There are no words in any language to describe such grandeur. Even the great literary works by men and women fortunate enough to have experienced this blissful state only paint a shadow of its glory. I don't know to this day where I was, I was no longer aware of my physical existence on earth, of my friends, my family, or my relatives. I was in a state that existed of nothing more than consciousness, but what a sublime consciousness it was! It was like a rebirth into another, higher kind of life.[15]

It seemed whole *Truths* revealed themselves to me. Waves of thought—ideas greater and purer than I had ever tried to figure out came to me. Thoughts, clear without effort revealed themselves in total wholeness, although not in logical sequence. I, of course, being in that magnificent Presence, understood it all. I realized that consciousness is life. We will live in and through much, but this consciousness we know that is behind our personality will continue. I knew now that the purpose of life does not depend on me; it has its own purpose. I realized that the flow of it will continue even as I will continue. New serenity entered my being.

As this occurred, an intensity of feeling rushed through me, as if the light that surrounded that Being was bathing me, penetrating every part of me. As I absorbed the energy, I sensed what I can only describe as bliss. That is such a little word, but the feeling was dynamic, rolling, magnificent, expanding, ecstatic—*Bliss*. It whirled around me and, entering my chest, flowed through me, and I was immersed in love and awareness for ineffable time.[16]

6. Experiencers describe **magnificent environments**, embellished with gorgeous unknown flowers and illuminated by colors of the most astounding beauty and intensity. These descriptions, based on sublimated earthly representations, seem to me to evoke a dimension that only becomes intelligible to the experiencer through the symbolic forms produced by his or her psyche. This interpretation was analyzed in my interview with Kenneth

Ring (see pg. 124). Below is the account, in its entirety, of a woman who had an NDE at the age of nine, as reported to Morse and Perry in *Transformed by the Light*:

> I got sick when I was nine years old for no reason that I knew of. My fever was about 106 degrees or above. I'd seen the doctor several times and when it became obvious that I wasn't getting any better he decided to put me in the hospital. That did no good. Over the course of the next days it went even higher. They did every test they could think of but they couldn't find the cause of the fever. Finally a team of three or four pediatricians decided that they had to bring the fever down or I would get brain damage. I was very weak at that point. I heard doctors express their concern that I couldn't stand this fever much longer. Finally these doctors decided to take drastic measures. They stripped me naked and wrapped me in ice cubes and a sheet. Then a nurse stood there and took my temperature every few minutes. When I got all wrapped up I passed out. I seemed like I was floating and everything around me was dark and pleasant. And then there it was, a tunnel of light with a very bright light at the end. I was being helped by someone to move up this tunnel. When I arrived at the end there was a lovely vista spread out before me. There were all fields with flowers and there was a nice road over on my right and the trees were painted white halfway up and there was a white fence. It was lovely. And there were the most gorgeous horses I had ever seen in the pasture off to the right. I would have to cross two fences to get to these horses but since I was nine years old there was no doubt where I was going. I started off that way and after a little while there was a white kind of light, a presence beside me that was friendly and not at all threatening. The presence said: "Where are you going?" And I said: "I'm going over there." And he said: "That's great. We'll come along." There were a lot of flowers that I had never seen before and I was asking him their names and picking them as we went along. And I was talking to this blinding white light that was all colors and no colors at the same time. And it didn't have a face or feature *per se*, but that didn't bother me. I remember looking back down

the tunnel at the people crowded around the bed and I didn't care that I was up there and my body was down there. I felt very good, as a matter of fact. So I was talking to this light and wandering over to these horses. I had just gotten my leg over the top rail of the fence and into the horse pasture when this voice out of nowhere said: "What is she doing here?" And the light answered: "She came to have the horses." And the voice said: "It's not right. It's not her time. She has to go back." At this point I was clutching the rail because I didn't want to go back. That was the *last* thing I wanted to do. And the voice talked to the white light a little bit more and they decided that I would have to go back. So I threw a tantrum. I pitched a royal fit. I grabbed onto the rail of the fence and wrapped my arms and legs around it and I wouldn't let go. The voice just laughed. "Look, you can have it later, but this is not the time. And throwing a tantrum is not going to do you any good." I found myself floating over the field and going back down into the tunnel. And I was screaming and yelling and kicking and biting and everything else, and this hand was just gently guiding me down the tunnel that I had come up. "Why *can't* I stay?" I yelled. "Because we have something for you to do," said the voice. I felt this hand gently guiding me back down this tunnel I had come up and I popped back into my body. I remember lying in my bed looking up. A frightened doctor was standing next to my bed. He sighed with relief and said to one of the nurses: "Oh good, she's back."[17]

7. Experiencers also tell us about a **city of light**, which they describe as follows in Ring's *Heading Toward Omega*:

Suddenly there was this tremendous burst of light and, uh, I was turned ... to the light. I saw at a great distance a city.... It's not like you'd look out of an airplane and see the layout of a city.... Even at tremendous distance, I realized that it was *immense*! It all seemed to have the same dimensions and there seemed to be nothing supporting it and no *need* for anything to support it. And then I began to realize that the light was coming from within this city and there just seemed to be a laser beam of light and in the midst of that, that was directed to me.... The first thing that I saw was this street. And it had such a clarity. The only thing I can relate it to in this life was a look of gold, but it was clear, it was transparent.... Everything there had a purity and clarity.... The difference (between things here and there) was also—you think of gold as something hard and brittle; this had a smoothness and softness.[18]

8. The being of light instills in experiencers not only a feeling of absolute love and unimaginable happiness, but also a sense of being able to access **universal knowledge**. The knowledge acquired during an NDE may manifest itself in various ways. In the words of one experiencer (Morse and Perry, *Transformed by the Light*):

Suddenly I was on the other side, and all pains were gone. I had lost my interest and attachment to my biological life. [I realized that] the boundary between life and death is a strange creation of our mind. It is horrifying and real when perceived from this side [the side of the living] and yet is insignificant when perceived from the other side. My first impression was a total surprise. How could I exist in such a comfortable way, and how could I perceive and think while being dead, and yet have no body?[19]

After returning to life, experiencers remember having had access to total knowledge, but no longer remember the specifics of it. In the words of two of Kenneth Ring's respondents in *Heading Toward Omega*,

It was not, she related, anyone she knew. She told him: "I know what's happened, I know that I've died." And he said, "Yes, but you aren't going to be staying because it isn't time for you yet." And I said to him, "This is all so beautiful, this is all so perfect, what about my sins?" And he said to me, "There are no sins. Not in the way you think about them on earth. The only thing that matters here is how you think." "What's in your heart?" he asked me. And somehow I immediately was able to look into my heart and I saw that there was nothing in my heart except love. And I understood exactly what he meant. And I said to him, "Of course." And I felt it was something that I had always known and somehow I'd forgotten it until he'd reminded me of it. "Of course!"

And then I asked him, "Since I can't stay, since I'm going to be going back, I've another question to ask. Can you tell me—what it's all about?" [Laughter from the audience. In other words, she was asking, she said, how does "the whole thing" work?] And he *did* tell me. And it only took two or three sentences. It was a very short explanation and I understood it perfectly. And I said again, "Of course!" And again, I knew it was something I had always known and managed to forget. And so I asked him, "Can I take all this back with me? There's so many people I want to tell all this to." And he said, "You can take the answer to your first question—which was the one about sin—but," he said, "the answer to the second question you won't be able to remember." [And she found in fact that when she returned to physical life, she could not.] And that was the last thing I heard ... [before coming back].[20]

And, the second most magnificent experience ... is you realize that you are suddenly in communication with absolute, total knowledge. It's hard to describe.... You can think of a question ... and *immediately* know the answer to it. As simple as that. And it can be any question whatsoever. It can be on any subject. It can be on a subject that you don't know anything about, that you are not in the proper position even to understand and the light will give you the instantaneous correct answer and make you understand it.[21]

Here is the astounding description of a city of knowledge, as reported to Kenneth Ring in *Heading Toward Omega*:

I moved closer to the lights and realized they were cities— the cities were built of light. At the moment I realized what it was ... we were there. There was no more traveling or floating along this path.

I stood in the square of a brilliant, beautiful city and I will describe the city. The building I went in was a cathedral. It was built like St. Mark's or the Sistine Chapel, but the bricks or blocks appeared to be made of Plexiglas. They were square, they had dimensions to 'em, except you could see through 'em and in the center of each one of these was this gold and silver light. And you could see the building—and yet could not for the radiance.... Now, this cathedral was literally *built* of knowledge. This was a place of learning I had come to. I could sense it. 'Cause literally all information—I began to be bombarded with data. Information was coming at me from every direction. It was almost as if I was stickin' my head in a stream and each drop of water was a piece of information and it was flowing past me as if my head was under it.[22]

This impression of having access to knowledge raises a number of questions. These are addressed in Chapter 5 and include the following: Is this knowledge to be found within ourselves? Is it inaccessible during ordinary consciousness, yet available in the state of consciousness inherent to the near-death state? Or does it come from some external source?

9. This momentary access to universal knowledge often has the effect, upon returning to life, of creating an enormous *hunger for learning*. Many experiencers have become avid readers and passionate seekers of knowledge. It is not unusual for them to go back to school in order to satisfy their need to learn as much as they possibly can. Quantum physics seems to occupy a special place among the subjects that interest experiencers, as well as all of the sciences that study the organization and functioning of the universe. The wife of an experiencer related the changes she noticed in her husband following his NDE to Kenneth Ring in *Heading Toward Omega*:

"What?" his wife asked.
"Quantum," repeated Tom. "Quantum."
"Tom, what in the world are you talking about?"
"I don't know," said Tom, as if to himself.[23]

His wife goes on to say,

Many times he says a word he has never heard before in our reality—it might be a foreign word of a different language—but learns ... it in relationship to the "light" theory.... He talks about things faster than the speed of light and it's hard for me to understand ... when Tom picks up a book on physics he already knows the answer and seems to feel more ...[24]

Here is another account on this subject, as related to Kenneth Ring in *Heading Toward Omega.*

My purpose and my outlook on life became from that point on a searching.... Books became my friends [before this, she said, she tended to read only escapist literature].... I found myself on a college campus, which was somewhere I had always wanted to be when I was younger, but I never got to do.... I went back to school.[25]

10. It is also interesting to note that **heightened intellectual abilities** occur during the NDE in the form of sharper and quicker thinking and reasoning. The following image will help to illustrate this unusual manifestation of intellectual ability: We know that in its usual mode of functioning, the human brain utilizes its faculties only partially, and we could say that during the NDE, it functions at full capacity, and utilizes the full range of its powers. However, I do not mean to imply by this analogy that the brain is functioning during a near-death experience. Indeed, everything seems to indicate that it is not, and this is definitely where the mystery lies.

One experiencer interviewed by Kenneth Ring had this to say:

By my side there was a Being with a magnificent presence. I could not see an exact form, but instead, a radiation of light that lit up everything about me and spoke with a voice that held the deepest tenderness one can ever imagine.... As this loving yet powerful Being spoke to me, I understood vast meanings, much beyond my ability to

explain. I understood life and death, and instantly, any fear
I had, ended.[26]

11. An **enduring feeling of self-identity** becomes
very evident during the NDE. Subjects are certain of being
themselves, of having retained their personality, their
character, and their life experience. Even more than this,
they firmly believe they have never before been so entirely, so completely themselves—the concentration, the
essence of their deepest and most authentic self. An experiencer interviewed by Morse and Perry in *Transformed by
the Light* puts it like this:

> It was hard to explain. It was a time when I was not the wife
> of my husband. I was not the parent of my children. I was
> not the child of my parents. I was totally and completely me.[27]

Two of Moody's *Life after Life* respondents give these
descriptions:

> I was out of my body looking at it from about ten yards
> away, but I was thinking, just like in physical life. And
> *where* I was thinking was about at my normal bodily
> height. I wasn't in a body, as such ...[28]

> My thought and my consciousness were just like they are
> in life, but I just couldn't figure all this out.[29]

12. During the NDE, experiencers often report feeling
**certain of belonging to a universal and harmonious
whole**. They are convinced of fitting into a cosmic logic,
even if this understanding is less clear upon returning to
life. Yet traces of the clarity that filled them during their
experience remain. Two of Kenneth Ring's *Heading Toward
Omega* respondents describe it as follows:

> It's as if by gazing upon this beautiful golden light the
> power that it was was revitalizing something within the
> depths of me. There was a transmission of a higher power,
> knowledge, understanding, and the "oneness of every-
> thing" through gazing upon the light.[30]

This magnificent light seemed to be pouring through a brilliant crystal. It seemed to radiate from the very center of the consciousness I was in and to shine out in every direction through the infinite expanses of the universe. I became aware that it was part of all living things and that at the same time all living beings were part of it.[31]

Another individual told Morse and Perry in *Transformed by the Light*:

The first thing I saw when I awoke in the hospital was a flower, and I cried. Believe it or not, I had never really seen a flower until I came back from death. One thing I learned when I died was that we are all part of one big, living universe. If we think we can hurt another living thing without hurting ourselves, we are sadly mistaken.[32]

13. **The perception of time is greatly altered** during an NDE. Experiencers' accounts evoke an atemporal dimension, or another kind of time, perhaps similar to the one theorized by quantum physics. Following is an account that addresses this subject, as reported to Raymond Moody in *Life after Life*:

The most striking point of the whole experience was the moment when my being was suspended above the front part of my head. It was almost like it was trying to decide whether it wanted to leave or to stay. It seemed then as though time were standing still. At the first and the last of the accident, everything moved so fast, but at this one particular time, sort of in between, as my being was suspended above me and the car was going over the embankment, it seemed that it took the car a long time to get there, and in that time I really wasn't too involved with the car or the accident or my own body—only with my mind.[33]

This altered perception of time continues well beyond the NDE. In fact, it seems to be one of the profound and lasting changes that characterize experiencers and changes their conception of life. It enables them to put daily events into perspective, to see them for what they are, and to relate them to a wider and more genuine whole. As described by one of Morse and Perry's *Transformed by the Light* respondents:

> When I came back to life I knew I had been to heaven. Things were very different for me from then on. I was much more easygoing than my sisters. They would get bothered by things like whether they had a date or not but those things never really bothered me. I think the difference in me was caused by the way I now saw time. It was very different after that experience. I realized that time as we see it on the clock isn't how time really is. What we think of as a long time is really only a fraction of a second. Thinking like that really made me less materialistic.[34]

14. Normal sensitivity to **gravity** also **changes radically** during an NDE. Subjects perceive themselves as either without a body, or with an extremely lightweight one, and are able to move at very high speeds. They find they can travel to different locations instantaneously, even those a great distance away, simply by willing it. It seems that during the near-death experience all of the laws governing our earthly existence are abolished, and just as in fairy tales, everything can come true with a wish. Here is a description provided by one of Kenneth Ring's *Heading Toward Omega* respondents:

> Then, after that, I realized that I was able to float quite easily, even though I had no intention of doing that.... Then I very quickly discovered also that not only was I floating and hence free from gravity but free also from any of the other constrictions that inhibit flight.... I could also fly at a terrific rate of speed with a kind of freedom that one normally doesn't experience in normal flight, in airplanes, but perhaps experiences a little more in hang-gliding and things like that.... But I noticed that I could fly at a phenomenal rate of speed and it seemed to produce a feeling of great joy and sense of actually flying in this total fashion.[35]

15. The impression of **phenomenal speed** reported by many experiencers during the passage through the tunnel raises a number of questions. Carl Jung, in particular, claims to have traveled an enormous distance at a dizzying speed during his NDE, and to have seen the earth from the vantage point of the astronauts. Let us hear the account of one of Kenneth Ring's respondents:

> Then all this time, the speed is increasing.... Gradually, you realize ... you're going [at] at least the speed of light. It might possibly be the speed of light or possibly even faster than the speed of light. You do realize that you're going just so fast and you're covering vast, vast distances in just hundredths of a second ...
>
> And then gradually you realize that *way*, way off in the distance—again, unmeasurable distance—it appears that it might be the end of the tunnel. And all you can see is a white light.... And again, remember that you are traveling at *extreme* speed. [But] this whole process only takes ... [say] one minute and again emphasizing that you might have traveled to infinity, just an unlimited number of miles.[36]

16. A number of experiencers report **not having had a body** during their NDE, but having been pure consciousness, or a powerful center of energy without a bodily capsule. Others claim to have had a lightweight body that was fluid, with indistinguishable lines. In thinking about the accounts of experiencers, it occurred to me that we might be able to draw a parallel to a phenomenon involving amputated limbs. Individuals whose arms or legs have been amputated continue to have feeling in the area of the amputated limb; in fact, they often feel a sharp pain in that location. Although the body that some experiencers felt themselves to have was not painful, but on the contrary, seemed less constraining than the physical body, I still wonder if the perception of this new body is not a residue of our usual body awareness, in much the same

way that an amputated limb remains part of our sensory perception. Here is an interesting passage from one of Raymond Moody's respondents in *Life after Life*—a man who lost part of his leg in an accident during which he had an NDE:

> I could feel my body, and it was whole. I know that. I felt whole, and I felt that all of me was there, though it wasn't.[37]

Experiencers seem to retain not a true body image—the material aspect becomes secondary at this stage—but rather what I shall refer to by analogy as a psychological image. Here is a passage from Moody's *Life after Life*, which illustrates this idea:

> [When I came out of the physical body] it was like I did come out of my body and go into something else. I didn't think I was just nothing. It was another body ... but not another regular human body. It's a little bit different. It was not exactly like a human body, but it wasn't any big glob of matter, either. It had form to it, but no colors. And I know I still had something you could call hands.[38]

An experiencer quoted by Morse and Perry in *Transformed by the Light* puts it like this:

> I also had a feeling that I didn't have a body but that I was a complete being.[39]

17. When experiencers **encounter deceased loved ones** during their NDE, they are always recognized by the deceased persons, and most of the time, experiencers recognize them in return. Here are the accounts of two individuals cited in Raymond Moody's *Life after Life*:

> I had this experience when I was giving birth to a child. The delivery was very difficult, and I lost a lot of blood. The doctor gave me up, and told my relatives that I was dying. However, I was quite alert through the whole thing, and even as I heard him saying this I felt myself coming to. As I did, I realized that all these people were there, hovering

around the ceiling of the room. They were all people I had known in my past life, but who had passed on before. I recognized by grandmother and a girl I had known when I was in school, and many other relatives and friends. It seems that I mainly saw their faces and felt their presence. They all seemed pleased. It was a very happy occasion, and I felt that they had come to protect or to guide me. It was almost as if I were coming home, and they were there to greet or to welcome me. All this time, I had the feeling of everything light and beautiful. It was a beautiful and glorious moment.[40]

Several weeks before I nearly died, a good friend of mine, Bob, had been killed. Now the moment I got out of my body I had the feeling that Bob was standing there, right next to me. I could see him in my mind and felt like he was there, but it was strange. I didn't see him as his physical body. I could see things, but not in the physical form, yet just as clearly, his looks, everything. Does that make sense? He was there but he didn't have a physical body. It was kind of like a clear body, and I could sense every part of it—arms, legs, and so on—but I wasn't *seeing* it physically. I didn't think about it being odd at the time because I didn't really need to see him with my eyes. I didn't have eyes, anyway.[41]

This recognition is usually mutual—the deceased person always recognizes the experiencer, since the deceased person is the one who comes to meet the experiencer, but is not always recognized in return. The deceased person may be an ancestor, for example, whom the experiencer recognizes only after the NDE by looking in a family album. Let us listen to the account of an experiencer quoted in Morse and Perry's *Transformed by the Light*, who had an NDE in his childhood:

I was rushed to the hospital as a child, after a bad fall while playing in a derelict building. During the night after I had been unconscious, I felt myself float out of my body and looking down at myself. I was convinced I was dead. Somebody came toward me and a voice told me it was my father, who had died before I was born. His arms were outstretched and there was a line in front of him. I was sobbing and realized that if I crossed that line there would be no going back.[42]

There are also cases in which the experiencer encounters a person whose death he or she is unaware of. Following is the account of a woman who describes her experience in Morse and Perry's *Transformed by the Light*:

> I began bleeding badly after the birth of my daughter and I was instantly surrounded by medical staff who started working on me. I was in great pain. Then suddenly the pain was gone and I was looking down on them working on me. I heard one doctor say he couldn't find a pulse. Next I was traveling down a tunnel toward a bright light. But I never reached the end of the tunnel. A gentle voice told me I had to go back. Then I met a dear friend, a neighbor from a town that we had left. He also told me to go back. I hit the hospital bed with an electrifying jerk and the pain was back. I was being rushed into an operating theater for surgery to stop the bleeding. It was three weeks later that my husband decided I was well enough to be told that my dear friend in that other town had died in an accident on the day my daughter was born.[43]

18. The **life review** is one of the most important elements of the NDE. The experiencer witnesses a three-dimensional and atemporal review of all the significant events of his or her life, from the most striking to the most ordinary. Experiencers are unanimous with respect to the essence of the message they received from the being of light—they should show love to others and increase their knowledge. Here is the account of one respondent from Kenneth Ring's *Heading Toward Omega*:

> He [then] asked me, "Do you know where you are?" ... I said, "Yes." ... And he said, "What is your decision?" When he said that ... it was like I knew everything that was stored in my brain. Everything I'd ever known from the

beginning of my life I immediately knew about. And also what was kind of scary was that I knew everybody else in the room knew I knew and that there was no hiding anything—the good times, the bad times, everything.... I had a total complete clear knowledge of everything that had ever happened in my life—even little minute things that I had forgotten ... just everything, which gave me a better understanding of everything at that moment. Everything was so clear.

... I realized that there are things that every person is sent to earth to realize and to learn. For instance, to share more love, to be more loving toward one another. To discover that the most important thing is human relationships and love and not materialistic things. And to realize that every single thing that you do in your life is recorded and that even though you pass it by not thinking at the time, it always comes up later.[44]

Following is an account from Raymond Moody's *Life after Life*:

When the light appeared, the first thing he said to me was "What do you have to show me that you've done with your life?," or something to this effect. And that's when these flashbacks started. I thought, "Gee, what is going on?", because all of a sudden, I was back early in my childhood. And from then on, it was like I was walking from the time of my very early life, on through each year of my life, right up to the present.

It was really strange where it started, too, when I was a little girl, playing down by the creek in our neighborhood, and there were other scenes from about that time—experiences I had had with my sister, and things about neighborhood people, and actual places I had been. And then I was in kindergarten, and I remembered the time when I had this one toy I really liked, and I broke it and I cried for a long time. This was a really traumatic experience for me. The images continued on through my life and I remembered when I was in Girl Scouts and went camping, and remembered many things about all the years of grammar school. Then, when I was in junior high school, it was a real big honor to be chosen for the scholastic achievement society, and I remembered when I was chosen. So, I went on through junior high, and then senior high school, and graduation, and up through my first few years of college, up to where I was then.

The things that flashed back came in the order of my life, and they were so vivid. The scenes were just like you walked outside and saw them, completely three-dimensional, and in color. And they moved. For instance, when I saw myself breaking the toy, I could see all the movements. It wasn't like I was watching it all from my perspective at the time. It was like the little girl I saw was somebody else, in a movie, one little girl among all the other children out there playing on the playground. Yet, it was me. I saw myself doing these things, as a child, and they were the exact same things I had done, because I remember them.

Now, I didn't actually see the light as I was going through the flashbacks. He disappeared as soon as he asked me what I had done, and the flashbacks started, and yet I knew that he was there with me the whole time, that he carried me back through the flashbacks, because I felt his presence, and because he made comments here and there. He was trying to show me something in each one of these flashbacks. It's not like he was trying to see what I had done—he knew already—but he was picking out these certain flashbacks of my life and putting them in front of me so that I would have to recall them.

All through this, he kept stressing the importance of love. The places where he showed it best involved my sister; I have always been very close to her. He showed me some instances where I had been selfish to my sister, but then just as many times where I had really shown love to her and had shared with her. He pointed out to me that I should try to do things for other people, to try my best. There wasn't any accusation in any of this, though. When he came across times when I had been selfish, his attitude was only that I had been learning from them, too.

He seemed very interested in things concerning knowledge, too. He kept on pointing out things that had to do with learning, and he did say I was going to continue learning, and he said that even when he comes back for me (because by this time he had told me that I was going back) that there will always be a quest for knowledge. He said that it is a continuous process, so I got the feeling that it goes on after death. I think that he was trying to teach me, as we went through those flashbacks.[45]

19. Apparently, the **last judgement** does indeed exist, but not as it has been described to us for centuries. According to experiencers, the being of light helped them to understand their actions—both the good, and especially the bad ones—and to realize the impact of their actions on others. The judgment did not come from the being of light, but from the experiencer himself. Following are two accounts from Kenneth Ring's *Heading Toward Omega* that will serve to illustrate this point:

You are shown your life—and you do the judging.... You are judging yourself. You have been forgiven all your sins, but are you able to forgive yourself for not doing the things you should have done and some little cheaty things that maybe you've done in life? Can you forgive yourself? This is the judgement.[46]

[In that experience] I sensed something so strongly that I just came back knowing there was a God. And it wasn't God like I had ever pictured God. When I was a little girl, I held strongly to the old-man-with-a-beard concept.... I saw nobody ... yet I would stake everything I have and wish that I could prove that there was something with me that was just wonderful. It was an all-encompassing energy. Even if everything I saw would have made me out to be evil, it would have been OK. Whatever this was that was with me just loved me the way I was.[47]

20. We now turn our attention to **the sense of sight**. Experiencers see their bodies from an external vantage point, usually at some distance above the physical body. An experiencer whose account appears in Raymond Moody's *Life after Life* informs us:

It was about two years ago, and I had just turned nineteen. I was driving a friend of mine home in my car, and as I got to this particular intersection downtown, I stopped and looked both ways, but I didn't see a thing coming. I pulled on out into the intersection and as I did I heard my friend yell at the top of his voice. When I looked I saw a blinding light, the headlights of a car that was speeding towards us. I heard this awful sound—the side of the car being crushed in—and there was just an instant during which I seemed to be going through a darkness, an enclosed space. It was very quick. Then, I was sort of floating about five feet above the street, about five yards away from the car, I'd say, and I heard the echo of the crash dying away. I saw people come running up and crowding around the car, and I saw my friend get out of the car, obviously in shock. I could see my own body in the wreckage among all those people, and could see them trying to get it out. My legs were all twisted and there was blood all over the place.[48]

Some experiencers report having had considerably more powerful vision than normal during their NDE. Here are three accounts from Raymond Moody's *Life after Life*:

I just can't understand how I could see so far.[49]

It seemed as if this spiritual sense had no limitations, as if I could look anywhere and everywhere.[50]

There was a lot of action going on, and people running around the ambulance. And whenever I would look at a person to wonder what they were thinking, it was like a zoom-up, exactly like through a zoom lens, and I was there. But it seemed that part of me—I'll call it my mind—was still where I had been, several yards away from my body. When I wanted to see someone at a distance, it seemed like part of me, kind of like a tracer, would go to that person. And it seemed to me at the time that if something happened anyplace in the world that I could just be there.[51]

Cases in which blind persons, or those with poor eyesight, have been able to see during their NDE seem to indicate that vision is not retained in the form of sensory perception, but is accomplished in some other way, at some other level. An account from Kenneth Ring's *Heading Toward Omega* will illustrate this point:

> I'm very nearsighted, too, by the way, which was another one of the startling things that happened when I left my body. I see at fifteen feet what most people see at four hundred.... They were hooking me up to a machine that was behind my head. And my very first thought was, "Jesus, I can see! I can't believe it, I can see!" I could read the numbers on the machine behind my head and I was just so thrilled. And I thought, "They gave me back my glasses."[52]

21. As regards **the sense of hearing**, experiencers seem to read the thoughts of others rather than actually hear sounds. There are two types of accounts that relate to this point. The first concerns the subject who hears **living persons** during the NDE. Such subjects often "hear" the thoughts of others before they are put into words. Incidentally, there have been many reports of experiencers who hear a member of the medical staff pronounce them dead. When they attempt to communicate with those around them, they find it impossible to make themselves understood. This is how one woman explained it to Raymond Moody in *Life after Life*:

> ... I heard the radiologist who was working on me go over to the telephone, and I heard very clearly as he dialed it. I heard him say, "Dr. James, I've killed your patient, Mrs. Martin." And I knew I wasn't dead. I tried to move or to let them know, but I couldn't. When they were trying to resuscitate me, I could hear them telling how many cc's of something to give me, but I didn't feel the needles going in. I felt nothing at all when they touched me.[53]

The second type of account having to do with **hearing** concerns communication, this time mutual, between the experiencer and **deceased persons or** between the experiencer and **the being of light**. This transmission of thoughts takes place without words, from consciousness to consciousness, as if telepathically, without going through the usual sensory channels. Understanding is apparently instantaneous, with there being no possibility of misunderstanding. Here are two accounts that appear in Kenneth Ring's *Heading Toward Omega*:

> I was asked if I was ready to stay. [Who asked you?] This light. [Was there a sense of a presence associated with this light?] Oh, yes. In fact, I should say that when I communicated … with the light, there wasn't a transfer of words. I mean, no words were spoken. It's like thinking a thought and having them know it and answer it immediately. I mean, it's transference of thought. It was instantaneous.[54]

22. One cannot use one's **sense of touch** during the NDE. Experiencers tell of trying to grab someone's arm, often to prevent them from continuing to work on their body, but they meet with no resistance and pass right through people and objects. Here is what two individuals interviewed by Raymond Moody in *Life after Life* have to say in this regard:

> The doctors and nurses were pounding on my body to try to get IVs started and to get me back, and I kept trying to tell them, "Leave me alone. All I want is to be left alone. Quit pounding on me." But they didn't hear me. So I tried to move their hands to keep them from beating on my body, but nothing would happen. I couldn't get anywhere. It was like—I don't really know what happened, but I couldn't move their hands. It looked like I was touching their hands and I tried to move them—yet when I would give it the stroke, their hands were still there. I don't know whether my hand was going through it, around it, or what. I didn't feel any pressure against their hands when I was trying to move them.[55]
> People were walking up from all directions to get to

the wreck. I could see them, and I was in the middle of a very narrow walkway. Anyway, as they came by they wouldn't seem to notice me. They would just keep walking with their eyes straight ahead. As they came real close, I would try to turn around, to get out of their way, but they would just walk *through* me.[56]

23. The other two senses—those of *smell and taste*—seem to play no role during the NDE. I know of no account that makes reference to these senses. We might note, in passing, that these are the only two senses that respond to chemical, molecular messages.

24. Experiencers often report seeing **a limit or boundary**, symbolized in various ways, which, if crossed, would make returning to the physical body impossible. The following two accounts cited by Raymond Moody provide an illustration of this:

> There was light—beautiful, uplifting light—all around me. I looked ahead of me, across a field, and I saw a fence. I started moving towards the fence, and I saw a man on the other side of it, moving towards it as if to meet me. I wanted to reach him, but I felt myself being drawn back, irresistibly. As I did, I saw him, too, turn around and go back in the other direction, away from the fence.[57]

> I had a heart attack, and I found myself in a black void, and I knew I had left my physical body behind. I knew I was dying, and I thought, "God, I did the best I knew how at the time I did it. Please help me." Immediately, I was moved out of that blackness, through a pale gray, and I just went on, gliding and moving swiftly, and in front of me, in the distance, I could see a gray mist, and I was rushing toward it. It seemed that I just couldn't get to it fast enough to satisfy me, and as I got closer to it I could see through it. Beyond the mist, I could see people, and their forms were just like they are on the earth, and I could also see something which one could take to be buildings. The whole thing was permeated with the most gorgeous light—a

living, golden yellow glow, a pale color, not like the harsh gold color we know on earth.

As I approached more closely, I felt certain that I was going through that mist. It was such a wonderful, joyous feeling; there are just no words in human language to describe it. Yet, it wasn't my time to go through the mist, because instantly on the other side appeared my Uncle Carl, who had died many years earlier. He blocked my path, saying, "Go back. Your work on earth has not been completed. Go back now." I didn't want to go back, but I had no choice, and immediately I was back in my body. I felt that horrible pain in my chest, and I heard my little boy crying, "God, bring my mommy back to me."[58]

25. The **return to life** may be imposed, requested, or left up to the initiative of the experiencer. There seem to be more imposed returns than requested ones.

The only apparent reason for an **imposed return** to life is that the subject has some unfinished business to attend to, such as a task to be accomplished, or a problem to be resolved. Let us listen to an account taken from *Transformed by the Light* by Morse and Perry:

In the midst of all this hospital chaos, I just zoomed out of my body and into a tunnel. I was walking down a tunnel with the most beautiful light at the end that was enveloping and warm. I could feel myself being surrounded by the most loving arms and my cheek could feel the warmth of a being against whose chest I seemed to be leaning. There were people in the distance and I wanted to go greet them. A man's voice, very warm and caring, held me back from going to the people. The voice seemed to be coming from whoever or whatever was holding me in that wonderful loving warmth. The voice said, "Suzanne, turn around." I turned around and I saw my children standing in midair. Then the voice said: "Go back and be a good mother."[59]

Experiencers accept a return to life that is imposed by the being of light more easily if they understand the reason behind it, as described by an experiencer who had a childhood NDE in this account taken from Morse and Perry's *Transformed by the Light*:

> When I was sixteen, I had a near-death experience while undergoing surgery.... All of a sudden I was traveling somewhere and then I was with a Being that radiated unmeasurable love. I felt comfortable and very glad to be with him. I thought about my young life and all the physical problems I'd had and said: "I'm glad to be done with that one." He didn't agree. "You didn't do much," he said patiently. Immediately I was filled with a sense of having a mission that was left undone. I said: "Oh you're right, maybe I should go back." And like that I was back in my body, full of pain. I felt so heavy and restricted inside a body. I was full of anger. I said, "Maybe I should go back." I didn't say I wanted to go back. I calmed down quickly. Since then I have always had a sense of a mission unfulfilled. I feel I am supposed to be doing something for mankind. I became a nurse but have not gotten over that feeling that I have yet to discover exactly what it is I am supposed to do.[60]

A **requested return to life** on the part of experiencers often springs from a desire to take care of loved ones who are dependent upon them, particularly children. One of Kenneth Ring's experiencers in *Heading Toward Omega* says:

> There was nothing but love.... It just seemed like the real thing, just to feel this sense of total love in every direction.
>
> [Later] I did feel, because of my children and the woman I was married to then, the urge to return ... but I don't recall the trip back.[61]

A woman quoted in Morse and Perry's work had this to say:

> It was a wonderful experience, but I suddenly had the feeling that I was leaving this world, that I was going to die. I didn't want to go! I had two children and I didn't know what would happen to them if I wasn't around. As though he could read my mind, the man with me laughed

and said: "You aren't dying. You still have not done what you are supposed to do." Something drew me back the way we had come. Then I regained consciousness.[62]

It may also happen that **experiencers are undecided** about whether to stay or to return to life, as described by one of Kenneth Ring's experiencers in *Heading Toward Omega*:

> And I was asked if I was ready to stay. And I didn't know. I really didn't know. And I was told that I would have to go and make up my mind. I'd have to go make a decision ... [Later] before making that decision ... I had the life review.[63]

In some cases, experiencers are **free to choose** whether to stay or to return to life, as described by an experiencer whose account appears in Morse and Perry's *Transformed by the Light*:

> ... I do recall the sense of having an option as to whether I wanted to go back or not. Somehow I do recall choosing to go back and re-enter my body.[64]

However, experiencers seem to have a free choice only if their business on earth has, for the most part, been completed. Here is how another experiencer describes it in Morse and Perry's work:

> I communicated with my grandparents but I didn't talk. I don't even remember thinking. But I was right there with them as they spoke. What did they say? They said I had solved most of my problems and could now go either way. That meant I could either stay with them in the light or go back to my body. It was up to me and it wasn't absolutely necessary to stay with them.[65]

26. Experiencers rarely describe the way in which they **reenter the physical body**. They usually say things like, "Suddenly, I was back in my body," without giving any further details. One experiencer who was inter-

viewed by Morse and Perry describes this last stage of the NDE more clearly:

> The next thing I knew, my life was flashing in front of my eyes, everything that I had ever done in my life. After that, I felt myself falling back down the tunnel, faster and faster until I was back in my body.[66]

27. *Difficulty returning to life* is another typical characteristic of the NDE. Although experiencers obediently accept the return to life (often imposed upon them against their will), they do so with a longing for that state of grace they enjoyed during the NDE. Once they have regained consciousness, there is no question of refusing the return to life, and they dedicate themselves to using the extra time they have been granted in the most generous way possible, usually in the service of others. Nevertheless, acceptance of the return to life may sometimes be preceded by a temporary, but violent period of revolt, such as the one described by an experiencer in Kenneth Ring's *Heading Toward Omega*:

> … and I realized that I was back in this *body*, this physical form. And all the pain was there again…. [How did you feel when you came back?] Ah, angry! Angry, angry, angry. [For how long?] Oh, for a good year. First of all, at having to come back—that I saw such a *beautiful, beautiful* place and, once again, I have no word to describe the beauty in the forms, in the peace, in the love, in the languages, in the music, in this being, in the wall, in everything. And the speed, the movement at will, without the limitations of this body! And to gain that kind of knowledge and then—It's like taking a backward step, you know? To have to come back to these limitations.[67]

A survivor whose account appears in Morse and Perry's *Transformed by the Light* describes a similar revolt:

> Suddenly I felt like I was being pulled down and thrown back into my body. I was angry. I don't think I have ever

before felt such a rage! I screamed and screamed in anger and rage because I wanted to go back to that place with the clouds![68]

28. Another characteristic of the NDE is its *ineffability*. Experiencers claim that they cannot find the words to express what they have witnessed, and that no one can fully understand them. In the words of one experiencer, "I have been where no one has ever been." Indeed, how can you share an experience with others when you think you're the only one who has ever had it? Everything points to the hypothesis that earthly space–time does not exist in the dimension where NDEs occur. It is very important that the consequences of this be taken into account. Experiencers really cannot use the same language we do, since our languages are based exclusively on concepts rooted in our three-dimensional space–time. This feeling of ineffability may create a feeling of loneliness for the experiencer. Below are the comments of two respondents whose accounts appear in Moody's *Life after Life*:

> Now, there is a real problem for me as I'm trying to tell you this, because all the words I know are three-dimensional. As I was going through this, I kept thinking, "Well, when I was taking geometry, they always told me there were only three dimensions, and I always just accepted that. But they were wrong. There are more." And, of course, our world— the one we're living in now—*is* three-dimensional, but the next one definitely isn't. And that's why it's so hard to tell you this. I have to describe it to you in words that are three-dimensional. That's as close as I can get to it, but it's not really adequate. I can't really give you a complete picture.[69]

> My experience, all the things that I was going through, were so beautiful, but just indescribable. I wanted others to be there with me to see it, too, and I had the feeling that I would never be able to describe to anyone what I was seeing. I had the feeling of being lonesome because I

wanted somebody to be there to experience it with me. But I knew nobody else could be there. I felt that I was in a private world at that time. I really felt a fit of depression then.[70]

The following account (*Heading Toward Omega*), talks about the difficulty of explaining the encounter with the being of light:

I had the warmth and love toward this person so intense, total trust, not like a love I've had for anything or anybody. It is so hard to describe 'cause it's hard to realize a total surrendering-type love, a total love that kind of immerses you. The kind that no matter what he would have told me, I'd have done.[71]

29. *Prophetic or precognitive NDEs* are intriguing because they call into question our usual concepts of space and time. Here again, quantum physics has some interesting theories to propose, particularly the one concerning a dimension in which there seems to be simultaneousness of all events, whether these be past, present, or future (see interview with Régis and Brigitte Dutheil, pp. 214–215, 224–225). During the life review, experiencers are sometimes able to see future events, as in this account, recorded by Kenneth Ring in *Heading Toward Omega* of a childhood NDE in which the individual had a vision of his own future:

1. *You will be married at age twenty-eight.*

This was the first of the "memories," and this was perceived as a flat statement—there was no emotion attached to it.... And this did indeed happen, even though at [my] twenty-eighth birthday I had yet to meet the person that I was to marry.

2. *You will have two children and live in the house that you see.*

By contrast to the prediction, this was felt; perhaps "experienced" is the correct term. I had a vivid memory of sitting in a chair, from which I could see two children playing on the floor in front of me. And I knew that I was married, although in this vision there was no indication of who it was that I was married to. Now, a married person knows what it was like to be single, because he or she was once single, and he or she knows what it's like to be married because he or she is married. But it is not possible for a single person to know what it feels like to be married; in particular, it is *not possible* for a ten-year-old boy to know what it feels like to be married! It is this strange, impossible feeling that I remember so clearly and why this incident remained in my mind. I had a "memory" of something that was not to happen for almost twenty-five years hence! But it was not seeing the future in the conventional sense, it was *experiencing* the future. In this incident the future was now.[72]

Morse and Perry also relate an account on this subject in *Transformed by the Light*:

My wife and I had been told that she couldn't have any more children. But then, in June 1959, I was involved in a serious pit accident at a coal mine. I was taken to the hospital and found to be dead on arrival. But somehow I was revived and remained in a coma for a week. While unconscious I had a vision of walking along the sun's rays and seeing a hand with a long white sleeve reaching down. I was almost touching the hand when I felt myself being pulled back, and I heard a voice say: "Don't worry. You are going to be all right and your son will be all right." A few months later we learned my wife was pregnant and our son was born almost a year to the day after my accident.[73]

30. Many experiencers develop *psychic abilities* following their NDE. These newly-acquired abilities include telepathy and prophetic or precognitive visions, as well as the ability to see at a distance, read the thoughts of others, diagnose illnesses, and even heal them. There are frequent reports of experiencers who see apparitions of loved ones at the precise moment of the latter's death. The following account, as told to Kenneth Ring in *Heading Toward Omega*, provides an illustration:

Latter part of July 1980—[A] friend with leukemia came to me in a sort of vision. I could see me with him. He said, "Come, my friend, walk with me." And we walked through a beautiful forest and came upon a ridge that looked into the most beautiful valley I've ever thought about seeing. It sort of glowed and sparkled. He said, "This is as far as you can go," and he walked off into this valley and I felt immensely peaceful. It still brings tears to my eyes; I will never forget it. The next day his daughter-in-law called and told me he had died the night before.[74]

Experiencers are often able to predict an accident or the death of a loved one. These premonitions frequently manifest themselves in dreams. In the words of a child who was interviewed by Morse and Perry in *Transformed by the Light*:

On a regular basis, I dream what will happen the next day. I'll often witness conversations in my dreams that actually take place the next day, or I'll dream events that happen the next day. For instance, I dreamed that I was going to meet a guy on the street and we would spend the entire day together. The very next day this happened. This kind of experience has happened to me over a hundred times, I'm sure. I didn't used to believe these were real until I dreamed my uncle's death. He was in perfect health but on this night I dreamed that he was going to die suddenly. The next day he died of a heart attack. When my parents told me I just said, "I knew it was going to happen." Since then I've always believed my dreams.[75]

One individual, whose account appears in Kenneth Ring's *Heading Toward Omega*, has found a way to put her talents to use by serving others in her job as a hospital nurse:

I find my own NDE helpful in my work.... In my work with patients who die slowly, I am aware of when they are "in their bodies" and when they drift "out." I even use various relaxation techniques with them to help them "get out" when uncomfortable procedures such as suctioning are being done....

When I'm in the emergency room, serving as a link between a patient who had [been] "coded" and the family, I'm often in tune with the part of the patient who is "over in the corner by the ceiling" during an NDE and telepathically send a message that he or she will just have to excuse our need to try and bring them back and that I'm aware of how nice it is "out there." I also let him or her know that I'm supporting the family. Frequently, in cases where the patient lives, when I visit later in the ICU, a patient may say, "I remember talking to you in the emergency room," or, "You look familiar. Do I know you?" or, "You're the one who was with my family." Of course, during the contact to which they refer, they were completely unconscious. I find that most patients seem comfortable in sharing their NDEs with me, perhaps because in some sense they are aware that I was aware of what they were experiencing.[76]

31. *Deathbed visions* are not a new phenomenon, but rather were considered by our ancestors as normal, ordinary manifestations. Our society's anxious and repressive attitude toward death certainly does not favor a calm and encouraging attitude in listening to dying persons. Yet their last words may bring great comfort to those they leave behind, if the latter know how to interpret them. My grandfather suffered in agonizing pain at the end of a prolonged and excruciating illness. Yet, only moments before his death, his facial expression suddenly softened as if he had seen something, and in a reconciled and peaceful tone, he said, "Oh, if only I had known that before."

Those who witness deathbed visions in others are often profoundly and lastingly marked by the experience. With this in mind, let us hear the words of an elderly woman whose account is given by Morse and Perry in *Transformed by the Light*:

Oddly enough, I have been able to cope with the death of my husband of forty-four years as the result of my niece's deathbed vision. She died at the age of ten after having cancer. She was so ill that she could not lift her head from the bed. Yet just hours before she died, she suddenly sat up in bed and told her mother: "You can't go with me! The light is coming to get me but you can't go! I wish you could see it. It's so beautiful!" Shortly after that, she died.[77]

We should never forget that experiencers who lose a loved one do not experience mourning in the same way we do. In fact, their experience is quite the contrary. Kenneth Ring in *Heading Toward Omega* relates the account of a woman who had an NDE while giving birth to her second child, named Tari. During her NDE, the being of light announced to her that Tari would die the fourth day after she was born, and this news filled her with great joy:

It would have been easier, I think, to try to forget my own name, than to forget that wonderful feeling, surge of sheer joy I had felt when he took my hand, and told me he had come for *my* child. That was the greatest moment I've ever known.... Well, I soon realized that my acceptance back into this world depended upon "pretending" to forget, and "pretending" to grieve the loss of my baby. So I did this for everybody else's sake—except my husband, who believed me, and gained some comfort from it, second-hand.... I had three more children after Tari's birth. My beloved husband died in my arms at home sixteen years later. My firstborn son lived to be twenty-five and was killed in a car accident (*instantly*—no time for pain or suffering) seven years after the death of my husband. My grief was softened and shortened each time. People said, "She's in shock now, she'll grieve more later." Later they said, "She must be a very strong person to live through what she's had to live through so calmly." Neither statement was true. It feels good to tell the truth to someone. They aren't dead. They are all alive, busy and waiting for me. Our separation is only temporary and very short, compared to all of eternity.[78]

Chapter Three

Testimony of Jean-Pierre Girard, M.D.

EEV: *Sir, you are a professor of medicine, your specialization is immunology, and you have a practice in Geneva. It is somewhat ironic that the accident that triggered the experience we will be discussing is closely related to your specialization. Can you tell us what happened?*

JPG: A few years ago, I suffered a heart attack as a result of a bee sting. I had been walking barefooted in my garden on some white clover that was in bloom, which bees like very much. One bee decided to respond to my aggression and stung me. I didn't think much about it, since I had already been stung before without incident, except for once when I had a minor reaction. Nevertheless, four or five minutes after this particular bee sting, I felt a strong itch traveling up my leg and spreading throughout my entire body. It was especially pronounced on my scalp.

Late Professor of Hôpital Çantonal of Geneva.

Almost simultaneously, I began to feel slightly faint. I decided to go back inside to give myself a shot of adrenaline, which is the prescribed medicine for this type of problem. The garden is some distance from the house, so it takes a few minutes to get from one to the other. By the time I reached my office, I really was not feeling well at all. The kits did not yet exist [at the time] so I had to break open a vial, fill up a syringe, and so on. Just as I began doing this, I was forced to drop everything as I was overcome by a wave of nausea and a strong need to vomit. I went to the bathroom next door and that's when I collapsed and lost consciousness. In the meantime, my wife had come home. She found me lying on the floor, but didn't know how long I had been there, so she went to fetch the town doctor, who lives close by. When the doctor arrived, he administered the necessary treatment and I came out of the coma perhaps twenty or thirty minutes later, though it's difficult to say exactly how long it was. To get back to the main point of our discussion, after I lost consciousness, I had a very powerful sensation of something pleasurable. It's difficult to describe, since our ordinary senses don't function in these cases—it was like floating in a sort of very white, very brilliant atmosphere. I also felt as though I was immaterial, and thus extremely light. This atmosphere of brilliance and lightness lasted for a period, which I recall as being extremely long. During this period, some things came to mind concerning my life, though afterwards I was not able to remember exactly what I had experienced. But I have a very clear recollection of having experienced episodes of my life, of having reexperienced situations in my life that I didn't really have any valid reason for experiencing again at that particular moment. Then, following the treatment I was given, I gradually resurfaced, and came out of this brilliant, luminous, and extremely light and peaceful atmosphere. I pulled myself up and found myself sitting on the ground against the tub in the bathroom, surrounded by the doctor and my wife, and the first thing I said was, "How simple it is to die!"

EEV: *You are familiar with the typical progression of an NDE. Did you go through what is known as the tunnel, or did you have an out-of-body experience?*

JPG: I did not at all have the impression of going through a tunnel. My first impression was one of being immersed in a very brilliant, very bright, luminous atmosphere, and I felt like I was floating. But I don't have any recollection of seeing myself lying on the bathroom floor.

EEV: *Did you hear any noise?*

JPG: I did indeed hear a noise that sounded like water running ... more like something resembling a waterfall.

EEV: *Did you come into contact with deceased persons or did you encounter the "being of light"?*

JPG: I had no contact with anyone.

EEV: *... nor telepathic communication with someone who was in the same sphere as you?*

JPG: There's just one thing that has stayed with me; it's related to the episode in which I reexperienced aspects of my life. I saw my mother again very clearly. It's the only concrete recollection that I have.

EEV: *... your mother who is deceased?*

JPG: Yes, she is deceased. I am convinced it was her.

EEV: *Did you have telepathic communication with her?*

JPG: Yes, probably so.

EEV: *How did you feel right after you regained consciousness?*

JPG: I had the most extraordinarily peaceful feeling. I had experienced something I considered at the time to be a sort of brief death that seemed to be extremely harmonious and happy. As I mentioned previously, my first words were, "How simple it is to die." In fact, the feeling that overtook me completely was: it's so simple, it's so easy, there's no problem.

EEV: *During one of our previous discussions, you told me that you were not very happy to have been brought back to life?*

JPG: In fact, I wasn't too sure why this experience came to an end so quickly.

EEV: *You were not too happy about this?*

JPG: … no, not too happy.

EEV: *Did you feel like talking about this experience to your family or friends?*

JPG: No, I didn't talk to them about it very much.

EEV: *Is it really possible to convey an NDE with words?*

JPG: No, I don't think so. The feelings and impressions are difficult to convey. It's likely that the sensory dimension is practically nonexistent at that moment. It is a message that is most likely conveyed through other means. The idea of describing it with words has always seemed to be very inadequate to me.

EEV: *I suppose that in your capacity as a physician, you had already been confronted with death before you had your NDE. Had you formulated any specific ideas about death?*

JPG: I had a spiritual concept of life and the afterlife that corresponds to who I am and to my needs, but I didn't have a very precise, determined concept of dying.

EEV: *Among your patients, is there anyone who has had an NDE and spoken to you about it?*

JPG: Yes, a very long time ago, when I was a young doctor. There was a young woman who was suffering from leukemia, and who had fallen into a coma for several hours during an acute episode. When she regained consciousness, she told me that she had experienced some wonderful moments, and that she was not at all happy to have regained consciousness, especially given the pain and suffering she would have to endure once more. At the time, I didn't really think about how to interpret that. I simply thought how nice it was that she had experienced it that way, nothing more.

EEV: *Before having this experience, had you read any books on the subject of NDEs, by Moody or Ring, for example?*

JPG: No, I read them after my NDE.

EEV: *How did you integrate this event into your concept of life?*

JPG: In my case, it was the catalyst for a very distinct improvement. I think there is a before and an after. I live now knowing that I am mortal and that I will die one day. I don't know when, but I don't have any apprehension or fear. I have seen a definite change in myself since this experience. In my case, it's very clear.

EEV: *Do you consider this experience to be important?*

JPG: Absolutely.

EEV: *Has your NDE had an impact on your way of living?*

JPG: Undoubtedly, in the sense that it removed my anxiety about the finality of existence, which had been part of my being and thinking. Whether we like it or not, we all have this anxiety, but it has definitely disappeared in my case. Any event or experience that eliminates a major source of anxiety cannot fail to have an effect on one's way of being and living.

EEV: *Do you view your role on earth differently since your NDE?*

JPG: I've always had the idea that I have a very specific role, but my NDE has altered and shaped this idea into a belief that I belong to a set of cosmic forces, a coherent whole, which was not at all evident to me before.

EEV: *Do you think you have been transformed by this experience?*

JPG: I consider it to have been very important.

EEV: *What were your religious convictions before your NDE?*

JPG: My Christian upbringing has left a definite mark on me; I have always seen it as representing what is essential, from the religious perspective. I never was a fervent churchgoer, but I think I have indeed developed a more distinct mystical approach since this experience.

EEV: *Has your NDE changed your relationship to church? Do you now consider it to be more like an intermediary?*

JPG: I wouldn't want to be presumptuous. I believe church is indeed essential and important, perhaps more so for some than for others. I think that one can also have a different, personal idea of what church is, one that differs from the building with a bell, clock tower, and sermon going on inside. I have a different idea of church: When I'm in nature, surrounded by beauty, I'm in a church. In fact, there is a sort of wider participation implied in the notion of the universe as man's church, or temple.

EEV: *In your opinion, do you think NDEs prove that there is an existence after death?*

JPG: This experience gave me the clear impression that death is not simply a total rupture and then nothing. As for what comes next, I think that is somewhat of an act of faith. Personally, I am convinced that certain forms of energy, emanating from man, live on after death, joining up with cosmic energy in some way or another. It's rather simplistic, but we don't really know much more about it than that. But I'm still certain that there is something like this, without being able to put it more concretely than that.

EEV: *Could we qualify it as "consciousness"?*

JPG: Perhaps ... yes, perhaps.

EEV: *If you were face-to-face with someone who knew he or she was going to die, what would you say to him or her?*

JPG: Actually, I've already been confronted with this situation. I would explain my personal experience and my belief that death is a transition from one state to another, since, in fact, there is no void. This is probably a very beneficial state for the human soul. I think that the energy system survives human beings to the extent that they accept death and know that they are part of a global system in which life and death are equally important, even identical. I would very simply explain my point of view on this subject to the person in such a way as to counteract, as much as possible, any fears he or she might have.

EEV: *How do you react now when someone informs you of the death of someone you know?*

JPG: The death of a close friend or relative is very difficult, in any situation. You feel their absence, someone you care about is taken away, you are robbed of an emotional asset. Yet having said this, I would then say that we perhaps tend to make too much of a fuss about death. Death is necessary, it must come—it can come more or less quickly, of course, but I think we fear it too much in our civilizations. We are afraid of it, and this fear results from the attitude of those who think that death is the end of everything. This, in turn, makes one's life seem all the more valuable, since there is an end to earthly existence. I think this is an erroneous attitude.

EEV: *Could we say that death is only sad for those who remain behind, not for those who die?*

JPG: Undoubtedly, for those who die, death can be—on the contrary—a release and a joy. For those of us who stay behind, it's normal to be sad when someone we love passes away. But, what doesn't seem normal to me is that this sadness should throw certain persons into the depths of despair, sometimes lasting an infinite amount of time. That doesn't seem right to me.

EEV: *If these persons knew that something happens after death, they would be sad, but they wouldn't wallow in despair?*

JPG: No, they probably wouldn't be at all as affected by it.

EEV: *Do you see the fact of having had an NDE as a privilege?*

JPG: I don't know if I have the right to consider myself privileged, but I do think I was fortunate to have had the experience.

EEV: *Do you consider the NDE to be important for humanity?*

JPG: I think that there is perhaps a certain determinism in it. If we look at esotericism throughout the history of man, death was never considered to be a misfortune, or an end in itself. On the contrary, the purpose of life for those who were spiritual, those who lived their lives in the belief of an afterlife, was to prepare oneself as best one could for that moment. There was no fear—man possessed within himself everything he needed in order to confront death in a perfectly appropriate manner, and to secure for himself, so to speak, a decent afterlife. Along with the decline in spirituality in our very materialistic society, which ultimately rejects everything that isn't visible and demonstrable, there has been a considerable increase in the fear of death in terms of an unexplained phenomenon. Man, or at least many men, are now completely detached from their genuine heavenly roots, if I dare say. I think this fear of death may be reduced by learning about the NDEs of those who have experienced them.

EEV: *How do you reconcile your tendency to reason as a scientist with the "otherworldly" aspect of the NDE?*

JPG: I don't think there is any incompatibility. The scientist's attitude should be extremely modest with respect to the marvel of creation, to all of the worlds that surround us, which we do not admire enough and do not revere sufficiently. What we know of science boils down to some facts, which are ultimately quite down-to-earth and practical. No, I don't think there is any incompatibility.

EEV: *What do you think about the fact that the psychic abilities of those who have had an NDE seem to increase considerably following this experience?*

JPG: Could it be that being at peace with one's afterlife, with the fear of death, allows people to retrieve behaviors from their unconscious that are usually blocked? I don't know, I can't really provide any explanation.

EEV: *Have you noticed this same phenomenon in yourself?*

JPG: In all modesty, what I can say is that I feel much more at peace with myself and with others, and that, in fact, life does seem to be different in that particular sense. If you want to introduce the word *psychic* into the discussion, then I would have to say "no."

EEV: *You haven't noticed any psychic abilities that you didn't have before?*

JPG: ... nothing that was absolutely clear, concrete, indisputable, and demonstrable.

EEV: *As a physician, you are familiar with hallucinations. Are NDEs hallucinations?*

JPG: I am convinced that this is not the case. Hallucinations imply a somewhat exaggerated, biased sensory functioning, but one that is nevertheless present.

EEV: *Do you think NDEs can be caused by a lack of oxygen in the blood or by a physiological disturbance at the time of death?*

JPG: I think that the existence of supraterrestrial energy does not depend upon oxygen in the blood!

EEV: *Could NDEs originate from the depths of the psyche, as a final defense mechanism against the threat of imminent death?*

JPG: I don't understand too well how they could be a defense mechanism.

EEV: *I asked you this because I just read the description of a negative NDE. A cardiologist named Rawlings tells about a man whose heart had stopped several times during a heart attack, and who lost consciousness several times during the resuscitation procedure. Each time he came back, the man claimed to have gone to hell, and to have had the most frightful, unbearable experiences, and he begged the doctor not to let him go back there. The doctor was very impressed since the man seemed to be genuinely terrified, as if he had seen the most frightening things. The doctor, who managed to save him, went to see the patient a few days later in his hospital room. He began speaking very cautiously about what had happened and was astonished to find that the man did not remember anything frightening. Much to the contrary, he had a few vague recollections of a rather positive, pleasant experience. We know that terrifying events can be buried in the unconscious and will not come into conscious awareness, for they pose too great a risk to the conscious mind. It was along these lines that I asked you this question.*

JPG: I don't have a very firm opinion on this subject. In my experience, the dominant impression is one of extraordinary serenity and peacefulness, of total peace. That's not something one experiences every day, is it?

EEV: *Do you think that our personality continues to exist after death, that it is not just an abstract, depersonalized cosmic energy?*

JPG: I think that there is some sort of personal guidance. Here again, if we look at Buddhist or Hindu esotericism, there are different levels, and I think that these levels exist, whether we like it or not.

EEV: *... levels of inner knowledge?*

JPG: Yes, of inner knowledge, in our thrust toward the absolute, toward the eternal.

EEV: *... of spiritual development?*

JPG: Yes, that's it. It is not at all out of the question for NDEs to be experienced differently depending upon one's level of knowledge or spiritual development. From my perspective, this would seem to be quite simple and natural.

Chapter Four

Testimony of Henry H.

EEV: *Please tell us who you are and what your experience has been.*

HH: My name is Henry H., and I'm thirty-seven years old. As for my educational background, I've studied psychology as a major and business as a minor in various universities. My interests have been in child development, and drug and alcohol counseling—I wanted to work with young people. From 1972 to 1975 I served in the U.S. Army. When I was eighteen, I had to return home because I received news that my only brother, who was one year younger than me, had died—he had committed suicide. This was the first time I had ever been confronted with the death of someone close to me. I was already into drugs at that time. The day of my brother's burial, his friends and I went to the grave site to talk to him. I even put some marijuana joints in the suit he was wearing in the casket, because I thought he might like to smoke some joints wherever he was going. As far as my near-death experience is concerned, it occurred on July 17, 1991. At the time, I was going through a divorce with my second wife, and I don't do divorces very well—I have a tendency to punish myself. This time I had slipped back into drugs. I've had a history of on-and-off drug use over the past twenty years since I was in the military. When I had the experience, I was alone in my apartment in downtown San José. That day I had taken both heroin and cocaine, like I had been doing for some time. I had never overdosed before in my life. It was about six o'clock in the evening when I got home, and I had gone into the bathroom. That's usually where I would mix my stuff. I was an IV drug-user. I had just talked to Caroline, my ex-wife and I felt bad. I don't know what happened. I had just purchased a quantity of heroin and a quantity of cocaine and was putting them in the spoon. I guess I must have accidentally dropped too much in the spoon because about ten seconds after I shot up, I knew I had done too much. I started to go into convulsions. From what I understand, doing too much cocaine actually gets your heart off rhythm and it just stops beating. Cocaine is a very powerful drug and it can stop your heart. That's what happened.

EEV: *You had a heart attack?*

HH: I don't know if that's the correct medical term or not. I didn't feel any of the symptoms, like pain going to the left side. I think it's more like your heart just stops at a given point. I remember I couldn't stand up anymore, and that's when I collapsed onto the floor. I hallucinated at this point, and I thought I saw six people coming into my apartment. At the time, it seemed very, very real.

EEV: *Who were these people?*

HH: They were either friends or neighbors of mine who knew that I was using drugs and didn't want to have a drug addict living in their complex. Now that I think about it, I believe they represented those who had loved me and worried about me all throughout my habit, and just couldn't bear to see the pain and suffering I was putting not only them through, but also myself. They came into my bathroom and physically started to beat me to a bloody pulp. I remember hearing the voices of these people making comments and laughing—something to the effect that they were just going to kill another dope addict, that they were going to teach me a lesson, that I had had every chance in twenty years to quit using this stuff and here I was still using it. When I was lying on the floor, I physically felt the blows coming to my face. After what seemed to be about ten minutes, but I'm sure it was only a minute or two, I remember lying on the ground and telling myself that I was going to pretend to be dead, because I thought that if I pretended to be dead they would quit beating me up. I was willing my heart to stop and was trying to stop breathing so they would think I was dead. I went through this three different times, and each time I would go through this process of wanting to just lay there dead so they'd quit beating me. At this point, I would see in my mind that there was a door. There was the light, which I interpreted as being God, and a very distinct voice. I could see myself lying on the floor, and at the same time I was walking up to the door.

EEV: *Was it a real or a symbolic door?*

HH: It was a symbolic door, representing death on the other side. I had the impression that I was out of my physical body, which still lay on the floor, and that my spirit was going toward the door to escape this life. I would go to open this door and this voice, which was the light, would tell me, "Henry, I'm not going to let you go through with this. You have a purpose on earth. I won't let you go through that door." When I attempted to go through the door three times, it was still me who was controlling things, the fact that I wanted this to stop. When the light, which I knew was God, said the third time, "No, you have a purpose here on earth, you cannot enter through this door yet," it was at that point that I said, "Okay, God, I'll do it Your way. You cease this pain I'm experiencing right now and I'll do it Your way." So after the third time of trying to do it my way, that's when I said, "Okay, just let me do it Your way." And today, one year later and ninety-five days of being clean and sober, what makes this so different from any recovery program I've been through is that I'm 100 percent committed to being open to doing it my higher power's way. Everything in my life right now is His way, and I really feel sincerely that it was this experience that I had a year ago that really validates my program of doing it His way, totally. And it works this way for me today. And then I came back, and the beating started up again.

EEV: *Was that the beating of your heart?*

HH: No. I tried to figure this whole thing out, and I think that while I was lying on the floor in convulsions, I was throwing my head back and was hitting it either on the edge of the tub or on the wall of my bathroom.

EEV: *Was this overdose a suicide attempt?*

HH: No, it was not. I knew the dealer, I knew he had good stuff. The "bag" I purchased that day must have been the second one, because I had already used some that morning. That day I had purchased what I normally purchased every day, which was $100 worth of heroin and $100 worth of cocaine. I remember my dealer telling me that day to be careful, because this stuff was pure. My grandmother had died in January of the previous year and had left me an inheritance, of which I had spent approximately $50,000 on drugs over the past five months.

EEV: *Tell me more about this voice. Was it a female or a male voice?*

HH: It was a male voice.

EEV: *And you saw a light?*

HH: I saw the light, yes, but I didn't see any form or anything. But the voice and the light and the power would not let me go past the door. This happened three times.

EEV: *When you tried to go past the door?*

HH: Right.

EEV: *What do you think would have happened if you had gone past this door?*

HH: I would have died.

EEV: *What happened after that?*

HH: After the third time, I remember that that was when I started making promises to God, saying, "If You just make them stop beating me, I'll do whatever You say."

EEV: *What did He want you to do?*

HH: He didn't spell it out specifically. All He said was, "It's not your time to go, you still have a purpose in your life for My good in this world."

EEV: *Did he tell you what that purpose was?*

HH: No, but I had always had a strong belief that there was a definite plan for me, according to His will.

EEV: *But your faith didn't help you turn away from drugs before you had your NDE?*

HH: Oh no.

EEV: *It had nothing to do with it?*

HH: No. Because a drug addict like me can make promises to God all day long and the reality of it is that the next day I'll wake up and shoot up again. Do you know that this is the first time I've ever really talked about this experience? It really is.

EEV: *And why didn't you talk about this before?*

HH: I never talked about it before because I feel it's like making a commitment or a promise. In my life, making and keeping promises has now become very, very important to me. I made a strong commitment to God that night, and He fulfilled his obligation, but I had not fulfilled mine since I was still on drugs. That made me feel guilty. I was derailed from the great significance of this event by my guilt at not having lived up to the promise I made that night.

EEV: *Now let me get this straight. When you dialed the emergency number, you told the operator that six people were beating you to death. But you know that these were hallucinations due to the drugs.*

HH: I didn't know it at the time.

EEV: *But you know it now?*

HH: Yes, now I know that this part of the experience was a hallucination caused by the drugs.

EEV: *But how do you know that your encounter with God wasn't also a hallucination?*

HH: I know that the encounter I experienced with the door and the light and God was not a hallucination. When I was lying there on the floor and willing myself to be dead so the beating would stop, that was a hallucination. I firmly believe that I was dead, or close to death, when I saw the door and the light. The difference is that this encounter was peaceful and good. The light was reassuring; it did not scare me. The hallucinations were fear, pain, frustration, and just wanting to give up. The door and the light were so peaceful that all I wanted to do was go through this door. In fact, when I came back for the third time, I understood that I couldn't yet go past this door, that my hour had not yet come, and that I must go back to life. It was only then, after seeing the light and after God talked to me, that I decided to get help. Before this encounter, I would never have gone to the phone, because I wanted to die. So this was good. The feeling that I had had an encounter with God was so strong that the three officers who came with the emergency staff to my apartment never gave me a citation for being under the influence of drugs, though it was obvious to them my condition was due to an overdose. I still had something very fresh and very real from this encounter with God, and they could sense it from me. They said, "Thank your lucky stars you're alive, and we hope that what you saw will help you continue living." Which I'm doing today, but I didn't do it the very next day after this experience.

EEV: *Did you go back to using drugs after your NDE?*

HH: Oh sure, because in my mind I had beaten death. I still had money left, and I decided just to be a little bit more careful so that this wouldn't happen again.

EEV: *Then, what impact did the NDE have, if you continued doing drugs?*

HH: I can look back now and I can see that everything is done for a reason and what it would have taken for me to quit using. The near death experience—that wasn't enough, as powerful as it was at the time. I first had to hit bottom.... I'm very spiritual today, but that dawned on me only ninety-five days ago when I quit using any kind of drugs. Today, I've got ninety-five days of being absolutely drug-free and it's the first time in twenty years.

EEV: *Do you think this change was brought about by your NDE?*

HH: I'm positive of that. It took some time for me to reach bottom. My NDE allowed me to turn my life around by seeing the isolation, the loneliness, and the not having friends or family, because by this point I had pretty much broken off with all of them. I was broke; I was doing things that weren't like me. I was getting good at going to the horse races. I won $20,000 during the month of February. Then I spent $20,000 dollars in three weeks on drugs. When I finally got to April, I was in my shop about three days before I decided to quit using. I wrote down on a piece of paper, "God, if You're watching, I need help." I asked for help. I tacked it up on the wall of my shop. It's still there.... I chose to quit using drugs on Easter weekend in April. I went to church on Saturday of Easter weekend, and I was still on drugs that day when I heard one of the best sermons I had ever heard in my life about the resurrection, the Second Coming of Christ. That was a very powerful message, and that's when I decided, on my own, that I was going to quit using. My ex-wife, who was with me that day, never knew the extent of my drug use, as she always saw me feeling fine, because I was always under the influence. With heroin, once you're strung out, you can perform normally and do your duties. So she never knew to what extent I was strung out. The following Monday, after twenty-four hours, I started going into pretty bad withdrawal and I was very sick. By chance, I had spent five days last November in a detoxification center in a Veterans Administration hospital in

Palo Alto, and after five days, I split, thinking that I was well. Normally, to get into any VA program, there are so many veterans with addiction problems that they have to sort out the ones who are sincere from the ones who just need three meals and a bed. What they do is they play this trick by telling you to call back the following week. And you pretty much have to do this each week for a month to show your sincerity, because they don't have time to mess with you. My ex-wife, seeing me in withdrawal, was so scared, she didn't know what to do. She had never seen me like this. She happened to find a business card and made a phone call to the guy who admits people to the Palo Alto hospital, where I had been last November for five days before splitting. So I talked to this guy named Kevin on the telephone, and I told him that I hadn't used drugs for two days: "I don't want to use them anymore. I'm tired of using. I turned my life over to the will of God." And miraculously, Kevin told me that I could come to the hospital the following morning.

EEV: *How many months passed between your NDE and the day you quit drugs?*

HH: Let me count ... nine months. That's exactly how long a person is in the stomach of a woman!

EEV: *Tell me more about how it happened that you changed so radically.*

HH: I was in five different drug and alcohol programs over the course of twenty years, and they never worked. Maybe they worked for a day or so, but then I went back into drugs right away. You see, I wasn't doing these programs for myself. I was on methadone for six years during the time that I was in school. I thought I was doing well, getting good grades at college, and then I got married and had two kids, but I was still on methadone, which is a powerful drug, you know. This time, the whole spiritual experience of choosing not to use drugs was the most moving thing in my life. Now mind you, I still had a little bit of money. I could have gone out and bought some drugs and felt good for just a little bit longer. But I chose to quit using drugs. In the period between my NDE and the day I quit using, I was convinced that if I went out in my truck, for example, and tried to kill myself, it would never happen, because somebody would intercede and not let me do it. And just talking about this near-death experience with you makes me think that it's because of this NDE, in which God told me that I couldn't will myself to die, that He wasn't through with me, and that He still had a job for me to do.

EEV: *But you don't know what job that is?*

HH: Oh, I know what it is.

EEV: *Can you tell me about it?*

HH: My purpose in life ... I can talk, I can sell, I can manipulate. I can get what I want and I have done it for bad. I think there is a yin and a yang, a good and a bad. Well, I was very good at being very bad, because I put the talents God gave me to bad use. I've known all along that there is a Christ. I know this in my heart. I might not have been acting on it, but I've known it in my heart since I was very young. But I let pride come in, and at the time I was more the type to say things like "Look what I'm doing, look what I have."

EEV: *And you don't have this need anymore?*

HH: No, I don't have this need anymore. Now, I can talk about feelings, and I have a clear understanding of the purpose of my life and can find my balance.

EEV: *Money is not important to you anymore?*

HH: No, no, I'm sure of that. Materialistic things have never been important to me. Obviously, I mean, look at all the money I've spent on drugs. But that's the sickness and the insanity of the addiction. Like when I was talking to you earlier about having a social, a physical, and a spiritual balance. I was interested in changing my behavior and my attitude, but I can't change my character. All I can do is to try not to manipulate people any more. What's different now is that I know God has given me a sign. Let's say that life is a road and you have a sign that says right turn and a sign that says left turn. Well, I have always chosen to take that left turn onto a dead-end street. God has given me so many miracles that now I want to give back some of that to others. I enjoy going to church. I opened up last Friday night and spoke about drugs to the young adults of our church, as I am speaking with you now.

EEV: *So, you work with young people now?*

HH: Helping young people is what the calling of my life has been. Ever since my younger brother died at the age of seventeen, I have always wanted to help young people. I was very rebellious; I always questioned why. I saw the hypocrisy of the Church in the late sixties and the early seventies, I saw all the divorces happening around me. I didn't know who I was, but I wanted to fit in with what I thought was "cool." This happened to be the opposite of my religious and moral upbringing. I have always had access and was taught knowledge about my higher power from a very early age. But it was only after the NDE that I was able to tie my beliefs in to how I really felt, and how God was important to my life. It's only been since this NDE that I have been able to look for things and read the Bible and have a real idea that, yes, this is happening to me. Before it was always a kind of fantasy story, something that's out there, that's not real. After this experience, everything is very real to me, but I didn't understand this right away. It's only been after a period of sobriety and being clean that I've been tying all this together, and now I look forward to reading inspirational words in the morning and having God's word and His will accompany me throughout my day.

EEV: *So now you try to live like an honest man?*

HH: Yes. Now I have a conscience. I don't even say bad words anymore. To me, if I say those words, it discounts a whole two hours of being real. It feels bad to me to say them. If you knew my past! That's a miracle! I know that I'm choosing not to lie. I try my best. I'm working now. It's like I can see every little thing and some big things. I lost my oldest son through custody during my first divorce. A week ago, my ex-wife sent my oldest son back to California, and I will now have full custody. I'm going down this weekend to see him for the first time in two years. God knows me, and He knows what miracles I need, because I am still an addict. I've made a 180-degree turn. I'm now into good feelings, good relationships, being honest, talking, and letting the control of my life be in the hands of God. And hey, it works! I'm still the person I have always been, and that's why drugs never filled up my spiritual void. I never felt as though I fit in. You know, I never fit in with the hard-core junkies, because I didn't pull off robberies and I didn't steal with guns, but I didn't fit in with straight people either. But you know, and I can say this honestly, that I haven't talked in depth like this with anybody since my NDE happened, until I met you.

EEV: *I suppose it's not an ordinary topic of conversation!*

HH: No! I didn't even know what an NDE was when I had this overdose. But in the treatment program I was in, it was quite common to hear people talk about nearly dying. It's the belief of treatment programs that you have to hit bottom before you can turn your life around. Now the bottom can come in the form of nearly dying, nearly killing yourself by not eating, or of putting yourself in situations where you have the shit beat out of you—there are a lot of near-death situations, but they are not near-death *experiences*. I never talked about my NDE before, because I still didn't understand what had happened to me until I met you. I've been in two different detox programs in the last year, and I met one person in particular who talked to me about his near-death experience. I wanted to hear how this person was able to change his life around. He is a Vietnam veteran. His near-death experience seemed so much more powerful than my little incident, but my little incident is very powerful to me.

EEV: *Has it changed your life?*

HH: Yes, it has changed my life.

EEV: *Do you believe now that there is something beyond death, or have you always been sure of it?*

HH: I was never really sure before, but I am sure today.

EEV: *Were you sure about this just after your NDE, or did it take some time?*

HH: No, it took some months. You see, I have always believed in heaven, but I never understood what heaven was like. It was always something intangible out there, something out of reach. Something you can read or hear about when you're growing up and imagine running around with lions and lambs. You know what I mean, that kind of neat stuff. But today, it's real. It's what this life and trials are all about—the final peaceful, wonderful place to spend eternity—after death's sting—here on earth.

EEV: *I have the impression that before, you wanted to die, and that now you are trying to live. What stopped your need for self-destruction? Love wasn't strong enough—you had two wives and two kids. So, what was stronger than that?*

HH: That's a good question. If I'm doing it for others, if I'm doing it for my wife, if I'm doing it for my kids, if I'm doing it for my parents, these are all the wrong reasons, you see. These were my reasons for wanting to get off drugs before. What's different this time is that I want to do it for myself. I'm beginning to know who I am. I've always loved giving and doing things for people, but it was always in a twisted way, when I was expecting something back. It wasn't pure giving or pure love. It was more or less conditional love, not unconditional love. What's different now is that I can unconditionally love myself, because God accepts me just the way I am. I can't do anything to earn the love of God. He loves me the way I am. Today, I really find pleasure in helping somebody without expecting anything in return, and this is how God loves me. By getting in touch with love and with God, He's showing me how to love others. But first I have to love myself, and it's kind of hard to love yourself when you're full of guilt, when you stick this stuff in your arms, and when you feed your head with a bunch of polluting stuff.

EEV: *Your brother's suicide seems to be the reason, or one of the reasons, for your drug addiction. Did you feel guilty for being alive when he had to die so young? Did you think that you had no right to live?*

HH: I didn't feel I had no right to live, but I did feel guilty. When my folks divorced, I took off and went to college.

My sister got married. My younger brother was left, flip-flopping between Mom's house and Dad's house, both of whom were remarried. I escaped by going to college when I was sixteen. By the time I was eighteen, I had joined the military, and had escaped again. I didn't know my brother very well for about a year and a half. I felt guilty because I had turned him on to smoking his first marijuana joint. I had pretty much been the guy in the family to forge the trail for my little brother, so he could do what I did. When I was given word in the captain's office that he had died, the first thing that raced to my mind was, "Oh, it was a motorcycle accident." I was the one who had talked my parents into letting him buy a big motorcycle. So right from the start, it was like it was *my* fault that he had died. Then I thought I had killed him by turning him on to drugs. And it has taken me twenty years of trying to escape getting in touch with the truth, which is that he chose to kill himself, and I admired him for it. He was not a people-pleasing kind of guy like I was, and if he wanted to do something, he just did it. I was hurt and lost because I wasn't around to talk to him. I thought that if I had been around, he wouldn't have done it. So that was another reason for me to think that I had killed him. Then I looked back at a fight we had had down in Mexico one time on vacation when we were pretty young. I used to have a real bad temper, and we would fight very violently. I remember that that day my sister had stopped us from fighting on the beach and had told me, "Henry, if you don't control your temper, your gonna kill him someday." That's another way, you know....

EEV: *I have one last question. Some people use psychedelic drugs to expand their consciousness. You have used just about every hard drug there is. Is that true?*

HH: Very true.

EEV: *Did your encounter with what you call God resemble what you experienced while being on drugs? Was it the same kind of spiritual state of mind?*

HH: No, absolutely not. The drugs are all manufactured chemicals. I never had a spiritual trip in my life. I saw things physically melting, I had very fearful trips; but the end result is that it doesn't make you feel good when you're off of it. It was just a real bad feeling for me. I didn't like it when I came back. But the NDE is very peaceful, very real, and very meaningful. The other, manufactured trips ... there's nothing there to talk about, unless you want to talk one hippy to another about how many times you saw a tree melt. You know, it has no substance. An NDE has substance.

Chapter Five

Dialogue with Kenneth Ring, Ph.D.

FREQUENCY AND NATURE OF NDEs

EEV: *How long have you been studying near-death experiences?*

KR: Fifteen years.

EEV: *How would you describe a typical NDE?*

KR: A typical NDE has several features: a feeling of tremendous peace and well-being; a sense of being separate of the physical body and being able to see the physical body from the outside; a feeling of moving through a dark space, sometimes described as a tunnel, toward a radiantly beautiful golden or golden-white light. An individual may have a panoramic life review. He may be asked to make a decision to return to the physical body or to go on, or he may be told to return to the physical body. There are other elements that define an NDE, but those are the main ones.

Professor of Psychology, University of Connecticut

EEV: *What is a core experience?*

KR: It is an experience that has most of these features, and a few others in addition, which together indicate an unusually powerful or deep NDE.

EEV: *What percentage of people experience an NDE while clinically dead?*

KR: I don't know, but I can give you another answer. It is often difficult to determine whether an individual is clinically dead from medical records, but of those persons who come close to death, whether they are clinically dead or not, the best estimate that we have at the present time is that roughly 30 percent of those individuals report an NDE. I am not talking just about those who were clinically dead, but of people who *come close to death*.

EEV: *According to your estimates and by extrapolation, how many Americans would you say have experienced an NDE?*

KR: Eight million.

EEV: *Are there statistically more NDEs among females or males?*

KR: There is no difference, but it seems that females are more likely to talk about their experience than men are.

EEV: *Which category accounts for the most NDEs: those induced by illness, accident, or attempted suicide?*

KR: Taking all the studies into account, there is no difference. It's roughly the same percentage of persons who report an NDE, regardless of the circumstances that bring them close to death.

EEV: *In your books, you give accounts of NDEs that occurred as far back as ten or twenty years ago. Don't you think these accounts are less reliable than more recent ones, since experi-*

encers have had the time to perhaps embellish their stories, gather documentary evidence, and interpret their experiences through those of others?

KR: These are not factors that distort a person's account of the NDE, because what many experiencers have told me is that their experience, although it happened twenty years ago, is just as clear in their minds as though it happened yesterday. I have also talked with many people over the years and heard them recount their NDEs on a number of occasions—for example, those who come to my classrooms—and it's almost always exactly the same. People don't embellish these experiences precisely because they leave such a strong and lasting impact in their minds. It's not a story that expands over time or where there is exaggeration. NDE accounts are very constant; there is a great reliability in these stories. And, therefore, although more recent experiences might in some way be fresher, they are not necessarily more accurate.

EEV: *Have you noticed a difference between recent NDEs and those that occurred many years ago?*

KR: I have noticed a difference only in one respect. There is now more evidence of frightening or distressing features in NDEs being reported. For many years, such experiences were not much talked about in the literature. But it now seems that there is a tendency for persons to give more emphasis to these aspects of NDEs. But, by and large, I've been impressed with how stable the experience has been during the time that I have studied it. It is essentially the same experience, and it is the same in many different countries the world over. So, overall, the similarities and constants in the experience are more obvious than the differences, with the one exception that I previously noted about frightening NDEs.

EEV: *Do subjects who believed in God, and in a life after death, before being in a near-death state, have proportionally more NDEs?*

KR: No.

EEV: *Do the NDEs of believers differ from those of nonbelievers? Or is there simply a difference with respect to symbolism, such as visions of heavenly beings?*

KR: There basically isn't a difference between the experiences of believers and people who are skeptical about religion. The difference is primarily in the interpretation of the experience, but the essence of the NDE seems to be much the same for both.

EEV: *Have you found there to be variations in the content of NDEs in terms of objective criteria, such as the experiencer's age; nationality; and intellectual, social, or cultural status?*

KR: I have not. For the most part, I find that the experience has a great uniformity across all the different variables that you mention. And although in my research I haven't studied children who have NDEs, other people have, and what has been found in about six different studies is a great continuity between childhood reports of NDEs and those of adults. Children tend to describe their experiences in simpler terms, in a more fragmentary way, in a more innocent way, but the elements that make up the NDE are much the same. And that's true for people of different ethnic groups, nationalities, and so forth.

EEV: *How do you explain this great similarity? Could it be attributed to the collective unconscious?*

KR: My feeling is that what happens at death is that we enter into a transcendental world that is structured like our physical world. And we simply experience what is there. I don't think it's just something in the unconscious. We seem to enter into what I call an imaginal domain—not imaginary but *imaginal*—which has properties that most people become aware of only when they come close to death. So I believe that they are experiencing a real domain, not in the physical world, obviously, but one that inheres in the transcendental order.

EEV: *Is it possible that NDEs are more or less the same because human beings all have the same basic constitution and therefore react identically in given circumstances? Or is this uniformity attributable to the fact that the NDE is an objective reality?*

KR: Of course, it's possible that the reason NDEs are much the same is because human beings are all the same—we all have the same nervous system—and the process of death in its ultimate stages may also be the same. However, I do not believe that that's the explanation. I think that there is an objective reality to these experiences, and that the fact that human beings are the same does not suffice to explain all the features of the NDEs. I do believe people are touching an authentic, objective reality, not in the physical world, of course, but in what I call the imaginal world.

EEV: *The testimonies of experiencers are, by nature, personal and subjective. What objective and verifiable data can be extracted?*

KR: The most objective data and the data that are also subject to verification have to do with the out-of-body aspect of the experience, where people report things that they claim to have seen while out of the body. In many instances where we've been able to look into this, people have made statements that could not have been made on the basis of ordinary perception and yet turn out to be true. There has been some careful work done on this already, and there will be more in the future.

EEV: *Have you ever met anyone who was blind from birth, and who saw colors for the first time in his or her life during an NDE?*

KR: I have not met such persons. I have heard such cases described by other researchers, but I don't know of a *documented* case in the literature where a congenitally blind individual is able to perceive colors. I know of a case of a congenitally blind woman, related to me by a physician named Fred Schoonmaker, who was at one time, and might still be, the chief of cardiology at Saint Luke's hospital in Denver, Colorado. Schoonmaker claimed that during the time of that woman's NDE, she had an out-of-body experience. She was able to identify the number of people that were in the room—there were fourteen of them. She was *not* able to see colors, but she was able to see objects during her experience. According to Schoonmaker, she was able to accurately describe what had happened in the operating room, as though she had actually seen it. This case, however, has only been described to me; I don't know whether it actually happened and if all these details are correct. I've heard of cases like this but never had the opportunity to study one myself.

EEV: *Does the nature of the NDE vary according to the reason for the near-death state?*

KR: No, it does not.

EEV: *Are the NDEs of suicide attempters different from the others?*

KR: They are not.

EEV: *Do individuals who are convinced they are close to death experience NDEs more frequently than those who are in real danger of death but are not aware of it?*

KR: I'm not sure if I can give you a definitive answer. We do know that people who believe that they are about to die—for example, those who are about to be in a very bad automobile accident, but who survive—can have the features of an NDE without actually being physically close to death itself. It seems to be just the threat or the expectation of death that can set it off. But I'm not sure whether the percentage of persons who are in that situation and report an NDE is higher than or different from that for persons who have no expectation that they are going to die.

EEV: *So, this means that an NDE can happen without any physical injury at all, just the threat of it?*

KR: That's right. For example, a person can be climbing in the mountains, take a fall that he or she believes to be life threatening, land safely, but in the process of the fall he or she has all the elements of an NDE. So you don't have to be physically close to death to have an NDE.

EEV: *An interesting point, mentioned frequently in the accounts of experiencers, is that they lose their sense of time or, more precisely, time seems not to exist where they are. This reminds me of quantum theory, which describes a dimension in which space and time do not exist. What do you think about this?*

KR: First of all, it's very clear that in this state time does not exist, or certainly it doesn't exist in the way that we normally think about it. Time seems to be a function of thought, an intellectual construct. I suppose one could say that time, in the sense of absolute time, is really a Newtonian construct. And in the case of the NDE, of course, we have to have recourse to ideas where such absolute conceptions of space and time are overthrown. Quantum theory gives us such an understanding of time and space. In this sense, then, this is the kind of theory that helps us to understand the NDE better than the traditional Newtonian view does. I also like the idea of a holographic understanding of the NDE, because that, too, is a perspective based on quantum physics that fits well with the NDE. At the very least, we certainly need new ways to think about this kind of experience, and we can get some good ideas from quantum theory.

EEV: *The precognitive visions that occur during the NDE are very impressive. I'm thinking, for example, of a young, single woman without any children who, during her NDE, saw herself in the company of her husband and their two children. Many years later, when she was with her husband and the children to whom she had meanwhile given birth, she realized all of a sudden that she was living exactly the scene that had appeared to her in a flash during her NDE. This corresponds to quantum theory in the sense that it describes a dimension in which there is no past, present, or future, but instead an absolute simultaneousness of all events. Is this proof that experiencers are really in another dimension, the one described by quantum theory?*

KR: I don't know if it's proof. What I would say is that here we have a kind of experience which, if it is authentic—and I believe that it is—violates our conventional understanding of the nature of time. There is a holographic simultaneity, as though we are aware of everything at once. So it isn't proof, but it is *consistent* with the ideas of time that we have in quantum theory. I feel that, as a psychologist, I'm probably not competent to comment on the linkage between NDEs and quantum theory. I can only say that the line of thinking that underlies this question is certainly beginning to be explored by persons who do have a background in physics and an interest in the NDE. The connection you point to in your question is very much worth pursuing.

EEV: *We also find precognitive elements in prophetic visions. One of Moody's experiencers speaks of something that occurred immediately after the life review. He suddenly felt that he possessed "total knowledge," which he described as including awareness of all events from the beginning of time and throughout the future. At this point, the experiencer had access to all the secrets of time and the universe. But at the moment he decided to return to life, this knowledge vanished instantly and was completely erased from his memory. It is interesting to note that the subject was obviously not meant to remember the teachings, since he decided to return to life. There must be something or somebody who gives the near-death experiencer knowledge, but who doesn't want him or her to take it back with them.*

KR: I'm not sure if that's the case. Maybe I would phrase it slightly differently. People in this state have access to total knowledge. I believe that knowledge is poured into them, is encoded into them. I don't believe that knowledge could be expressed in a simple way through our ordinary language. But the knowledge is there, I'm not sure that it is withheld. I think it's more a matter of it being state-dependent, by which I mean that in certain expanded states of consciousness—for example, in mystical, religious, or even psychedelic experiences—a tremendous amount of information pours in. The knowledge is rooted in a particular state of consciousness. In that state you have that knowledge. But when you fall out of that state, the knowledge is lost to you, but you know that you've had the knowledge. I don't think it's necessarily meant to be taken away from you, but simply that when you are no longer in that state, you can't have access to it.

EEV: *Does this mean that total knowledge is encoded into all of us from the very beginning, but that we have access to it only in a particular state of expanded consciousness?*

KR: Yes, and I think that it is very similar to what Plato meant when he said that essentially all knowledge is remembering. The knowledge is laid down on us, and in these expanded states of consciousness, such as an NDE, that knowledge is unfolded to us and is deployed, as it were, into our consciousness. We have access to all knowledge or at least to great realms of knowledge, but when we come back to our limited, contracted, egoistic selves, we lose contact with that knowledge. It might still be within us, but we can no longer have access to it.

EEV: *Many experiencers tell us that during their encounter with the "being of light," they had access to total knowledge. Everything becomes evident, comprehensible; all things have meaning and are integrated into a perfect logic. When they come back to life, they seem to retain, if not total knowledge, then at least the calm assurance that everything is all right, complete, and as it should be. Is this why experiencers seem to be reconciled with life regardless of what might happen to them?*

KR: This is a very interesting question. I would say that this kind of total knowledge, the knowledge that everything is sort of perfect in the way that it is understood in the NDE, is a powerful source of consolation and equanimity for many people who have had these experiences. But maybe it's not necessary to get that total knowledge in the NDE in order to feel this, because there is something about the NDE and its feelings of peace, love, and acceptance that is profoundly reassuring. So this may be one factor that is responsible for those feelings of at-easement in the world, but it may not be the only factor.

EEV: *Are the NDEs of children different from those of adults? We talked about this before—would you like to add something?*

KR: No, they are not. But there is one way where they are different statistically. And that is that children are less likely to report the panoramic life review phenomenon than adults.

EEV: *Is that because their lives are so short?*

KR: Yes, perhaps, since they don't have much of a life to review.

EEV: *The phenomenon of the NDE is relatively recent and dates back to only about twenty years ago. Do you think people also had NDEs in the past, and that it is only thanks to modern mass communication that this phenomenon is more widely known? Is its greater frequency simply attributable to modern resuscitation techniques? Or do you think that there is a profound reason for its emergence at this particular point in time?*

KR: I think that NDEs have always occurred throughout history. We have some fragmentary evidence for these experiences in historical records. But it is certainly true that advances in modern resuscitation technology have made it possible for many people to survive near-death encounters and, therefore, to report them. In addition, within the last twenty years, we've had a body of researchers, investigators, and chroniclers of these experiences, who have given us the possibility of knowing much more about these experiences. So, yes, resuscitation has made it possible for a large number of persons to have and survive this experience. But I am also inclined to think that there are larger reasons behind the emergence of this phenomenon, as I have written in my latest book. I feel that there seems to be a higher orchestration of these experiences on the part of what I would call a planetary intelligence. And that, just as each of us has an internal guidance system that tries to enable us to act with wisdom (e.g., in the help that we may receive from dreams or through other experiences that seem to be guided by some beneficent force within ourselves), I feel that the earth also has such a regulating mechanism as well, a planetary mind or a planetary intelligence, as the expression of our deepest yearnings and perhaps of our deepest fears. And the NDE is a part of it. I feel that this earth intelligence is benignly disposed toward the earth's welfare and is very concerned about the fate of the earth. So, considering that the destruction that's ravaging the planet caused by various kinds of environmental irresponsibilities and by wars has reached such an incredible pitch in the twentieth century, it seems natural that this planetary intelligence, this mind at large, would create the conditions whereby many people would have these kinds of awakenings— awakenings to the need for wholeness, for harmony among people, for a heightened ecological sensitivity— because if we, as a human species, do not awaken to this, then we might not have a habitable home to live in any longer. We may be irrevocably poisoning our own planet, and it's the only planet we have. We have to be able to make it a place where we can sustain life. And, as far as we know, now perhaps more than at any other time in human history, we are in danger of undermining our own habitat. I found, in my studies, that experiencers become much more ecologically sensitive than they were before their experience, much more concerned with the welfare of the planet, and with a much heightened "reverence for life," as Albert Schweitzer would say. If we had a world filled with these people, we probably wouldn't be seeing the environmental destruction and planetary degradation we are witnessing today, we wouldn't be burning down the rain forest or depleting the ozone layer, because the consciousness wouldn't allow it. So, we may be seeing so many of these experiences today not merely because of the resuscitation technology but also because the planetary intelligence—assuming that there really is one— sensing how imperiled the fate of the earth is, has decided to do everything it can in order to create mass phenomena to produce many people with a new ecological consciousness. Of course, there are many ways to become more ecologically minded, and many people in the world are becoming so. It's obvious that you don't have to have an NDE to feel this way about the earth. But the fact that experiencers feel so strongly about this following their NDE suggests that there may be more at work here than just the effects of modern medical technology.

EEV: *And people nowadays dare to talk about it, without fear of being considered crazy?*

KR: Yes. We now have a climate of acceptance, at least in certain Western countries. And this makes people feel more at ease to talk about these unusual experiences now, more so than fifteen or twenty years ago. This certainly helps to bring out these accounts.

EEV: *Research on NDEs is fairly recent, having begun only a few decades ago, following the publication of a book in 1975 by physician and psychiatrist Raymond Moody entitled* Life after Life *(an inappropriate title, in my opinion), which is more anecdotal than scientific. Moody began the research for his book following the account of an NDE by George Ritchie, a professor of psychiatry, which he related to his students. George Ritchie had come down with double pneumonia in an Abilene military hospital as a young soldier. He was presumed dead and would have been buried alive if it hadn't been for an attentive hospital employee who noticed his hand move. At this, he was given an injection of adrenaline, which saved his life. All recent scientific research into NDEs traces its origin to this particular near-death experience. Cardiologist Maurice Rawlings published a book in 1978 entitled* Beyond Death's Door. *Your book* Life at Death *was published in 1980. Your second book* Heading Toward Omega, *dealing more specifically with the implica-*

tions and the aftereffects of NDEs, was published in 1984, and your last book The Omega Project *came out in 1992. Cardiologist Michael Sabom began studying NDEs in order to prove that there is a scientific, rational explanation for this phenomenon. His initially negative attitude quickly turned into a growing interest, which led to the publication of his book* Recollection of Death *in 1982. In 1985, a British psychologist, Margot Grey, who had had an NDE herself, published a book entitled* Return from Death. *Have I mentioned all the leading books in this field?*

KR: I would say those were the main books. In that particular period, there was another book, not as well known, by Charles P. Flynn called *After the Beyond*. It was a book that also dealt primarily with the aftereffects and religious significance of NDEs. Those were the main books that were written between 1975, with the publication of Moody's book, and the next ten years in this field.

EEV: *There is also abundant esoteric literature dealing with the passage from the material to the spiritual world. Are there some common elements between this literature and the scientific publications mentioned above? If so, what are they?*

KR: Oh sure, there is an obvious connection. The spiritual traditions that speak about the passage from life to death and the research on the NDE or the clinical death experience coincide in that they're talking about the process of death, the transition into death. The trail of the NDE leaves off, of course, at the moment of death, and it talks only about what happens then and maybe immediately thereafter. That's where the similarities cease because the esoteric literature talks also about what happens afterward. For example, *The Tibetan Book of the Dead* has many features—the out-of-body experience, the primary light, the seeing of blissful and wrathful deities, and so on.

There are many commonalities between what *The Tibetan Book of the Dead* and what the experiencers say happens at the moment of death. But this book, of course, goes on to talk about the various *bardos* and the various stages that people go through, which usually culminate in the process of rebirth. The NDE doesn't deal with these issues. So, there are similarities, because they both talk about the transition into death. But there is no information from the standpoint of the NDE about what happens afterward. For that, one would have to rely on the esoteric traditions.

EEV: *Esoteric literature often mentions the "silver string," which is said to tie the physical to the spiritual body. Did any of your experiencers see such a thing?*

KR: Yes, one or two. I asked about this in my first study, *Life at Death*, but not many people commented on that particular point. It is possible that if researchers were to ask that question more systematically, we would have a greater number of positive responses. What I've been told by people who have had out-of-body experiences (some of which have many similarities with the NDEs) is that you have to turn around, you have to look back in order to see that thread or that cord. If you don't, you miss it. It's not surprising that many people haven't commented on it. But there are at least a few cases where that is mentioned.

EEV: *Why don't you ask those who are able to induce out-of-body experiences at will to have a look?*

KR: I recently met a person from Sweden who had many out-of-body experiences—about seventy or eighty—and she specifically commented that, at least on one occasion and maybe more, she did see something like a silver cord or a thread. I haven't talked with many people who had multiple out-of-body experiences, but I suspect that many of them would mention the silver cord or the silver thread.

EEV: *These people saw the silver string without particularly advocating esoteric arguments or being influenced by them?*

KR: Many people probably saw this and then became interested and tried to learn more about it and, only afterward, discovered the esoteric and metaphysical literature that talks about it. So they were not preconditioned to see it. And according to cross-cultural anthropologic research (and cross-cultural research of other kinds), it is well known that the tradition of something like a rope or a cord or a silverlike substance joining the physical body to a subtle body is found in many cultures throughout the world. And, in many cases, this is also true for preliterate cultures which, of course, have no written tradition of this kind of material. So this seems to be a universal human experience that many people have when they find themselves outside of the physical body, either as a result of going through a near-death crisis or for some other spontaneous reason when an out-of-body experience occurs.

EEV: *Observations of dying persons have led to important research, in particular to the publications of Elisabeth Kübler-Ross, William Barrett, and Karlis Osis. I think the NDE could be viewed as the continuation of the deathbed vision. What do you think about this and how valuable do you find it?*

KR: I would phrase this slightly differently. The deathbed visions that were studied by the individuals you mentioned are similar to, but not exactly the same as, the NDE. They are protracted experiences of the transcendental world; people go back and forth, in and out, in the process of dying. The NDE is a sudden thrust into that particular domain as a result of a violent accident, or an impulsive suicide attempt, or a sudden cardiac arrest. Whereas those who are in the process of dying, whose physical bodies are deteriorating but whose spiritual senses are alive, have what we may call gradual immersions into that other world. They would fall in and out of it. So they are very definitely related processes, with the difference that the NDE is a sudden, almost an explosion, into that world, and the deathbed vision is a gradual awakening into that world.

EEV: *In his book* Closer to the Light, *Melvin Morse studies the phenomenon of visions. He tells of a nine-year-old boy, suffering from leukemia, who was greatly distressed when his physician told him that his last chemotherapy treatment had not been successful. While riding home in the car with his mother, he fell asleep and dreamed that God came to see him and told him to stop the treatment, which was pointless since the hour of his death had already been determined. During the next few months before his death, he had many visions, both while awake and asleep. He met God and had a glimpse of the afterlife. These visions gave him the strength to face his death, which he knew was at hand, with calmness and serenity. They also had an extremely positive effect on his parents. Our first reaction would be to consider these visions as very strong unconscious desires. But perhaps this interpretation is too simple? Do you think that these visions are real, that they actually provide access to another world, and, in some way, are precursors to the NDE?*

KR: I would respond positively to all those last questions. I do think that interpreting these experiences just from a conventional psychodynamic perspective, say from a psychoanalytic theory, does simplify and distort these experiences. I do believe that these visions, whether they take place in children who are on the verge of death or in elderly people, are intimations of another dimension of reality. And people can tap into that. Many people, for example, know when they're going to die and they turn out to be right. Now how can somebody know that? They never died before! It's as though they have access to a kind of information that's irrefutable. I think we have to expand our notions of what is possible, to find new ways of thinking about these experiences. Not simply to dismiss them, in a psychiatric sense, as hallucinations, but truly to talk about them as visions that inform, that give us a sense of the transcendental order, that give us an idea of where we really belong, where we come from, and where we're going. So I take these experiences seriously. That doesn't necessarily mean that I always take them literally or always think that they're true. But I think it's a mistake to just reduce them to some kind of psychological framework and not to consider their implications. I'm basically sympathetic to the interpretation that Morse gives to these visions in the cases of the children that he studied.

EEV: *Apparently, in the past, dying persons often saw angels, God, Jesus, or deceased loved ones, who made their death easier, and who helped them to face it more calmly. Today, these visions are considered hallucinations, and patients are given doses of medication in order to suppress them. Do you think that modern medicine obstructs natural phenomena that could assist people in the process of dying?*

KR: I think modern medicine as a whole is not particularly attuned to the dying process because it's well known that the patient who is dying in the hospital tends to be neglected and, even to a degree, feared. Since, from the medical standpoint, death is the ultimate enemy and victor, it's avoided. But it seems that the results of the NDE research are giving us a different, better, and more humane way to understand not only what death is but also the process of dying. And, therefore, it forces us to look at death not as an end but as a transition. Once that begins to take hold within medicine or begins to be a strong countercurrent against the main tendencies in modern medicine, there will be more and more people who will be attentive to the process of dying, who will not sedate patients, but will stay with them and encourage them to let go, to release into this kind of experience, so that they will be able to experience, as fully as possible, the ecstasy that often attends the process of dying.

EEV: *How do you define the difference between a coma and a near-death state?*

KR: A coma, as I understand it, has certain distinctive physiological or neurological properties. There are certain brain states associated with it, whereas a near-death state is a much more generalized condition. A comatose state is a specific state, and even in a comatose state one is not necessarily in a near-death state; that is, people may be expected to come out of a coma. But a coma can give you access to the same realm of information, the same kinds of knowledge and experience, that can occur in an NDE. So there are some similarities, but they are not the same.

EEV: *Is it possible to have an NDE while in a coma, and if so, are such NDEs similar to those experienced during a near-death state?*

KR: The answer to both questions is "yes." I've talked to people who have been in a comatose state and, in that state, they did experience an NDE. Those NDEs were not different in any substantial way from those that occur under other circumstances.

EEV: *Does the duration of the near-death state have a direct implication on the depth of the NDE, in terms of the number of NDE features?*

KR: There is some relationship, but it's complex. There isn't a one-to-one correspondence between the length in terms of clock time of an NDE and the depth of the experience, because in some cases you can have experiences that seem to be very short in terms of clock time but very profound in terms of what is experienced there. However, I have looked into this question, as have some other researchers, and there is a modest relationship between the two factors. In general, people who seem to be clinically dead longer have deeper experiences, but there are many exceptions to this generalization.

EEV: *There are other phenomena, besides near-death states, that resemble NDEs at least partially. I am thinking in particular about OBEs (out-of-body experiences), certain states of deep meditation, and of directed dreams. Do you see a parallel between these phenomena and consider them valuable?*

KR: Absolutely. In fact I think it's unfortunate that the term *near-death experience* has become as popular and as widely used as it is, because it implies that there is a unique state of consciousness that is associated with the onset of death. There is a very distinctive state of consciousness that occurs when people come close to death, but it's not unique to near-death crises. There are many other pathways that lead essentially to the same state of consciousness. Out-of-body states, meditative and spiritual disciplines, yoga, shamanic journeys, psychedelic experiences, lucid dreams, spontaneous mystical and religious experiences—all can lead to an encounter with the light, to a feeling of ineffable joy, of well-being, of total knowledge. So I consider the near-death crises to be only one of the many pathways that lead to these same realizations, these same states of consciousness. Perhaps a more dramatic pathway because of the circumstances that are associated with it but, essentially and in terms of what is learned, no different from the kind of knowledge that can be accessed through many different ways.

EEV: *Experiencers often talk about their ability, during their NDE, to pass through persons and objects. They describe, for example, wanting to grab the arm of their physician to make him stop working on their body, since they are at peace and quite happy the way they are. But these attempts are in vain, and they have no means of communicating with the physician. Do the experiencers feel themselves to possess a nonmaterial body, or do they conceive of themselves as "pure consciousness"?*

KR: Both. Sometimes people have a sense of having some kind of a subtle or nonphysical body of light, but very often they are not aware of being embodied. They are just aware that they are whole, that they are complete, that they are basically just a center of consciousness. They find themselves in such an odd state, that to make it less odd, they may have to give themselves a spiritual body or a body of light, just because it's so difficult for us to think of ourselves in a disembodied way. And somehow, as they get used to this condition, they see that the spiritual body is just like a crutch—so to speak—that they supply for themselves, but that they don't really need.

EEV: *The public at large is becoming increasingly well informed about NDEs. Logically speaking, people who know about NDEs before their own near-death state should make up the majority of those who experience one. Oddly enough, according to statistics, this is not the case. On the contrary, these persons experience proportionally fewer NDEs than those who were not previously aware of the phenomenon. How do you explain this fact?*

KR: That's an interesting question. I'm not sure if subsequent research would show that people who know less about the NDE would actually be more likely to have one. The difference was statistically slight in the first place. I think that maybe if a person is familiar with the NDE and has thought about it, they don't necessarily psychologically need it as much when they actually come close to death, because they already worked through the process. For example, Dr. Bruce Greyson and other researchers who have specially focused on suicide-related NDEs, find that the life review is not as common among people who have attempted suicide and have NDEs as it is for people who have NDEs in other ways. This is the case perhaps because if they already have done the work to think about their lives and prepare for suicide, they may not need it. But I think there are many other factors that are associated with why some people have the experience and some do not.

EEV: *It seems to me there is a contradiction here. You say that if people have thought a lot about the meaning of the near-death experience, they will not have a great psychological need to have one at the time of their death. But wouldn't this mean that NDEs are not an objective reality, but rather a psychological need?*

KR: No, it doesn't necessarily mean that. It means that maybe there are certain conditions that make that particular objective reality available to people. And for people who do not have a need for it, their filters would be such that they would screen it out because they've already done it. And we already know that not everybody who comes close to death has an NDE. Some people are more likely to have this experience than others. We now have studies done on exactly this question—why do some people have this experience and others do not? And this is the issue we probably should talk about in order to try to address the question you're asking.

EEV: *I would conclude, therefore, that someone like you, who knows NDEs well, would be less likely to have an NDE than a person who had never heard about this experience. But at a certain point, you, too, will have access to this objective reality. Let's say that an NDE is a trip to another dimension that is more immediately necessary for those who have never really thought about these things, and who need this information. Those who have already formed an opinion on the subject will have less need for the experience because they will have already done part of the work. But at the time of death, everyone enters into the objective reality of the other world. So how can this phenomenon, on the one hand, depend upon our psychological needs, while at the same time be an objective reality that we all experience eventually?*

KR: I can speculate why some persons will have a delayed reaction and others will have it more immediately. There are many factors involved. But one of the things that we have learned in our recent studies is that those persons who come close to death and remember having an NDE are distinctive in certain ways compared to those who come close to death and don't remember these experiences. The persons who are more likely to be immediately aware of an NDE at the time that it happens are those who as children have become, for whatever reason, sensitive to what I call alternate realities, sensitive to the psychic realm. One of the factors that now seems very clearly to be implicated is the presence of child abuse, trauma, stressful childhoods, childhoods with illnesses. These are circumstances that make a child more likely to dissociate from the ordinary physical world and to tune into other, alternate realities, especially in response to trauma. And, later, they are likely to sensitize those individuals to the domain of consciousness in which the NDE is embedded because, of course, the NDE is a major trauma, the trauma where you are threatened with bodily annihilation. If you have a history of dissociating into alternate realities in response to trauma, because of your childhood back-ground for example, you're more likely to enter sponta-neously into those states of consciousness when you come close to death. Therefore, you are more likely to register this experience as a conscious event. Somebody who doesn't have this kind of background, who doesn't have these sensitivities, who is more plugged into the physical world, who is very fearful, is more likely to screen out that experience. So there are various filters that would have to be demolished before people can become aware of and register the experience. For most of us, it takes, I think, a powerful thrust, an agent, to knock down the walls, the barriers to our perception; and when we can see, and once we see, then we are aware. But persons who are naturally sensitive would almost immediately find themselves in that realm. Although we can't say this from the standpoint of the scientific research on the NDE, I think that eventu-ally everybody awakens into this particular state. The important thing in life is to try to eliminate the filters, the attachments, the blindnesses, the fears, and everything that block us from what I call the *imaginal vision*. This is a whole process—of awakening to these experiences before you die so that when you do die, you can enter into them fully, and you understand what is happening to you.

EEV: ... *and you're not too frightened.*

KR: ... You're not too frightened, and you've already done your work. In a way, it is similar to what Plato says—that the whole purpose of philosophy, the whole purpose of the dialectic was to prepare for death, was basically a rehearsal for death. I think the NDE and the knowledge that is coming out of this experience may be helpful for people in preparing for death, by giving them an idea of what really happens. Although there are individual differences in sensitivities, I think eventually everybody will enter that state.

EEV: *What do you think of the arguments of skeptics who deny the existence of NDEs? Let's take the case of persons who, while under anesthesia during surgery, hear and see the medical team working on their body. Skeptics attribute this to a state of semiconsciousness, due to insufficient anesthesia. That might be a possible explanation, but the fact remains that experiencers feel no pain, situate themselves in a corner of the ceiling, and view their bodies from above!*

KR: I'm not particularly interested in trying to prove the existence of the NDE. There will always be skeptics. There are certain models that have been offered by skeptically oriented psychologists and others, like Susan Blackmore for example, that can explain away these experiences, at least to their way of thinking. I have not found these explanations plausible. I'm not interested in trying to engage in debates, or in winning arguments, or in convincing people. What I'm interested in doing as a scientist and as an investigator of the NDE is to offer the information, to invite people to explore it.

EEV: *Another argument offered by skeptics is that NDEs are dreams. It is a fact that the impression of floating, or of flying, is one of the basic symbols of dreams. But can this fact explain the whole complexity of NDEs?*

KR: No. Anybody, even a skeptic, who looks into NDEs would very quickly dismiss the idea that these are dreams. Experiencers almost routinely emphasize the fact that this experience was more real than any dream could possibly ever be real. Talking about the experience is less real than the experience itself was. There are so many aspects of this experience that are undreamlike (like the out-of-body state where things can be verified), that are so beyond anything we understand as dreams—even lucid dreams—that the dream hypothesis is ultimately untenable. People who just don't want to believe in the NDE call it a dream—it's one of their last refuges; they use it as an epithet, as a term of dismissal. I don't believe that anybody who looks into this experience with an open mind would conclude that it's a dream. But people will conclude what they want to conclude, and they will selectively evaluate the evidence that supports their interpretation.

EEV: *Skeptics are very categorical with respect to those who believe in God: Their experiences are nothing more than a desire to see their beliefs come true.*

KR: How would that explain frightening NDEs? How would it explain the experience of a person who attempts suicide, who wants and believes that it's only going to be an annihilation afterward, and who tries to attain the state of extinction, to be fully and forever unconscious? How would it explain the experiences of extremely young children who can certainly have no expectations about what the afterdeath state is like? How would it explain the experiences of people who are reared in a particular tradition, such as the Catholic tradition, for example, and who say that nothing in anything that they were taught, or trained, or led to believe about the nature of the afterlife was at all like what they experienced?

EEV: *One of the arguments against the validity of NDEs is the hypoxia theory, which assumes that NDEs are a state of delirium caused by a lack of oxygen to the brain. What do you think about this?*

KR: It's certainly the case that in many instances of NDEs, there would be an interference of blood flow to the brain, except that in many other instances it seems very clear that this is not the case at all—it's been monitored, and people still have the same kind of experiences. You can't explain a constant by a variable; and hypoxia is a variable, the NDE is a constant. Therefore, it's not a sufficient explanation.

EEV: *Another argument against NDEs is the fact that experiencers cannot tell us anything about life after death, since they haven't really been dead. Upon initial consideration, this seems to be an irrefutable argument, but in fact it isn't! We do have testimonies of individuals who actually died during their NDE. I am referring to recordings of past lives under hypnosis. These testimonies are very similar to those related by near-death experiencers. What importance do you attribute to them?*

KR: I met a man who told me that he had done exactly this kind of work. He has worked as a past-life therapist. He told me that in his case, he tried to find out whether persons who reported their own death in past lives had heard anything about NDEs. In a number of cases, they seemed to be ignorant of this, and yet they reported experiences that were very similar. So I think that this is another sign that these are authentic experiences. I do have a certain sympathy, though, with the skeptical side of the question. I myself believe that NDEs are not afterdeath experiences and that, in themselves, they can't tell us anything from the scientific point of view about a life after death. That is not to say that the persons who have these experiences aren't convinced that there is a life after death. They are convinced of that, and they feel very positive about what that may be. But this is something that stems from their experience, it's a state-specific knowledge. For the rest of us, we can only wonder about what happens after death. But these experiences are very suggestive about life after death even if we can't always talk about what form it takes. Another thing that also connects with your question is this: In a number of studies (including the one that I've most recently done, and in a study done by an Australian sociologist by the name of Cherie Sutherland), there is strong evidence that people who had NDEs are much more inclined to a reincarnational view of life; they believe that we live more than once, and that we will live again. There is something about the NDE that seems to conduce people to this kind of belief. This, again, is something that needs to be looked into further—why does the NDE so often lead to a shift in a person's worldview that embraces reincarnation?

EEV: *Could the fact of having narrowly escaped death be such an enormous psychological shock that it would explain the radical changes in personality that take place in near-death experiencers?*

KR: No, not in itself because I have done studies that show that just coming close to death, which of course is a shock, does not bring about the full gamut of changes in the person's life afterward, that there are many changes that seem to be unique to remembering an NDE at the time. So it's not just the coming close to death that makes the difference. It's coming close to death *and* having an NDE that makes the difference in many cases.

EEV: *I think that the only accurate measure of the value and dimension of NDEs is their impact on the experiencer's life. As the saying goes, "You judge a tree by its fruits." What is your opinion?*

KR: I agree 100 percent.

WORKING HYPOTHESIS: NEAR DEATH EXPERIENCES ARE
A DEFENSE MECHANISM OF THE PSYCHE AND REPRESENT
UNCONSCIOUS DESIRES

EEV: *We have seen that about 30 percent of persons in a near-death state experience an NDE. Do you think that everyone experiences an NDE under these circumstances, but that only 30 percent of them remember it?*

KR: Yes, something like that. The actual experience may often occur, but the recall of it may be limited to a relatively small number of persons. NDEs are not dreams, but an analogy can be made to dreams. Not everybody who dreams (and almost every normal person does dream at night) remembers the dreams in the morning. That doesn't mean the dreams haven't happened.

EEV: *One could suppose that only those who experienced a positive NDE would remember it, since it is well known that the mind can refuse to allow a traumatic experience into consciousness, keeping it buried in the unconscious. I would like to cite an account reported by cardiologist M. Rawlings describing a dramatic case of resuscitation.[1] A man suffering from a heart attack had lost consciousness several times during efforts to revive him. Each time he regained consciousness, he claimed he had gone to hell, had had the most terrifying, unbearable experience, and begged the physician not to let him go back there. Rawlings was very impressed, as the man truly appeared to have seen the most terrible things. Since the resuscitation effort was successful, Rawlings went to see the patient a few days later in his hospital room and began to talk very cautiously about what had happened. He was astonished to discover that not only did the patient not remember anything frightening, he also seemed to recollect a rather positive, pleasant experience! This is a good*

*example of a terrifying event that is unconsciously repressed.
Could this be why there are so few negative accounts of NDEs?*

KR: I've met that man, and I met Rawlings. I also saw a
videotape in which this man appeared and talked about
this very experience. I can acknowledge that this man had
a frightening experience that he didn't remember, and I
certainly can acknowledge the general principle that traumatized experiences often are repressed, or that they are
otherwise unavailable to consciousness. I don't think,
however, that this is the most significant factor associated
with the relative paucity of frightening NDEs. I think,
rather, that people are aware of them but are reluctant to
talk about them, because they think that if a bad thing
happened to them, then they are bad. In other words, if
you have a positive kind of experience, as long as you feel
comfortable in talking about it, you will do so, because it
seems to say that you are the kind of person who deserves
it, or that, in some way, it's consistent with your character.
If you have an experience in which you feel you've experienced something extremely negative, that you've been in
a very dark, very frightening state, you may think it may
say something about your character. So you may be reluctant to talk about that.

One of the things that has been true about NDEs is
that there has been an emphasis on the positive experiences and not so much on the frightening ones. And that
makes it even more difficult for people to talk about them.
So, although I acknowledge that what Rawlings talks
about can happen, I don't think it is a significant factor. I
can draw an analogy with psychedelic experiences. These
are often unpleasant, frightening, terrifying. But there is
no particular evidence that immediately after these experiences people repress them. On the contrary, they remain
available for a time in consciousness. I don't think the

psychodynamics of an NDE are that different. Yes, in some cases, people may forget. But I've also heard of cases in which people had a very positive experience, shown by the ecstasy on their faces at the time, as reported by witnesses, but when those people were asked afterward, they also did not remember. So it's not that just the negative is repressed. It may be that the experiences that don't fit in with the person's particular point of view are forgotten. I'm not persuaded that Rawlings is right in terms of a general principle. He's got this one case; he shows the same man over and over again. It's not clear how representative it is of the whole of people who report NDEs. The problem with Rawlings is that he has particular religious views that certainly influence his position. There has never been an independent replication of this work that has found anything like the percentage of frightening NDEs that he reports. He may be right, but we have to wait for an independent investigator to come up with findings such as he reported. He does have a case that probably frightening NDEs or frightening aspects of NDEs are underreported for a variety of reasons, but I don't think the reasons are necessarily the ones he supposes.

EEV: *Does he report the greatest number of negative NDEs?*

KR: He says that frightening NDEs are just as common as the pleasant ones. But he is not a rigorous researcher; he collects his data from all sorts of sources and doesn't necessarily investigate them personally, though in some cases he does. There are statements in his book that are known not to be true. For example, he states that every suicide experience is negative. That's definitely not true on the basis of a number of other reports. It seems that at least some of the statements that Rawlings makes come out of his religious views of the experience rather than from the standpoint of actual meticulous and impartial investigation.

EEV: *Is it possible that the 70 percent of persons who report having been in a near-death state without experiencing an NDE actually had a negative NDE that was so terrifying that they unconsciously repressed it?*

KR: No. I'm quite convinced that this is not the case. Some of those persons may have had a frightening NDE but nothing like 70 percent of all of them having had frightening NDEs that they repressed.

EEV: *I think that many more negative NDEs would be reported if those who had experienced a near-death state could be interviewed shortly after the event, before unconscious defense mechanisms had a chance to repress it. Could time perhaps be a factor in this sense?*

KR: Yes, but this works both ways. People might also repress or not be aware of the positive aspects of the experience and, frankly, from a both humane and ethical point of view, it would be injudicious and imprudent to try to interview people immediately after their experience. They have just been through a near-death crisis, and they are in such an emotional state that it would be inappropriate to try to extract research information under these circumstances. But even if one could, I'm not entirely convinced that people would be closer to their negative experience at that time. Some people might, but some people might forget the positive sides, too.

EEV: *As a psychologist, you are well aware of the defense mechanisms that may be activated by the psyche when faced with a threat to its equilibrium. This is even more true when it is faced with something as extreme as being in danger of dying. Are*

*positive NDEs the final gift from the unconscious to help indi-
viduals deal with the dramatic experience of dying?*

KR: I don't think it's a gift from the unconscious or that it
exists just as a protector or a defensive device. I think it is a
blessing rather than a gift as such, or a consolation, or
something that protects the integrity of the ego. It is more
a revelation that occurs at the point of death. Herman
Melville in his most famous book, *Moby Dick*, says: "And
death which alike levels all, alike impresses all with the
last revelation which only an author from the dead could
adequately tell."[2] I think what these people are getting at
is the last revelation. I feel that it's simply too easy for
psychologically minded individuals to assume that this is
only a defensive maneuver from the ego to shield the
person from the threat of imminent death. It's an easy
argument to make, and it's not altogether untrue, because
there certainly are defensive aspects of the out-of-body
experience. You can see how an out-of-body experience is,
for example, like parachuting out of a plane—you para-
chute out of your body for safety because you are threatened. There can be certainly defensive actions that take
place. But once those defenses occur, the individual is free
to experience what is really there—the transcendental
order, not just a consoling hallucination.

EEV: *The NDE isn't inside, it comes from outside?*

KR: It's hard to say inside or outside. But it's not purely
psychological. It's a revelation of the true nature of things.
A crisis that threatens either the body or the ego may
trigger it, but it's not the full explanation for what the
experience is. I'm opposed to a psychiatric or a psychoanalytic interpretation of these experiences if those interpretations purport to be a total explanation for the NDE.

They are partial, they are not comprehensive, and they have a tendency to distort and to reduce the experience to only a psychodynamic aspect. This is unfair both to the experience and to the experiencer.

EEV: *Could we say that it's a higher dimension within ourselves that isn't normally accessible?*

KR: Yes, we could say that. It's an aspect of the true nature of things from which we are blocked, but something else is shown when one comes close to death, which shuts down the sensory systems and begins to interfere with our normal cognition. As an analogy, if we are functioning in ordinary, daily, solar consciousness, we do not see the stars; we are only aware of the sky and the sun. The light of the sun blinds us, but when sunlight is absent, then the starry heavens are revealed. Likewise, when ordinary consciousness is taken away from us, then we can see something far beyond it. At death, we see the equivalent of the starry heavens, and what we see is not just this earth, not just the sun, but large areas of the cosmos are revealed to us and we begin to experience our infinitude. That's the poetry of the NDE, and the psychoanalytical orientation would never allow us to see it or even suspect that it exists.

EEV: *Melvin Morse states in his book* Closer to the Light *that 40 percent of children decide during their NDE to come back to life, whereas only 20 percent of adults make the same conscious decision. Do you think this can be attributed to the strong bonds between children and their parents?*

KR: No. In my own studies I found that roughly 40 percent of adults who had NDEs made decisions to return. So I don't think there is any difference between children and adults.

EEV: *Experiencers often encounter deceased relatives during their NDE—their parents, for example. These are joyful encounters and are described as absolutely idyllic. The psychological explanation for this appears quite simple at first sight: The blood bond is very strong, and experiencers simply wish to encounter their parents and relatives. We have known since Freud's time that the unconscious is very powerful and complex, so why not simply assume that experiencers see those persons they wish to see?*

KR: Because it is not necessarily so. Children often don't see parents because, of course, their parents aren't dead, but they see other people, and that is a surprise to them. Also, sometimes people see individuals whom they don't even recognize but who seem to know them, and when they come back and describe the individual, a relative would say: "That's your great grandfather! Let me show you a picture." And the individual would say: "Oh yes, that's the person that I saw." So this clearly cannot be simply on the basis of expectation. It may often be influenced by expectation, but again, that can't be the complete answer. Some people have very frightening visions, not paradisiacal visions. These could hardly be on the basis of desire. We don't desire to find ourselves in a frightening environment, and yet we sometimes do. There was a man who had a heart attack and nearly died. He had an NDE. He had two brothers, one who had died thirty years before, and the other who had died only recently, but so recently that he didn't know he had died. When he came back from this experience, he reported the presence of his two brothers. He was not surprised to see the brother who had been long dead, but he couldn't understand what the other brother was doing there. That didn't make sense. So, again, here is something that is not just meant to console; it's a surprising element, and yet it's consistent with what we find in the NDEs. There are mysteries to the NDE for which every rational explanation cannot fully account. I don't think these experiences are just on the basis of desire. I'm not saying that there couldn't be psychological reasons associated with some of the perceptions that occur, and desire may influence in some way, but these are not sufficient explanations for some of the phenomena that occur during this experience.

EEV: *It is just one of the aspects?*

KR: Yes.

EEV: *Another point concerning deceased relatives is that parental relations in "our world" are not always as harmonious as those described by experiencers. Imagine someone who has suffered throughout his entire life from a conflictual relationship with his parents (and these cases are not rare). This person would not necessarily explode with joy upon encountering his parents during an NDE, especially since experiencers' personalities appear to remain unchanged during the NDE, and so, theoretically, do their prior earthly conflicts. How do you explain this magic ability to suppress all conflicts and problems? Is this due to an expanded awareness of the reasons for the earthly conflict, like an instantaneous and 100-percent-successful psychoanalysis?*

KR: First of all, of course not everyone who has an NDE sees a deceased relative. And those who see deceased relatives would not necessarily see their parents. The main thing that seems to happen in these experiences, if the individual does perceive the spirit of a loved one, is the love bond between them. That's the important thing. You are drawn to those with whom you are kindred, those with whom you resonate in love. However, during the life review phase of the experience, you can have an encounter that allows you to see exactly and with complete compassion why your parents may have mistreated you in the way that they did. For example, one person I know was badly abused when she was young; when she had a life review, she saw her parents and the way they treated her, and she understood what they did; she even saw some things that she didn't remember and she said to herself: "No wonder I'm the way I am." She was able to understand and have compassion toward her parents, regardless of what they did to her. In other words, she could see that even though they treated her in that particular way, she could still, with compassion, understand and see who they really were and love them for that, even love them for the danger and for the harm that they had done to her—not because of it, but in spite of it. So the kind of expanded understanding that you can have in this state is such that you can learn to forgive all the harm that was done to you and see the essential love that might exist between you and somebody who has damaged you, even if inadvertently, in your life. So both things are true: You don't always see your parents; you see people that loved you and whom you loved. And even if you do see them, you see them with this kind of expanded, compassionate understanding that allows you to see the love in them.

EEV: *So, an NDE could have something in common with a psychoanalytic treatment, in the sense that it helps to increase your understanding?*

KR: Yes, some persons have compared this to a very accelerated psychotherapy session, in which you understand in an instant outside of time what maybe five years of psychotherapy would not have been sufficient to instill in you. It's a very, very powerful healing, a cleansing, psychotherapeutic experience for those who really can understand and integrate what has happened to them. It's cheaper than ordinary psychotherapy, although it does nearly cost you your life!

EEV: *Experiencers always meet deceased relatives during their NDE, never living ones.*

KR: Not true. Sometimes they do.

EEV: *Can we say that most of the time they meet deceased relatives?*

KR: Yes.

EEV: *So, there is nothing amazing about them meeting deceased relatives during their NDE. Nevertheless, it is more intriguing when experiencers meet deceased relatives whose death they were unaware of. This can happen, for example, in a car crash involving an entire family, in which family members have no knowledge of the status of the others. During an NDE, it sometimes happens that an experiencer will encounter a member of his family who died during the accident. Do you know of any such cases?*

KR: I've heard them described by Elisabeth Kübler-Ross. I never had a case in which there were multiple deaths and a person who survived would describe that. I've heard it described in combat situations, in which a soldier would nearly be killed, and would have an NDE and see the spirits of his comrades who just died in the same battle, apparently existing in a kind of in-between state. I've never actually talked directly with a person who had this kind of experience, but I know other NDE researchers who have, such as cardiologist Michael Sabom.

EEV: *To come back to what you said earlier, if an experiencer encounters a living person during his or her NDE, does this mean that that living person has entered the other world, the imaginal domain, as you call it?*

KR: Sometimes persons seem to see individuals who are alive. But it's rare. There have been studies of this. For example, if people who are alive and not in a near-death crisis have apparitions of others, they tend to be of living persons. Those who are close to death ordinarily see apparitions of people who are dead. But not always. Sometimes they actually see living persons. For example, the apparitional body of a woman I know who had an NDE was projected to the home of one of her sisters. The dying individual saw her living sister, but she didn't see her in the imaginal realm.

EEV: *Do you think they see the living individual in our world or in another dimension?*

KR: I think it's possible that sometimes a person who is dying may see a living individual in that other domain, because that living individual may have a subtle body that is elsewhere. We know that people who have out-of-body experiences sometimes seem to enter into this other world, but they can't stay.

EEV: *So you think that the encounter between a living and a dying person is located in the hereafter, and not in our physical world?*

KR: That can sometimes happen. A dying individual, the person who has an NDE, may sometimes see an individual who is known to be alive and may sometimes see that individual in spiritual form in the other world. This could happen because that living individual may be having an out-of-body experience.

EEV: *Certain experiencers feel the presence of a relative or of the "being of light." Others see them and are able to provide details, such as the supernatural radiance of the "being of light," which corresponds to religious symbolism, or a deceased relative wearing the same clothes he or she did during their lifetime. Can we assume that there is some sort of visual support that allows the dying person to become acclimated to another dimension? And that this dimension is actually unimaginable and incomprehensible without this visual support, which serves as a link between the material and the immaterial worlds, similar to a computer interface?*

KR: You are saying that the scene may be structured with images or familiar features that would help an individual understand what's happening, to get acclimated to a very unusual domain. Yes. In the esoteric literature, it's mentioned that these beings present themselves in a form that can be recognized by the individual in terms of his or her own background. To what extent, however, is one actually seeing what is there objectively, and to what extent are they symbolic representations of the experience? This is a very important question. It's obvious that there is symbolism in these experiences, that it's not just a literal readout of what is happening. These experiences tend to be presented in ways that would be familiar and understandable in a symbolic form and with a meaning for the individual's unconscious, so that he or she can relate to it more easily. It is probably tailored to that individual by the intelligence that is behind all of this.

EEV: *It is amazing to note that children often see an old man with a beard during their NDE. Do you think that the persons encountered during an NDE correspond to our expectations or, more generally, do NDEs correspond to our desires?*

KR: They clearly don't always correspond to our desires or expectations but what is given in the NDE does seem to fit the individual. I wouldn't want to say this literally, but it's almost as though there is a higher part of ourselves, that we're not in touch with, which is designing this experience. The same part that perhaps produces a dream that's meaningful or even the NDE. I don't know how often children see an old man with a beard; they often seem to see a woman, actually, who is a guide. But whatever the intelligence is, whether it's our own higher intelligence or the intelligence of a higher self that's designing the experience, it is presented in such a way that the individual can assimilate it. And that, again, suggests that the experience shouldn't be taken literally, but that it has an important symbolic aspect.

EEV: *I would like to cite an experiencer whose account appeared in Melvin Morse and Paul Perry's* Closer to the Light. *He talked about the therapeutic, almost providential effect of his NDE. He explained that he often wondered if he might not have brought about his own NDE. He believed NDEs might be a sort of "shock treatment" created by some individuals, whose clinical death acted as a form of self-therapy, rendering a person more conscious. Incidentally, the NDE of this person was not induced by an attempted suicide. What do you think about this?*

KR: I agree with that. I've heard the same thing said to me by people that I've interviewed. I asked them: "Do you think that, in some way, you may have brought this on, or that you may have instigated this, some higher part of you?" And they would say: "Oh yes, definitely. My life was going offtrack. I needed to get back on course. This is the best kind of therapy. It was similar to a shock treatment, and it really put me back on course in a way that I don't think things in my life would have. It's like a treatment of the last resort. If you don't wake up in other ways, then the NDE will help to wake you up." I wrote an article called "Amazing Grace: The NDE as a Compensatory Gift," in which I talked about the seemingly providential character and timing of these experiences, how they seem to occur at a critical time in an individual's life and in such a way so as to put the individual back on course.

EEV: *NDEs induced by landslides, automobile accidents, or other circumstances that could lead to an immediate death are different from those induced by illness or a heart attack with regard to the perception of time. The subject's unconscious dilates time, slows it down, and sometimes stops it momentarily. The life review takes place in a few seconds that seem to last for a very long time. The subject knows that he or she will die in seconds; time, therefore, becomes the main threat. The unconscious produces an actual space–time distortion, thus warding off the reality of death.*

KR: Are you talking about different ways in which a person can come close to death with respect to what happens to time?

EEV: *Yes.*

KR: I'm not convinced that the temporal aspect or the atemporal aspect of the NDE is that much affected by the circumstances that bring it about. And I'm not sure if I agree with the premise of the question.

EEV: *Let's take the example of a person who takes a fall in the mountains; ten seconds remain before he will hit the ground, and yet he still has enough time for a life review. This person has less time available than a person who dies in his bed. Time becomes the chief threat he has to face.*

KR: Time does, in a sense, slow down. You have all the information that you need because you transcend time, you go outside of the time dimension. What was the last part of the question?

EEV: *The point of this question is time distortion. The subject knows that he or she will die in seconds, and time becomes the main threat. The unconscious produces a real space–time distortion and thus wards off the reality of death.*

KR: That's one way to think about it. You can say that the subconscious does it, you can say that the superconsciousness does it, you can say that the being of light does it. But in any event, the individual is protected and given exactly the information he or she needs in order to be able to see what is required in that situation. This is ultimately as unanswerable as trying to know what the agency behind the experience is. If you take a psychological approach to it, then you phrase it in terms of the subconscious and the kinds of gifts or benefits that the subconscious could confer on the individual to spare him some kind of pain. If you look at it from the standpoint of a superconsciousness or a higher agency of the self doing it, then the phenomenon is the same, but the understanding of what's responsible is different. I don't know how you would decide between those two alternatives. But I agree that there certainly is a time dilation in these experiences, and that a tremendous amount of information can be given. In fact, I have referred to a physician who, upon his return from a trip, was attacked in his own home and was stabbed thirteen or fourteen times; as the stabbing took place, time slowed down and it actually stopped; it froze, and he was able to see many things about his life. After all this, time began again and the attack continued. But he survived. How time freezes, what mechanism is responsible for it, and what purposes it serves are conjectural questions.

EEV: *Contrary to the case discussed previously, a near-death state induced by illness or heart attack finds its source of threat not outside but inside the body. The unconscious reacts to this threat by unlocking the process of decorporation. The threat of death is then reduced to the destruction of the body, which will not affect the personality, since consciousness detaches from the physical body that is heading for destruction. This is a way of denying that death can get to us.*

KR: I am not sympathetic with this particular interpretation, because it sounds like it's simply a defensive maneuver on the part of the ego to deny death. But death is not a reality, except from an external perspective. We see the death of the body; we never see the death of the individual. So you could say that the individual is being insulated or protected against the alienation of death by this particular mechanism; you could see it as a mechanism of defense. But you could also see it as a revelation of what is. And again, the reader will have to decide whether it is a psychological reaction, a protective defense function, or whether the defensive function that may occur is a doorway that allows you to see what really is there. One could only decide by having the direct experience him- or herself and then drawing one's own conclusions. It's always possible to interpret these experiences within a psychodynamic framework. Having thought about that framework, and having talked with so many people who had these experiences, I am convinced that this is not a sufficient explanation but just part of it. A lot of your questions are asking whether this could be a psychological defense mechanism of some sort. Yes, it could be, but I don't necessarily think that it is, both from my studies and particularly from the many people I have talked to who have had this experience. I can see how people could take that view, but that's a view mostly of those who are studying the phenomenon from the outside. My suspicion would be that if you could take a thousand people, including psychologists, who could really talk with hundreds of persons who have had this experience and who could get into this deeply (not just read books about the experience), I think that relatively few of them, regardless of what their initial preconceptions might have been, would end up with a purely psychological interpretation of these experiences. They would see that it's not in itself sufficient.

EEV: *Will the interpretation of NDEs always remain subjective?*

KR: It is always an enigma. It is always a mystery. It is always susceptible to multiple interpretations. It will not give you any clear-cut answers. It will give you hints, it will give you clues, it will give you things that strain a particular type of interpretative framework but won't necessarily crack it. Therefore, it is always going to be up to the individual how he or she is going to relate to it. And some individuals, who make up their minds pretty early on the basis of a superficial exposure of this material, will find that they are compelled to go into it more deeply, and these are the ones who will really explore and come to some meaningful interpretation. I find this all the time with the students in the NDE course that I teach at the university. We deal with it pretty extensively over the course of the semester. Now, many students are open to it to begin with and become more persuaded of the authenticity of the experience afterward. There are always some who have a more psychological interpretation, but I respect that, because at least they have opened themselves up to it. I don't think that the NDE is ever going to compel any particular interpretation. The importance of the experience to me is not what the explanation of it may be but what the person does in the process of exploring it.

There are two ways to go about this. You can say that this is a problem, a puzzle, and as a scientist I am attempting to solve this puzzle; and the way I can solve this puzzle is to give it a coherent explanation that would be consistent with our understanding of the conventional scientific theory, and that would fit our understanding in terms of the reigning scientific paradigm. That's one way of approaching it. But I'm saying something different. I'm saying that a more useful way to approach it is not by trying to explain the phenomenon but by exploring it, entering into it, trying to understand it from the inside as much as possible. Because in this way one will be enriched as a person. We will not be able just to file this on some shelf as a phenomenon to be explained, but we will deepen and grow through the exploration of the experience. There are mysteries that are meant to be solved, but there are also mysteries that are meant to be explored. I think that the NDE is the latter kind of mystery, a mystery to be explored.

EEV: *We could advance a psychodynamic theory to explain the euphoric nature of NDEs. When persons in a near-death state stop fighting and accept the idea of their death, they renounce their future and automatically turn to their past. This could explain the life review, which often begins with very early childhood, and shows essentially happy events. As with elderly persons who are simply tired of living, persons in a near-death state let go, stop projecting themselves into the future, as we all do continually, and hence turn towards the past. Resigning oneself to passivity leads to the acceptance of one's destiny, which in turn leads to a state of joy, as is well-known in psychodynamism.*

K.R: Nonsense! This is a very lovely psychodynamic theory, but it founders on the grounds that it just doesn't fit the data. For example, it's not true that the life review is always a very pleasant event. It can be extremely traumatic. And it's also not true that the life review only focuses on the past, because in about 10–20 percent of the life reviews there is a preview—you find yourself projected into the future, you see what is going to happen to you in the future if you make the decision to go back. So, you can try a psychodynamic gloss on this experience, and you can make a good case for it, but if you really begin to look at the details rather than the generalities of this experience, you find that it just doesn't fit. Again, this is not just a partial explanation; it's a distorted one. These explanations cut out parts of the NDE that don't fit and just deal with the parts that fit. This is not fair either to the experience or to the experiencer.

WORKING HYPOTHESIS: NEAR-DEATH EXPERIENCES ARE REAL AND OPEN THE DOOR TO THE HEREAFTER

Examination of Their Impact on the Lives of Experiencers and of Their Spiritual Dimension

EEV: *I would now like to discuss ego death. Stanislav Grof and Joan Halifax have studied the moment of ego death, which sometimes occurs as a prelude to a deep mystical experience. During this profoundly emotional experience, the subject "dies as an individual" upon entering the transcendental state, which is normally inaccessible. Following this experience, the subject is "reborn" and becomes open to the idea that consciousness is independent of the body and will continue to exist beyond physical death. Of course, what is sought in the mystical experiences is transcendence, not death. Likewise, during an NDE, experiencers become aware of transcendence, of their unity with the cosmos, and of their immortality.*

KR: There are connections between the ego-death experience and what occurs in the NDE. In fact, what is critical about the NDE is exactly the ego death. You die to yourself, and you are born as a cosmic being. You understand that you are a part of the cosmos, that there is an aspect of you that is beyond birth and death, that is eternal. Any experience that brings about an ego death will also bring about many of the same perceptions and insights as those that occur to near-death experiencers. Ego death is really a doorway, or, better said, a key that unlocks the door to the transcendental world and shows you who you really are and what the nature of things is.

EEV: *I cannot hear or read experiencer accounts without being profoundly touched. Yet, because these narrations all sound basically alike, one would think that one's emotional reaction to the phenomenon would diminish once the phenomenon became familiar. But, I never get bored with it! There are two possible explanations for this. One is that these accounts resonate with some deep, ancestral knowledge—an absolute truth that we all carry inside. I know instinctively that it is true, authentic, and essential, the same way I unhesitatingly recognize someone to whom I am attracted, or with whom I could have a close relationship. The other is that—and this explanation should not be neglected—these testimonies simply respond to a need, or to a very strong desire, to believe in the experience as a response to an existential quest. What do you think about this?*

KR: There is something in us that does respond at such a deep and almost primordial level to these experiences that there is a resonance. It's as if we know within ourselves the truth of these experiences, even if we haven't had an NDE ourselves. Something clicks. You see this when you listen directly to persons who have had NDEs. Something in us responds, something says "yes" to these persons. It's almost impossible to suppress that reaction, even if you want to deny it afterward. It's similar to fairy tales. NDEs, of course, are not fairy tales, but recall how we love to hear fairy tales over and over again, because we realize that even though they are just stories, there is something archetypically true about them. This is the way we respond to NDEs. We love to hear those stories, because we recognize there is truth in them. On the other hand, there is something in us that yearns for this to be true. And that probably opens us up to these accounts in the first place. But it connects for many people not as a function of desire but as a function of the truth of these experiences.

EEV: *The fact that we need it convinces us that it is true.*

KR: Influenced by Freud, many people have said that because we desire something, we have to begin to suspect it. We may, indeed, need it (or rather want it), but just because we desire something, it doesn't mean that there isn't truth in it. The fact that we want it to be true makes us open to it. And then when we are open to it, we recognize that it is true.

EEV: *Quite ordinary people can have an NDE. Initially, these people are no different from you and me. But when they come back to life, they are transformed into the precursors of a new race, with an expanded consciousness—mutants, so to speak. As an illustration, I would like to cite a passage written by William James in 1908 in his book* The Varieties of Religious Experience: *"[O]ur normal waking consciousness, rational consciousness as we call it, is but one special type of consciousness, whilst all about it, parted from it by the filmiest of screens, there lie potential forms of consciousness entirely different. We may go through life without suspecting their existence; but apply the requisite stimulus, and at a touch they are there in all their completeness, definite types of mentality which probably somewhere have their field of application and adaptation. No account of the universe in its totality can be final which leaves these other forms of consciousness quite disregarded."*[3]

KR: I've used that quote many times in my own lectures on transpersonal psychology and altered states of consciousness. What the NDE shows is that there are other states of consciousness entirely unsuspected by us. But, as soon as you come into the proximity of death, and you vault out of yourself and leave your ordinary consciousness behind, you discover entire new worlds—worlds of transcendental beauty, of wholeness, of perfection, of unconditional love. James was especially a psychologist of extraordinary states of consciousness. If he were still living today, he would probably have a very deep interest in the NDE, and might even be one of the leaders in this field! So, yes, there is a great similarity between what James said and what people learn during an NDE.

EEV: *I know that you stay in contact with your experiencers. Since the first recordings date back to approximately fifteen years ago, it would be interesting to examine the long-term effects of the NDE on these individuals. I think we can summarize the main characteristics of near-death experiencers as follows: a thirst for learning and understanding; an enlightened intellect; a feeling of love toward others and toward humanity in general; compassion, tolerance, and patience; profound inner peace; total lack of fear of death; a deep concern for the environmental state of our planet; and a marked indifference toward material acquisitions. Do these characteristics fade, remain the same, or improve over time?*

KR: I've looked into this in my most recent book. I divided people according to the length of time that separated them from their original experience. I wasn't able to look at all of those factors, but the ones that I examined indicate that the changes occur relatively soon after an NDE and remain stable for a long period of time, for as long as thirty years. I'm not saying all of them do equally; that certainly wouldn't be true. But many of the changes that seem to come about in the aftermath of an NDE seem to be enduring. They are definitely not just transitory changes. Most of them last for a long time and have a profound effect on people's lives over the long term.

EEV: *Could the fact that the transformations seem to last, and to improve with time, provide real depth and authentic value to the NDE?*

KR: Yes. The experience of coming close to death is one of great beauty, peace, and sublimity, but the real value of the NDE is its power to change lives in positive ways. As you said before, it's by the fruits of the experience that we evaluate its authenticity. We can debate for a thousand years interpretations of the NDE, but we can easily document its effects on people. It's real in its effects, and so the importance of NDEs rests precisely in the kinds of changes they bring about in people's lives.

EEV: *Plato once said, "Love yourself and others will love you." This seems easy, and yet the failure to apply it is the source of many conflicts. Those who don't love themselves, or accept themselves the way they are, will always have difficult and often conflictual relationships with others. The encounter with the "being of light" seems to transform experiencers in this regard. Since the "being of light" accepts and loves them the way they are, with all their inadequacies and imperfections, experiencers are then able to love themselves as well. This acceptance seems to allow them to open themselves to others, and to offer their calm assurance and support. What has been your experience in this regard?*

KR: What you said is right. I've talked with a fair number of persons who have told me how they felt liberated from the tyranny of their own previous judgments about themselves, of the feelings or opinions that others may have had about them, because of the unconditional acceptance that they received from the light. They feel that if the light can accept them with all their faults and shortcomings, then regardless of whatever doubts they may have about themselves, they know that they are an okay person as they are. That's a tremendous liberation. It's not that you would put on airs or think that you are a special person; but you know that you are absolutely okay, that you are loved just the way you are. This is one of the great and abiding gifts of the NDE. I would also add that this is true not only for the experiencers (although they learn it in a very compelling way because of the experience), but also the truth of their experience is valid for everyone. So, potentially, everybody can have this kind of knowledge, either through an NDE or in some other way.

EEV: *In fact, in a very imperfect way, that's what parents are supposed to do for their children.*

KR: Yes, to create a sense of unconditional acceptance. God is often thought of as the father, so to the extent that parents or anyone really expresses the love of God, then the child would be able to feel it. We are imperfect beings, but to the degree that some parts of the divinity show through us, to that same degree we will be able to respond to people in an unconditional way. This is one thing we can learn from experiencers.

EEV: *The encounter with the "being of light" is free of judgment. During the life review, the experiencers understand, with the help of the "being of light," every one of their actions, both good and bad, and feel the pain they have caused others. The compassion of the "being of light" helps experiencers endure this process, which, given its negative aspects, might otherwise be unbearable in terms of their self-reproach and remorse. The aim of the life review is apparently to help experiencers understand their faults and to make them into better persons, without judging them or making them feel guilty. This is far different from the approach taken by many religions, which threaten the sinner with punishment!*

KR: Yes. This is the beauty of what one gets from the life review, especially regarding the judgment of one own's life. People don't feel guilty, they just see with compassion and understanding how what they have done has affected others. I can give you an example. A friend of mine, when he was a young man, was very hot tempered and often got into trouble and into many fights. One day he was driving very fast and recklessly, and he nearly hit a pedestrian. He stopped his car, a fight took place; he knocked the pedestrian unconscious, left him lying on the road, and drove away. He was soon overcome by fear of the consequences of what he had done, so he reported this incident to the police (nothing bad happened to him). Years later, the same man, my friend, had a life review, during which this particular scene was shown to him. He found himself with a dual consciousness—one part of him seemed to be high above, in a building, watching the fight take place in the street below him, but another part of him was actually in the scene. Except that, this time, he was the other man, and he felt all thirty-two blows (he was able to count them) that he himself was now receiving as the *other man*. And like him, he also finally fell unconscious to the ground. But there was no judgment, just a complete understanding of what the effects of his actions were on others. What one can draw from this is that the Golden Rule is not simply a prescription for conduct, such as "Do unto others as you would have them do unto you," but it's actually a description of *the way things work*. Because what we do to others, we really do receive ourselves, as shown by this example and many others. And yet, there is no judgment, there is no God judging you, but you see the consequences of your actions and you learn that what you do, and even what you think, has effects on other people. To have this kind of understanding is a tremendous illumination; it's another of the great gifts that is conferred by the NDE.

EEV: *The "being of light" is often compared to an extremely powerful and loving energy. What do you think of this concept of energy?*

KR: It's a little vague. It's hard to know what to make of the being of light, except that it's a radiant intelligence. It seems to know everything about you. Maybe it's an aspect of your higher self, maybe it's an emanation of God. I think that it's more than just an energy. It has an energy, but it's an intelligent energy that has wisdom and a knowledge about you. It's more than just an energetic phenomenon.

EEV: *I would like to discuss the question of faith in more detail. According to the testimonies that I have heard or read, there seems to be no difference between believers and nonbelievers— either in terms of the likelihood of their having an NDE, or in terms of the nature of the NDEs they do have. Have you come to the same conclusion?*

KR: Yes, I find that what a person believes about life after death, about God, what his religious views are make no difference with respect to the likelihood of having this kind of experience. Those who are not religious, who are atheists or agnostics or skeptics, are just as likely to have the experience. What the experience creates is not faith afterwards but a knowledge of what is, a knowledge that there is a spiritual dimension to the universe. There is a famous film of Carl Jung, who himself had an NDE, where he is being interviewed, and he is asked whether he believes in God; he pauses, as I remember, and he says that he doesn't believe, but that he knows, he's had the direct experience. Near-death experiencers would say the same thing. Regardless of what they believed before, they know afterward that the spiritual reality is there and they cannot deny it. They don't care what others think; they know that it's true for them. And so for the experiencers, it creates not a faith, because faith is something you have to accept, but it creates a deep inner knowing based on direct experience.

EEV: *It is more a fact than a belief.*

KR: Yes, exactly. It's more a fact than a belief.

EEV: *Following their NDEs, it seems that experiencers distance themselves somewhat from religious practices of any kind. They give the impression of being in direct communication with God and don't seem to pay much attention to churches, for example, which become a sort of intermediary from their point of view. Their attitude toward life and others seems to be more important than sterile worship. Did you get this same impression from the experiencers you encountered?*

KR: One woman who had an NDE was told by her minister: "You don't have to come to church anymore, you have the church within you." Experiencers have told me that they may like to continue to go to church, but if they don't find that the experience they have in church resonates with their own knowledge gained during the NDE, they don't stay there. Of course, many churches are social organizations, or they preach a particular kind of dogma. The experiencer gains this universal understanding that all religions have their own truth, their own beauty, and their own value. But it's almost impossible for an experiencer to look at one's particular religious tradition as being the only way or the best way. I remember Alan Watts, who was quite a controversial yet great comparative philosopher of religion, and who was also an Episcopal priest at one time. He said that he often had a hard time finding God in church, but he could always find God in nature. Experiencers would feel very much the same way—everything becomes sacred, everything is holy, you don't have to go to a particular place called a church or a synagogue, or some house of worship, to be able to be in communion with that. Because they have experienced the light, experiencers bring that light back with them, and the light is God for them. Like the woman I described who carries the church everywhere within her, we don't have to go to a specific location in order to be able to be in touch with that divinity.

EEV: *But experiencers seem to really want to do something with their faith; they want to help people.*

KR: Yes, this is right. They act on the traditional Christian ideals of charity and service to others, not because they feel it's the right thing to do, but because they understand that it's the way it's supposed to be. We are here to help others and to express kindliness in our relations with others and with all life—to be stewards of the earth and not just its exploiters. It's the natural way to be for them. These individuals are very Christian in their understanding of the value of being charitable and of service to others. They know that service is the natural expression of love: If you really love, then you want to help others; it's natural, of course, how could you do anything else? Those who have this experience have what can be called a religious conversion, not in a narrow religious sense, but a spiritual conversion. Someone who used to be a gangster, a criminal before his NDE, said after his NDE that "to help others is more real than this world is real."

EEV: *I would like to go back to some of the main elements of a typical NDE. Concerning the life review, it is interesting to note that apparently insignificant events, which seem to be buried in the past, come to the surface during an NDE. This raises the issue of* memory. *Research in neurophysiology has indicated that we have something resembling an internal computer that records the tiniest details of our lives, which are usually* inaccessible. *These events reappear in part, and seem to be chosen by accident during the NDE. What purpose could this unceasing collection of data throughout life serve, if not for use in the realm beyond earthly existence?*

KR: David Lorimer, an English writer on NDEs, has explored the question of the life review and of the panoramic memory. Its importance is not just in the stored information itself, but in the ability to see this information in a holistic way, to see it with the understanding of the whole web of the life that you have led and of how this life has affected others. The meaning of your life does not come just from the experiences in themselves, but from how these experiences are woven together in your specific life pattern. It is a revelation for people to see this during their NDE. And assuming that the NDE is a prelude to what happens at death, then we may say that at death we may have a fuller life review. It seems that everything that is important about us is stored in that information. It is fine to compare this mechanism to a computer, because it is what gives us the output. But what is really important is what we do with the output. We could say that it's a teaching device, that it's the soul's gift to individuals in order to allow them to really understand what life is all about. The life review is an extremely important feature of the NDE. Perhaps the most important one is the feeling of love and that we are all part of that love. But the life review cannot be overrated in terms of its personal significance for the experiencer.

EEV: *An out-of-body experience can occur in other circumstances besides those surrounding the near-death state, and certain persons can even induce it deliberately. Is this proof that consciousness is not necessarily linked to the physical body?*

KR: It's not necessarily proof, it's evidence that suggests that there is a separation of consciousness from the physical body. The difficulty is that these experiences, of course, take place while the individual still has, and returns to, a functioning brain, which means that we cannot know for certain from these kinds of experiences whether consciousness can exist permanently separate from the body. But those who have these experiences are convinced that this is the case.

EEV: *We have many accounts of decorporation, but practically none of reincorporation. Survivors usually say, "And all of a sudden, I was back in my body." Can you provide an explanation for this?*

KR: Your statement is accurate, but I don't really have an explanation for it. Most people have a good sense of what the trip out is and usually not much sense of the trip back. Sometimes people do talk about the experience going in reverse; they go back, they pull back from the tunnel. But time seems to be dilated during the outward trip. An analogy could be a rubber band being stretched to the point of its maximum tautness—that can take a long time, but when it snaps back, it's in an instant. All the information is contained in the outgoing trip; there is essentially no new information on the way back. The experience is so profound going out that it may obscure the return trip because, psychologically, it's not as important for the individual to be aware of the return trip. It could be compared to a tape that's played, and when all the information is played, the tape recorder can be turned off. In fact, I've heard one or two people say that it's like a click in the ear; it just shuts off and that's it.

EEV: *Many experiencers develop psychic abilities after their NDEs. What is your experience concerning this fact?*

KR: There have been about six or seven different studies now, including the one I just completed, that show very clear evidence that individuals who had an NDE are much more likely to claim to have gained, afterward, a variety of psychic sensitivities or paranormal abilities, having more instances of telepathy, clairvoyance, precognition, especially precognitive dreams, out-of-body experiences, and so on. These claims, however, have never, to my knowledge, been tested in an objective way. We don't know whether these individuals are actually having more of these experiences or just becoming more sensitive to these experiences but that they had them all along. My studies have shown that people who are prone to NDEs are often individuals who are sensitive to the psychic realm to begin with, as children. So both might be true: There might be people who are very psychically gifted to begin with, and there are people whose gifts are enhanced by the experience. But there is no doubt that there is a relationship between having an NDE and having these enhanced paranormal sensitivities or awareness.

EEV: *Because these individuals seem to be prepared for such experiences?*

KR: Yes.

EEV: *In your opinion, which transcendental element is the catalyst for transforming the experiencer? Is it the fact of having narrowly escaped death, of having experienced the separation of consciousness from the body, the encounter with the "being of light," or the feeling of immortality?*

KR: I really don't have an answer to it. It's very difficult to separate these elements and say what leads to what, because they are all mixed together, and they are all important. But I can say that people who had out-of-body experiences often report some of the same effects as people who had NDEs, even though their experiences are far more shallow in many ways. They also often lose their fear of death, and they're often convinced of a life after death. So the fact that one could find oneself separated from the physical body probably carries a lot of weight in itself. But I can't really give you a definitive answer to this question.

EEV: *I would now like to discuss the instant of death, something that haunts us all and is a source of unbearable suffering when it concerns a person we love. Given this, it is essential to listen to experiencers when they tell us that the way death appears is very different from their experience of it. What we see from the outside doesn't concur with what the dying person feels. In fact, what the dying person feels is exactly the opposite of what the observer sees. Could you elaborate on this fundamental point?*

KR: In many ways the experience of death is the opposite from the appearance of death. What we see when we observe a dying person is a half-truth, as it leaves out something very important. It leaves out the interior part of the experience. Joseph Campbell says something to the effect that seen from afar, death is a horrifying specter, but seen up close, it has the face of the beloved. It's the face of the all-embracing, all-accepting beloved. That's what we don't see when we look at death from the outside perspective of the spectator. When we experience the process of death, then death, which has seemed like an enemy before, becomes a welcoming friend. So we need to have a full understanding of death and of what death has to teach us, not only about death but also about life. We can't deny the physical side of death, which is ugly, degrading and often hideous. But we can't let that facet of death blind us to the interior, beautiful, and sublime side of death. We need both perspectives to give us a fuller understanding of what death is.

EEV: *Could we interpret the accounts of experiencers as follows: The death of a loved one will always be painful, because it deprives us of an essential presence, but we shouldn't be sad for the person who leaves, only for those who stay?*

KR: Exactly. Experiencers would say, "I miss my mother, or I miss my husband deeply; nothing can replace him or her. But I'm perfectly okay about where he or she is right now. I'm not worrying about them. I'm just worrying about how I can get on with my life with that essential person missing."

EEV: *The thought of death is constantly present in our unconscious, since it sets the limit for all our hopes in time, and, ultimately, makes all our efforts seem absurd. If, on the other hand, all our actions, joys, and pains could extend infinitely, and if the purpose of our life were not measured solely in terms of our earthly existence, then might everything once more assume its true meaning?*

KR: This question really relates to the existential and transcendental perspectives of life. If life is terminated with death, as it may seem, then somehow all our actions in the end seem futile, life seems to be a cruel joke, nothing is forever, and one doesn't feel his or her existence as a reality. But if you take the view that comes out of the NDE, then there is no death, what we call life is only a prelude to true life, what we do here carries over to what we are there, and there is only a discontinuity, but there is no end, no annihilation, just a transition. Therefore, what we do here has enduring significance, because it does not cease when we cease bodily; it continues. Everything that we do, everything that we create, all of our actions continue to find a home in some place beyond death. So this gives a different perspective on life. It gives a sense that perhaps it's not as arbitrary or as absurd as many postmodern thinkers feel it is. In this respect, the NDE is almost subversive, because it gives rise to a wholly different set of values for living than those that dominate our contemporary materialistic culture, and because it undercuts postmodern secular thinking. It suggests that perhaps some of the teachings of the spiritual traditions and the universal parts of religious traditions still have a relevance in these times after all; they aren't just things that need to be discarded. Many people may have a difficult time relating to the NDE from the standpoint of modern consciousness, precisely because it doesn't seem to accord with current intellectual fashions. But the very fact that it will not go away, that it stubbornly persists as a phenomenon, a phenomenon that is gaining increasing interest, suggests that we will see a change in some of these postmodern worldviews to incorporate the spiritual dimension.

EEV: *In your book* Heading Toward Omega, *you carry your investigation further than simply describing and statistically registering NDEs. You try to show their deep significance for humanity and to give real meaning to this phenomenon, which in itself is anecdotal, but which becomes highly significant both quantitatively and qualitatively speaking.*

KR: The implication of the transformations that come about because of an NDE is that if you look at the NDE not merely as an experience of individual transformation but as a collective mass phenomenon, and if you note the kinds of changes there are occurring on a mass scale to millions of people across the world who have had this kind of experience, and who have undergone its transformative energies, then what the NDE collectively may represent is an evolutionary thrust toward a higher consciousness for all humanity. In other words, it may be a factor that serves as a catalyst that accelerates the growth of human consciousness toward higher and higher levels of functioning. So I see the NDEs as being potentially very important, not just for the individuals who undergo them but for a new planetary awareness, a higher level of consciousness for the human species as a whole.

EEV: *The number of experiencers will inevitably increase in the coming years, thanks to advances in medicine, especially in the area of resuscitation technology. As a result, there will be more and more experiencers in the future. Do you think they will have a real influence on society and maybe even lead to the transformation of humanity as a whole?*

KR: The fact that there is such a high rate of these experiences, and that many more people will have these experiences in the future, suggests the existence of an increasing current of evolutionary forces working through these experiences. That current has the power to push humanity toward higher levels of conscious functioning, so that humanity itself, not just experiencers, but humanity as a whole, as influenced by the river of NDEs, begins to act in ways similar to how experiencers behave—more compassionately, more lovingly, with greater wisdom. For example, I found in my most recent studies that not just people who have NDEs change in the ways that we've talked about but also people who become interested in the NDE, and who become absorbed in it, begin to show the same kind of value shifts—shifts in belief systems, in how they view the world—and they also show a loss of the fear of death and an increased conviction that there is life after death. They talk like experiencers and yet they have never had the experience. So, as publicity about this experience begins to spread (not just resuscitation technology creating more people that have the experience) and more people become familiar with the experience, it becomes like a secondary mass phenomenon. And a mass phenomenon has a lot of implications for planetary transformation. So I'm hopeful about the long-term consequences, and that's why I invite people to ponder the experience, to explore it.

EEV: *I would now like to discuss a childhood suicide attempt. Melvin Morse relates the case of a seven-year-old girl who tried to kill herself but was saved by a miracle. In describing what she learned during her NDE, she said: "When you hurt yourself, everything is hurt."*[4] *This is such a beautiful sentence one might think that the child had "supernatural" knowledge. Yet, one might also think that the psychological suffering leading to her suicide attempt also led her to obtain wisdom not often found in such a young child.*

KR: You could say that her suffering developed her wisdom, as wisdom does develop from suffering. But I also think that in these experiences—whether they are brought about by suicide, by some other crisis, merely by an accident, or an illness—there is a kind of knowledge that's conferred on the experiencer that, especially in the case of children, belies the age of the child. The child seems to be wise beyond his or her years. This is what seems to have happened to this child. And there is at least one other example in Melvin Morse's book about a child who attempted suicide and learned a great deal from that. There are many other examples from his studies of children, and from other people who study NDEs in children, that suggest that great wisdom comes through these experiences and that children are improbable, but nevertheless very persuasive, voices of that wisdom.

EEV: *Because the near-death experience seems so marvelous and the return to life so difficult, either for the sick or injured individuals who return to their physical suffering through reincorporation, or for the suicide attempters who find the same psychological conflicts as before, it would seem logical for them to attempt to regain this peaceful state as soon as possible. However, that isn't so. Experiencers tell us that, naturally, they are not afraid of dying anymore, but that they are not tempted to do anything to bring on death. There seems to be a moral interference, a sudden awareness that life is a gift we have no right to disdain. Where does this "inspiration" come from?*

KR: Whether someone comes close to death through a suicide attempt or in some other way, that person will realize in an incontrovertible sense of inner certitude that there is a meaning and purpose for his or her life. They find themselves part of a greater unity. They know that life is a gift, and that that state of wholeness and perfection during their NDE will be there for them when they die. They also see that, as a part of the meaning of their life, there is a design for it, there is a reason why they are alive. So if they were to die before their time, they would not be able to fulfill that purpose. The sense of purpose is very strong in experiencers, and the sense of an incomplete purpose would be obvious if their lives were to be prematurely shortened. Therefore, even though many of them may come back with illnesses as a result of what brought them close to death or with physical handicaps as a result of accidents, most people are grateful still to be here. They feel that they have a reason to be here, often to serve others or to contribute in some particular way. What happened at the point of death serves as a tremendous consolation and incentive for them, but it doesn't serve as a temptation to go back to one's death before one's proper time and before one has fulfilled one's purpose.

EEV: *Are there any elements in the accounts of NDEs that might give us a clearer understanding of life in the hereafter?*

KR: I don't think so. I've asked experiencers about this and, for the most part, they are very cautious about this subject. They say that they don't know exactly what life afterward will be, but they know that it will be beautiful, and that they will be happy there. Or they say that they know that it's something beyond the power of their imagination to conceive, even having had this experience. I don't think it's helpful to speculate about this too much. One thing that does seem to be implicated in many of their accounts is that there may be some reincarnational basis to life, that we may stay a while in an in-between state and then some aspects of ourselves may reincarnate.

EEV: *The majority do not say that, do they?*

KR: Actually, in one study, 78 percent of the persons who had NDEs believe in some form of reincarnation after their experience compared with 34 percent before their experience. In my most recent study, *The Omega Project*, I also found that a very considerable proportion of people shifted in the direction of being more open to reincarnation. This doesn't necessarily prove anything, but there is something about the experience that suggests this view. There seems to be nothing else, however, in the accounts of experiencers about what that life would be. To know more about this subject, we would have to turn to the esoteric and spiritual literature.

EEV: *Esoteric authors claim to know what happens after death, but they really don't know any more about it than we do.*

KR: Some of the people who haven't had these experiences can't necessarily accept as valid the claims of some authors who claim to know without having had an experience themselves. The reason that the NDEs have the compelling power to make us believe that there may be something authentic about this phenomenon is that the many thousands of people who have reported these experiences are, for the most part, ordinary people. And they all say very much the same thing. So it doesn't depend on the authority of any one man or woman. This may be the reason that we believe in their reports more easily.

EEV: *And even more so as they never claim to possess the truth; they just say, "I don't know exactly what's behind all this; I'm just telling you what happened to me."*

KR: Yes, they are generally unassuming. They usually do not have a dogmatic position that would fit one of the traditional belief systems, unless, of course, they are strongly committed to one of them.

EEV: *... and they don't try to persuade you.*

KR: They generally offer the information they have in a spirit of sharing what they have received, allowing others to draw their own conclusions. They usually don't talk about this indiscriminately, but if someone expresses an interest, they would say something like "This is what happened to me; I can only speak from my own experience."

EEV: *They don't write books and try to have people come and listen to them.*

KR: They are not trying to become spiritual leaders; they don't claim to be gurus.

EEV: *I would like to talk about the representation of consciousness during the NDE. One survivor described it as "... some-*

*thing loaded with emotions and the carrier of my whole person-
ality, directing itself toward a big light." Does this description
concur with the ones provided by your respondents?*

KR: I would say something slightly different, according to
the many narratives given by experiencers. The experiencers seem to have felt that they were more themselves,
an expanded version of themselves, as though their personal egoistic self was only a contracted or limited aspect
of their full being. People in this state seem to be able to
think more clearly, to have an expanded range of understanding, of consciousness, of wisdom. They seem to be
the essence of who they really are. I remember more than
one person saying, "Now I finally know what it is to be
alive." They knew it only on the moment of their apparent
imminent death. So it seems that, in this state, we expand
into the true essence of who we really are, and we are
flooded with a universal knowledge. Whether the knowledge comes from outside or whether it was inborn and we
simply recover it, it's hard to say.

EEV: *At the moment they leave their bodies, subjects experience a
moment of confusion. They see their inert body below them and
cannot understand how they can be physically dead, yet whole
in their psychological perception, at the same time. Does this
mean that the personality survives physical death intact?*

KR: I've found in my research that there seems to be a
persisting sense of personal identity following the onset of
the NDE. People seem to feel that they are themselves, the
essence of themselves, but the sense of personal identity is
not lost during this experience, it's retained. However,
from another point of view, we know that personal identity, in the sense of one's ego, is an illusion, a construction,
something that we build up; there is nothing solid to it;
it's just a bundle of thoughts and ideas and impressions,

all strung together and attached to a particular name. In speculation, what may happen following physical death is that the essence of one's self does continue, but the personality—which is not the essence or is only one expression of this essence—may eventually disintegrate or fall away because it is not essential. What is true and essential about ourselves, our real identity—that persists. But the personality, with a name, a history, and all the things associated with it, which we think are so important because of our being on earth—I doubt it survives intact. Because there is nothing solid to the ego, it doesn't have any permanent identity. I believe that this is an experience of eternity—eternity not in the sense of everlasting time but outside of time. The ego is in time, and anything in time will die. The body dies; no one says the body continues after death. So it seems that the ego, although it may persist for a time, will also undergo a death, and what will be left is the true essence of the individual, the self, as opposed to the ego. [*Pause*] You don't seem to be too happy with my answer.

EEV: *No, I am not. I'm trying to understand. When you say the essence, you mean just the fact of being a human being?*

KR: No, because the essence of ourselves is unique. There is something unique about all of us.

EEV: *But it's personal then, it's my personal history.*

KR: No. That's also unique, but that's not the uniqueness that I'm speaking of. If we were able to dissolve our personal history, if we just obliterated it but still persisted in some state, not necessarily on the physical plane, there would still be something unique and distinctive about us that would be apart from our personal history. There would be some essence, some emanation of our particular energetic component, of our intelligence, that would persist. It would be a soul essence rather than a personality essence. This is what would continue. The personality is like an artifact, it's what we have become identified with, it's an expression of our essence, but it's not the same as our essence. Instead of personality I could say "ego." The ego is put together for defensive purposes. We think it insulates us, we see it as our covering. Once the body dies and the ego has no reason to try to defend itself, there is no place for it, and the person undergoing an ego death would see that he or she is much more than the ego. But I don't mean to imply that we just dissolve into some kind of cosmic undifferentiated substance. Individuality is an important point for us in the West. I agree with the poet John Keats about this. Maybe we are just a little bit more narcissistic.

EEV: *We are very individualistic.*

KR: Yes, and we like that. And there is some truth to our sense that we are individuated beings. But this doesn't mean that our fundamental identity is tied up with our personality. Our fundamental identity is the individualized true essence of ourselves, and it is inextinguishable within us. It's something that existed before we were born and that continues after death. And if reincarnation does happen, it would probably be out of that essence. But I don't know what the experiencers would say. This is more speculation on my part.

EEV: *The personality is the ego, then?*

KR: Yes, the personality is like a covering. Do you know where the word *personality* comes from? It comes from the Latin word *persona*, which means mask. The personality is the mask that we wear in the play of life. We present ourselves in a particular way. And we have many different personalities. The study of multiple personalities has become fashionable in the United States. It's now obvious that we all have these different facets of ourselves that can be organized as personality. We don't have a single personality. But, underneath all these different personality expressions, there is an essence, not our personality, but there is something unique about us that nobody else has, or ever could have, and that will persist.

EEV: *But is it really unique? Don't we just dissolve into a cosmic wholeness?*

KR: No, I don't believe that. I believe that once an individual essence is formed, like a soul, it remains. Even though each of us is going to die as a body, none of us will ever be an "endangered species" (a species that is threatened with extinction) in terms of our essence. That essence, once it exists, will always persist and find some way of expression. So, no, I don't think that we just go back to the primordial soup or dissolve into an undifferentiated cosmic energy. And I don't think there is anything in the literature of the NDE that suggests that either.

EEV: *Could you call this essence the soul?*

KR: Yes. And there could be other terms.

EEV: *Many survivors have prophetic visions. What is the content of these forecasts, and what value do you attribute to them?*

KR: Generally speaking, people who have prophetic planetary visions see widespread ecological disasters, earthquakes, floods, hurricanes, economic collapse, everything bad. Then they see it followed by a kind of a Golden Age, an age of human brotherhood, of harmony, of a long time of peace, and so forth. It's basically the death and rebirth of the earth, almost like a planetary NDE. These experiences are important, but I certainly don't take them literally. I don't believe that people are tapping into a predictive future or that they have necessarily seen what is going to be the state of our planet. The significance that I give to that is that these are people who see the need for the planet to undergo a profound transformation. And they are experiencing this in a sort of geologic imagery, the expression of an archetype, the archetype of death and rebirth. Many prophets often have these same kinds of experiences in cultures that are undergoing severe crisis. They have these same kinds of cataclysmic visions of death and rebirth of their particular cultures. If we assume that the planetary culture is in crisis, then the experiencers are serving a prophetic function, collectively. They see the need for a transformation of our earth if our earth is to survive. So I read a more ecological message into these experiences, the need of an ecological and environmental reform so as to live in harmony with the earth. I don't see these visions as portending any kind of natural disasters on a mass scale but, rather, the death of the planet in a spiritual sense if we don't wake up to the requirements for living in harmony with nature and with one another.

EEV: *Do you think that some prophets, and maybe even Jesus, had NDEs?*

KR: One can only speculate about this, but certainly Paul (who was then Saul) had an experience on the road to Damascus that essentially led to his conversion and the establishment of Christianity as an institutional religion. I wonder whether Mohammed might have had one of these experiences, I wonder about Saint Francis, who was very ill. I've heard that Mary Baker Eddy, the founder of Christian Science, may have had an NDE. It wouldn't surprise me that some of the religions, both of ancient and modern times, were significantly influenced by experiences of this kind. Even in the studies of early forms of Buddhism— Buddhism of the fourth and fifth century in China—it's known that some of their religious leaders had what we today call NDEs or deathbed visions. To what extent they played a significant role in the development of some of the ideas of these religions is hard to say. But my feeling is that experiences of a transcendental kind, whether an NDE or some other, rest in the heart of many of the world's great religions and spiritual traditions. It would be interesting for somebody to do a study of this in the light of modern knowledge about the NDE, going back to the archival documents about the founding of some of these religions to see whether or not these experiences played a cardinal role in the lives of their founders.

EEV: *Some prophetic, planetary visions indicate several possible alternatives, several trajectories leading toward the future, but the experiencer doesn't know which one will ultimately take place. Consequently, free will remains, since man is able to choose from among the various possible alternatives.*

KR: From the standpoint of the NDE, there is the sense of alternate futures. In other words, the future is not fixed. We are the ones who, in our very actions, are determining our future in a particular way, as an outcome of many different individual choices. The prophetic aspect of the NDE does not imply that the future has a fixed course. There is nothing fixed about anything, and certainly not about the future. The future is up to us.

EEV: *In your book* Heading Toward Omega, *you draw an interesting parallel between Sheldrake's theory of morphic resonance and the impact of NDEs on humanity. Can you summarize this idea?*

KR: I can try. The theory of morphic resonance is an attempt to try to understand why certain things that occur in the world tend to persist, or tend to be learned more easily than others. Rupert Sheldrake, who is the inventor of this theory, says that once a certain behavior occurs in the world, it creates an invisible field, a morphic field, a field that has a particular kind of structure to it. And once this field is established, it's easier for the behavior it represents to occur again or to be learned. So, what we call the laws of nature are, in a sense, really only habits. Regarding the NDE, we know that millions of persons already had this experience, and more and more persons are having it. The more this experience takes place, Sheldrake would say, the easier it is for it to occur again because of the morphic field that was formed, which creates a resonance with these experiences. So the easier it is for these experiences to occur, the more they spread and the stronger the field becomes. Moreover, it's not just that these experiences would occur more easily, but there is another morphic field that has also begun to develop for the kinds of changes that are brought about in people by these experiences. It is the morphic field for the transformative aspect of the NDE. As more and more people undergo these kinds of transformations, the field becomes stronger, and even people who have not had these experiences can nevertheless be directly affected by that field and, therefore, begin to act in ways similar to individuals who actually had the NDE. It is a kind of contagion effect—the spreading of the NDE—not just because more people are having the experience, but because this morphic field exists, and it amplifies its transformative energies throughout the world. This is one of the chief mechanisms that has the ability to foster a new kind of consciousness throughout humanity.

EEV: *NDEs all over the world seem to be very much alike. Does this mean that each civilization has created its own religion, according to its beliefs and peoples, but that there is only one universal truth?*

KR: I'm inclined to think that however different the exoteric teachings of different religions and spiritual traditions may be, still, at the core, there is only the light, there is only God, there is only a universal intelligence. That intelligence is refracted through different belief systems, through different traditions, through different cultures. It may look very different by the time it is refracted into the cultures as a whole. In other words, the light goes through a prism and it comes out violet in one place, red in another, green in another, and so on, but there is only the light. This is what people touch in an NDE, they get to the universal core that lies within all the religious traditions. The way that core is expressed is as variable as people are variable and as diverse as cultures are different. But the implication of the NDE is that there is an underlying unity.

EEV: *In which direction is NDE research heading? Now that the phenomenon has been studied from the psychological perspective, should research now focus on the physiological aspects?*

KR: Yes, it seems that it's moving toward further studies of the neurological and the biological aspects. In the latest studies that I've done, for example, I found clear indications that people who have NDEs report consistent changes in their physiological, neurological, and brain functioning. Other people are reporting similar physical effects. There are a number of Russian scientists who are very interested in doing such studies. There are neuroscientists, also in the United States, who are interested in trying to study brain functioning and changes during and following NDEs. There is enough evidence now on the psychological aspects of the NDE and on the transformative aspects. Most of the work that has been done so far, even if it has been done by physicians, has been research on the phenomenology of the NDE and its effects, but not medical research. We still know relatively little about what really underlies this experience at a neurological level. This a very interesting and important frontier for scientists to explore. And I think this is a direction in which we ought to move. The existence of the NDE has been established beyond any doubt. Whatever you make of the experience, whatever your interpretation of it is, you can't deny that this experience happens. It has happened to a great number of people, and it has profound effects on their lives. Now that the phenomenon has been established, it needs to be reckoned with. And if science wants to have a say in this, it needs to use its methods of investigation to look at further aspects of the NDE. So I think that the neurological study of the NDE is perhaps one of the most promising and exciting of the avenues that beckon to us researchers as we move into the last years of our millennium.

Chapter Six

Dialogue with Louis-Marie Vincent, Ph.D.

LIFE

EEV: *Professor, today we will be exploring the subject of the near-death experience (NDE) from the standpoint of information. You have devised a new theory, which you are developing in conjunction with doctors, physicists, and biologists as part of GREC.B* (Groupe d'études des champs biologiques), *of which you are the founder and president. What would lead a biologist, who by definition studies life, to be concerned with subjects that essentially have to do with death, such as resurrection and NDEs, and what connection do you make between the two?*

LMV: NDEs are often referred to as "journeys to the threshold of death." The question as to whether or not the

Ph.D., Biology and Physical Chemistry; M.S., Electromechanical Engineering; Former laboratory director, Centre d'Etudes Nucléaires de Saclay; Former professor, University of Paris VI; President/Director GREC.B traveler crosses this threshold is one that is still being debated. The answer depends, to a certain extent, on one's particular point of view. Resurrection, by definition, is not ambiguous; it means a return to the land of the living. These questions fascinate me from the dual perspective of a biologist and a believer. To claim that an individual, whose bones, in the words of François Villon,[1] are nothing more than "ashes and powder," will come back to life, is nevertheless quite a strong statement! So strong, in fact, that even theologians tiptoe around it. As I stated in my book,[2] it would have annoyed me greatly as a Christian to be forced to believe something which, as a biologist, I would consider ridiculous! That's why I decided to take a closer look and, speaking as a biologist, realized that not only do we not really know what life is, but we are not quite sure what death is either.

EEV: *Before discussing the phenomenon of the NDE, I would like for us to talk about life. I think we can safely say that the life of an individual begins well before conception. Its life is already potentially present in the genetic information contained in the DNA molecules of the parents' chromosomes.*

LMV: Life is a chain which, according to Bergson (and I quote this from memory) links one germ to another, as it passes through bodies.... Biologists have long made a distinction between *germen*, the uninterrupted chain of life, and *soma*, the body, or more precisely, the individual. Yet, it is not certain—whether molecular biologists like it or not—that all genetic information is contained in the DNA molecules. We are just beginning to understand the role of cytoplasm,[3] but other types of information storage are also conceivable. As for the individual, he or she definitely originates upon conception, being the result of the fused genetic capital of the father and mother. This is true of sexual reproduction, although in nature there are plenty of other methods of reproduction to which the notion of the individual does not similarly apply. Let us take, for example, the case of asexual reproduction by simple cell division, in which the parent cell divides into two, identical daughter cells. There is no dead body, so we can say that the cell is immortal. But we can also say that the parent cell has ceased to exist as an individual in order to give birth to two daughter cells, which will in turn flourish and then grow old.... There is also the case in which the two daughter cells differentiate; one becomes male, the other female. They then unite to form a new cell, whose *genome* is different from that of the three preceding cells. Another case in point is that of snails, which alternate between male and female, and between fertilizing and being fertilized.... Entire books have been devoted to such subjects as the sexuality of mushrooms. It's not exactly erotic, but it is extremely fascinating!

EEV: *We have seen that the beginning of life does not correspond to a specific point in time, but rather to a series of successive stages in which a possibility becomes a reality, or a potential is actualized. It would therefore be quite surprising to find at the other end of human existence, that is, at death, an abrupt and total rupture at a specific point in time. It would seem logical for death, like the actualization of the life potential, to instead be a transformation from one state to another, and, why not, in this case as well, a transition from a less-evolved to a more highly evolved state, since the general evolution of nature is always toward an ever-higher, never lower order, even if that sometimes takes millions of years!*

LMV: A distinction must be made between life in general—including its nature and origin—and the life of an individual. Each individual human being is unique in the history of humanity. Even if humanity were to survive for billions of years more, there would never be two perfectly identical human beings. Not at the time of their birth—even in the case of identical twins—and much less at the time of their death, since they will not have had identical life experiences. An individual is somewhat like a novel written with the words of the dictionary; the same words can be used to write an infinite number of novels. The words belong to everyone, but the novel is unique. It does not exist before it is written, but once written it will always exist, if only as part of the history of humanity, even if it disappears from memory.

EEV: *If we follow this reasoning, we find ourselves going as far back as the origin of living organisms, or even farther still.... We know that the atom, and thus energy, is the basic building block of matter, whether living or inert. As the physicist Lupasco has shown, this energy is subjected to a cycle of potentialization and actualization. The elementary particles of the atom—the electrons, neutrons and protons—have an unlimited existence. They cannot be destroyed; they can only change states. Can we, in your opinion, extrapolate from this and say that life has no beginning—or end?*

LMV: I am not a physicist. You mentioned Lupasco, but there are others, such as Jean Charon, David Bohm, Régis Dutheil, not to mention Teilhard de Chardin, who have also studied this question. In order to know if the beginnings of life may exist at the atomic or particle level, one must first define what is meant by *life*. And that is quite a task! Life is not a substance, or a fluid, as was once held by the vitalists. As for myself, I have shown that life may be understood as a state of matter (it is actually a metastate), which is defined by its properties, in the same way as the liquid or gaseous state. We know that in these states, the constituent atoms are more or less closely linked. The living state corresponds to a certain arrangement of atoms in space and in time. If you incinerate a flower, you can gather back up, in the form of ashes, all the atoms that once constituted it, but the flower and the life will have disappeared. Therefore, in my opinion, life is, first and foremost, information that structures matter in a specific way. An individual human being is a particular living structure among all possible living structures. However, information is more than letters written on paper or signs represented by molecules; it is also the meaning conveyed by these letters and words. Meaning is something abstract; it is different from matter and exists only at the level of consciousness. I believe it is the second constituent of the universe. We can think of it as the *logos*, the very thought of the great architect! This point of view will, of course, shock the materialists. In order to explain the extraordinarily complex structures of living matter, without allowing for the existence of a creative intelligence, they are forced to rely upon chance. There's just one problem: We don't know what chance is either!

EEV: *Do you see life as a closed circle without beginning or end, or rather as a line emerging from the dawn of time and extending out into infinity?*

LMV: I think that inasmuch as the beginning of the universe may be traced back approximately 14 billion years, it is reasonable to think that life also had a beginning and will most likely have an end, at least as concerns the earthly form in which we know it.

MATTER, INTELLIGENCE, CONSCIOUSNESS

EEV: *Modern physics is increasingly looking to the mind, rather than to matter, to answer many questions. Interestingly, recent studies are tending to show that elementary particles are en-*

dowed with something akin to intelligence and approaching consciousness.

LMV: It is typical that physicists, especially quantum physicists, are the ones currently theorizing about the existence of a form of intelligence within matter, even at the most elementary level of particles, while quite paradoxically, biologists, who by definition study the phenomena of life, are the ones still operating under a completely reductionist or materialistic model of molecular biology. I am not sure we can talk about intelligence at the particle or atomic level. At the level of the cell, the building block of living organisms—yes. Great physiologists such as Louis Lapicque or, more recently, Paul Chauchard, have come out on the side of the existence of consciousness at the cellular level. They concur in this regard with the brilliant intuitions of Teilhard de Chardin. However, I think it is better to speak of intelligence [rather than consciousness] in order to avoid confusion with human reflective consciousness. However, "intelligence" refers not only to the storage but also to the processing of information. This also requires an operator, in the mathematical sense of the term. In my opinion, it is the mind, or the self, which plays this role.

EEV: *How do you define consciousness, and how does it fit into your theory of information?*

LMV: That's a very difficult question, and I am not actually qualified to say what consciousness is. That question would better be put to philosophers, since the term is used in different ways by different people. One can speak of consciousness, intelligence, the mind, the psyche.... In my opinion, aside from its moral or religious aspects, consciousness is basically the possibility of receiving, storing, and processing information in order to produce new information.

EEV: *Is consciousness located on the material or nonmaterial plane?*

LMV: Actually—and I think we will have the opportunity to come back to this point—the word *information* is itself ambiguous. Information consists of a material component or medium, which is the message. The message may take the form of letters written on paper, electromagnetic signals, sounds, or molecules. Keep in mind, however, that these signals have a meaning, and it is this meaning that constitutes the nonmaterial component. Information is therefore complex (mathematically speaking) in nature, being at once material and nonmaterial.

EEV: *We can assume that the atoms that make up our bodies while we are alive are going to survive us "eternally." Clearly, this is small consolation. Whether we disappear completely or whether we survive as electrons—these are equally joyless prospects! Of course, this is not what the world's religions mean by the afterlife. In the Letter on Eschatology, for example, the Church affirms the survival after death of a spiritual element endowed with consciousness and will in such a way as to preserve the human self. Are the scientific and religious viewpoints mutually exclusive, or do they complement each other?*

LMV: This is yet another formidable question, and the answer will depend upon one's philosophical orientation. As for myself, I think these ideas complement one another. Of course we know that atoms, like energy, are indestructible, and that the atoms from which we are made will survive us. And yes, it would indeed be small consolation to imagine our survival as electrons. However, there are two things that should not be confused: On the one hand, life itself as something very general, such as a state of matter, and on the other, the life of an individual. Life may perpetuate itself, but the individual will remain unique. The Letter on Eschatology describes it well when it says that something unique will remain after the dissolution of the material body.

TIME

EEV: *When we speak of "resurrection" and of "eternal life," we call upon the notion of* time. *Yet quantum physics describes an atemporal dimension in which there is absolute simultaneousness—the past, present, and future no longer exist. It seems to me, therefore, that from this perspective, the notions of "eternal life," "eternity," and "immortality" are devoid of meaning, since they are bound by the notion of linear time.*

LMV: Yet another difficult question to answer. I am not certain whether even the greatest specialists have a definitive answer. There is in effect a contradiction inherent in this concept of eternity. Historically, the notion of eternity has been understood to mean a very long time, time which goes on forever. This concept goes back as far as the epic of Gilgamesh, the Sumerian hero who sets off in search of the plant of immortality. However, certain physicists find it tempting to consider that the realm of the mind is located in another space–time, one in which time does not flow. Eternity may therefore be understood as an eternal present, where there is virtual synchronicity of all existing information and data. It is similar to spreading a movie film out before you and simultaneously viewing all of the frames versus seeing it on a screen, where the frames are viewed successively as the film advances. Nevertheless, where I see a contradiction, or at least a problem in interpretation, is in the fact that, according to the Catholic religion (the Letter on Eschatology is absolutely categorical), not only does that which survives death—the soul, or whatever name it is given—maintain its personality, it moreover possesses true life. This implies that there is in fact life in the spiritual realm. But life necessarily connotes a certain dynamism. Living beings (whether material or nonmaterial) typically evolve and perform actions, so there must be a temporal element, a before and an after; there must be a passage of time. Thus, rather than an absence of time, might eternity perhaps correspond to a time that is different from our earthly time? I do not know. This is a question to ask of physicists.

EEV: *The concept of time has been the subject of countless studies, as much from the mathematical, or physical, as philosophical perspectives. Five types of time may be distinguished: conceptual time; physical, or relativistic time; thermodynamic time; physiological, or biological time; and perceived, or psychological time. Can you briefly summarize the characteristics of these different types of time? Let's begin with conceptual time.*

LMV: The mere fact that we speak of these different types of time is, to my mind, proof that we do not really know what time is. Let me try to define them. Conceptual time is the time of the "Euclidian universe," in which time passes or flows completely independently of what is happening in space. Imagine a room with a wall clock. Two people come into the room. The clock will show the passing of an hour no differently if the people remain seated, walk around and talk, or leave the room entirely. Likewise, "Euclidian space" is conceived as a sort of box into which objects may be placed or not placed, but in any case the space exists. In my example, the dimensions of the room will remain the same before and after the people come in. In summary, conceptual time refers to a time conceived of by our minds, which does not necessarily correspond to reality. As a matter of fact, the theories of relativity, which were first developed by Einstein, have revealed the error of this view by showing that space cannot exist without matter. Indeed, it is matter, and ultimately energy, that creates space, and in any case, if there is no space, then there is no time either. This is more or less what is meant by "relativistic time."

EEV: *What about thermodynamic time?*

LMV: This is a third type of time, based on a rather recent concept attributed, in particular, to the Belgian physicist and Nobel laureate Ilia Prigogine. Prigogine links this type of time to the chemical reaction process. We know that any exchange of energy, any chemical reaction, results inevitably in the production of entropy—a degraded form of energy that is no longer useful in any way. According to Prigogine, thermodynamic time is in fact synonymous with this chemical reaction process. If one were to freeze a reaction, time would no longer flow. This model of time is quite different from the preceding ones since, if you think about it, it means that time is something that does not exist. It is as much a convention as the time indicated by the clock. Clocks do not in fact produce time; we may notice the movement of the hands around the dial, but time itself is something completely relative and subjective.

EEV: *This leaves physiological, or biological time, and perceived, or psychological time.*

LMV: These last two types of time are somewhat closely related to the ideas of Prigogine, with the only difference being that they more specifically concern living beings. As for thermodynamic time, it can be viewed in the context of a quite ordinary chemical reaction occurring *in vitro*.

Physiological time is the time during which biological processes occur. This notion of biological time was discovered by physician and biologist Pierre le Comte du Nouy. While caring for the wounded during World War I, he noticed that identical wounds would heal at different rates depending upon the age of the patient. He then deduced, with mathematical formula in hand, that time did not pass uniformly for living beings, the way it did for physical phenomena, such as the rotation of the earth around the sun. He concluded that each living being had its own time. At the end of the work he devoted to this subject, *Le temps et la vie* (*Biological Time*), Pierre le Comte du Nouy[4] wondered if ultimately, by analogy with the theory of relativity, life were not a particular deformation of space–time. Psychological time has been the subject of various studies, including the work of Lévy[5] which, mathematically speaking, is extremely well founded. He shows that our perception of time depends upon the number of events we register. If we were to stay in a room in which absolutely nothing was happening, and without any frame of reference, we would not have a clear idea of the passage of time. The time would seem to pass either very slowly or very quickly. Consequently, what gives rhythm to our perception of time is in fact the unfolding of events accessible to our consciousness. This is why time can seem to pass very slowly if we are waiting for something, or inversely, very quickly, if we are experiencing strong stimulation.

EEV: *Which of these five categories of time best fits your conception of resurrection?*

LMV: Once again, this is difficult to answer. In fact, I conceive of two kinds of time: the time corresponding to the spiritual or mental world, which Nobel-prize winner John Eccles refers to as "the number two universe," and the time in which physical bodies move. By the way, theologians became aware of this difficulty very quickly and came up with a kind of time they call *"aevum* time," which is specific to extraterrestrial entities and angels. We can surmise that this time is different from earthly time, and that it is located in the space–time of consciousness. The features of this type of time will, of course, depend upon the physical hypotheses that can be made concerning the nature of these abstract entities, these types of consciousness—in particular in the context of superluminal physics. It must be noted, however, that other theories are also possible.

EEV: *It is therefore not necessarily one of these five types of time that will best describe the dimension that interests us?*

LMV: Correct. It is not necessarily one of these five types of time, or rather four types, since we have seen that conceptual time does not exist. We also know that relativistic, thermodynamic, and biological time refer to the world of matter, whether inanimate or living. We can very well allow for the existence of yet another type of time, which precisely concerns the realm of consciousness, or of the psyche, such as I have just described.

THE SURVIVAL OF PHYSICAL DEATH

EEV: *Let us now turn to what happens at the moment of the near-death experience. Life has left the physical body, all physiological functions have stopped, brain activity is nonexistent. Yet, the experiencer's consciousness is functioning, since he or she perceives and registers the events of the NDE, which he or she can recall after returning to life. My first question concerns the notion of clinical death. I suppose that at present it is still very difficult to determine the precise moment of physical death, since*

*the corresponding criteria (respiration, heartbeat, brain activity,
etc.) have changed over time. Can we say that the experiencers
were actually clinically dead during their NDEs* according to
our current clinical criteria, *but that these criteria are, in fact,
erroneous, since these persons came back to life?*

LMV: That is, no doubt, the main issue concerning NDEs,
and I must say that I do not agree with what I have read on
this subject in various publications, because they always
question whether the experiencers were truly dead or not.
This question is flawed in two respects: First of all, before
we can say if someone is *truly dead*, we must have an exact
definition of death, which is not at all simple. As I mentioned earlier, in order to do this we must define what *life*
is. Allow me to come back to this point for a moment. I
consider life to be a state of matter. A state is defined by its
properties: A gas is compressible; a liquid is not, but it can
flow, unlike a solid, and so on. In the same way, a living
being can be defined by a *set of properties*, such as its
consumption of various forms of energy, its ability to
reproduce itself or to move about.... Some systems exhibit
the properties associated with life, without, however, being alive. An automobile moves and consumes energy, but
it does not produce baby automobiles. A mule is definitely
a living animal, but it does not reproduce itself either! A
virus can be crystallized, yet it reproduces itself, and so
on. These few examples illustrate the fact that these issues
are not simple. The boundary between the living and the
nonliving is not as clear-cut as one might think. To simplify greatly, one could say that things are more or less
alive! Let us say that death is the state of something that
once was alive, but no longer is. Second, death in human
beings is neither instantaneous nor uniform. Let me explain. While an experiencer's brain activity may be considered nil (a flat EEG), can we really be sure of this?

Clearly, the main physiological functions, such as blood circulation, breathing, and so on, have stopped. The human being is dead as an individual, as an *organized unit*. But its components, its organs and cells, are, for the most part, still living. And they continue living for a certain amount of time, as evidenced by organ transplants. Total, absolute death will not occur until the last cell has ceased to live. Death is therefore not instantaneous, or uniform, since certain tissues and organs are more fragile than others. Take the brain for example. As the greatest consumer of oxygen, it is the first to be adversely affected. Yet there is another question more important than determining if these individuals were truly dead or not—at any rate, we know they've come back. What is essential is to determine whether or not death is a *reversible phenomenon*. We could say that these individuals were not really dead, because death was not total, but we could also say that they were actually dead but came back to life, because death is a reversible phenomenon. Take the simple example of an iron bar which, when heated, lengthens and dilates. If we let it cool, it will contract and return to its original size. This is what is meant by a reversible phenomenon. There is nothing to prove that death is not a reversible phenomenon. None of these questions has been resolved, so before asking if someone is actually dead, we must first know what we are talking about.

EEV: *We can agree that, at a given moment, the physical body actually ceases to function, even if current criteria used to ascertain this moment are perhaps not exact. Yet, how can we, from the biological standpoint, conceive of the existence of consciousness without a material medium?*

LMV: The answer will depend upon the philosophical orientation of the person to whom the question is put. If you look at it from a materialistic viewpoint, if you believe thought, psychic phenomena, and mental activity to be solely the result of neuronic activity, then you would say that whatever images may have been seen by experiencers were attributable to residual activity in their nervous systems or brains. This undetectable residual activity would then be classified as hallucination. On the other hand, if you take an openly spiritual standpoint, as I do, you would arrive at the conclusion that there is something beyond the physical body, and that consciousness exists even outside the physical body. This is the theory held by such scholars as John Eccles, Karl Popper, and Karl Pribram. According to John Eccles, the brain does nothing more than decode messages, or information sent to it by consciousness, so that these may be perceived by the physical body. Clearly then, in such conditions, even if the physical body is inactive, a consciousness existing independently of the material body may very well continue to function.

EEV: *If we admit that consciousness, will, and personality survive death, then there must be a "memory" of some kind somewhere. This "memory" cannot be contained in living matter, since matter is destined for complete disintegration. How can we conceive of this "conservation of the past"?*

LMV: This is indeed one of the basic questions that is likely to perplex confirmed materialists. I think that in describing NDEs we have perhaps not given enough attention to this problem of memorization. Indeed, in order for experiencers who come back to life to tell about what they have seen or heard during their journey, they must have memorized it somewhere. In the case of those in a state of clinical death, it is quite difficult to hold, as reductionists do, that this memorization occurs only at the level of the neuron, whether in the physical form of electric impulses, or in the molecular or chemical form. Keep in mind that clinical death is precisely the lack of brain-wave activity. Thus, we are forced to conclude that there is something else, possibly physical in nature, but belonging to a different kind of physics—quantum physics for example—that serves as a medium for the storage of these data, enabling the experiencer who comes back to normal life to recall and report them.

ENERGY

EEV: *We have known since the time of Einstein and his theory of relativity that matter is energy, and that it cannot be dissociated from space and time. Thought is also energy. Is energy that transforms itself into tangible and visible matter the same type of energy that transforms itself into invisible but omnipresent thought?*

LMV: What I am about to say is my own personal opinion. Energy is one, and I think that thought is indeed a specific form of energy. According to certain recent theories, thought and mental activity are located in a different kind of space–time in which elementary particles travel faster than the speed of light. Relativity experts can explain it much better. As for myself, I go even further in these assumptions. In an article, I once referred to a statement made by Teilhard de Chardin in *The Phenomenon of Man*, I believe. He says that love is the most formidable and mysterious form of energy. He obviously meant that in a symbolic sense, but I decided to perform a little exercise and take it literally, that is, to conceive of love as an actual form of energy, as understood by physicists. I was quite surprised to find that this led to conclusions that were not all that incoherent. We know that energy generally assumes more or less noble forms. Heat is the most degraded form; it is energy that can no longer serve any useful purpose. The most noble form of energy is light; it can be transformed into electricity, electricity can be transformed into movement, movement into heat, and so on. These transformations are not free; there is a price to pay and that price is the production of *entropy*. Accordingly, we can very well conceive of love as being the highest form of energy, as capable of being transformed into light, electrical energy, mechanical energy, and so forth. One may object that love is a human feeling and has no relation to physics. But that remains to be seen! In order to change heat into electricity, you need a turbine. In order to change electricity into heat, you also need a machine; it's called an electric radiator. Both of these are manufactured by man. So why couldn't man be the machine needed to transform love into other types of energy?

EEV: *But here you refer to love in a concrete sense, since you relate it to energy and heat, which are concrete data.*

LMV: Yes, energy, electricity, and heat are perhaps concrete things, but the boundary between what is concrete and what is not is rather difficult to establish. When we examine matter using progressively more powerful means of investigation, we see crystals, then atoms, then particles. Finally, at a certain point, it occurs to us that matter is a wave of probability. Matter dematerializes progressively, the closer we look. Therefore, the idea that thought, or let's say mental activity and feelings, including love, are forms of energy, does not particularly shock me.

EEV: *Does this mean that the realm of consciousness, in which love and feelings may be included, has a direct effect upon the material world?*

LMV: I am absolutely convinced of it. There is abundant proof; just think of psychosomatic illnesses.

EEV: *We are quite familiar with the physiological functioning of the brain, but much less so with the origin of thought, emotion, and intelligence. Where do you see the connection between physiological and psychic functioning?*

LMV: I am not qualified to answer this question. I would advise you to put it to neurophysiologists or psychologists. I would simply say, on the basis of my theory of information, that emotions, like sensations, represent the abstract side of information, in the same way that the sensation of the color red corresponds to the meaning of a message conveyed by an electromagnetic wave of a certain frequency, or that the sensation of sweetness is the meaning of a message conveyed by a certain molecule. I also think that, to a certain extent, emotions are meaningful aspects of information, no matter what kind of stimulus provokes them.

EEV: *The brain, which is the physiological medium of the mental dimension, obeys the laws of matter, as do all parts of the human body. And matter, being highly condensed energy, obeys the laws of thermodynamics. We know that energy cannot be destroyed; it can only be transformed by changing states. This is the basic principal of the conservation of energy. We have seen too how thought might also be energy. What happens at the time of death? How can we envisage these changes in the state of energy, given the fact that energy cannot be destroyed?*

LMV: We must come back to Eccles's model in which the brain acts as a detector or a decoder of information transmitted by an independently existing consciousness. If upon death the brain begins to deteriorate, then all the chemical processes involved in the decomposition of matter will obviously take place, in keeping with the usual laws governing the conservation of energy. However, this happens independently of the existence of consciousness, which, as we have seen, can position itself on another physical plane and remain unaffected by the physical alterations of the brain. As for the first part of your question, to say that the brain is a machine that obeys the laws of thermodynamics is true. To say that the thinking brain consumes energy is true; this has been proved experimentally. But a radio receiving a signal also consumes energy. Therefore the fact that the brain consumes energy is not proof of the material nature of thought.

INFORMATION

EEV: *We know that information is contained in the genetic code of DNA molecules. At the time of death, these molecules disintegrate. What happens to the information at this point? Is it not also necessarily doomed to destruction?*

LMV: If you look at a textbook of molecular or genetic biology, nearly every page will contain the word *information*. We talk about storing it, transmitting it, and so on, as if it were a thing in itself, a piece of candy to be offered or tasted at will! It is easy to show that, in fact, information is very complex in nature. It is made up of a material component (the paper and words written on it) and an abstract component (the meaning of these words or the thoughts of the person who wrote the message). This meaning exists only at the level of the consciousness of the writer and the reader of the message. Therefore, the answer is clear: DNA is like paper! When the molecules disappear, it is the material component of the information that disappears.

EEV: *If meaning is not contained in molecules, that is, in matter, then where is it contained?*

LMV: Meaning belongs to the mental realm, which brings us back to hypotheses concerning the existence of a super-luminal realm. There are, however, other possibilities, such as other space–times, or perhaps storage by electrons, although I find this last idea less attractive than the others.

EEV: *Your theory is based on the premise that information is made up of two components: the first, DNA, is a material medium; the second, meaning, is the abstract element residing in the consciousness of the transmitter. In order for it to be decoded by the receiver, he or she must have prememorized the meaning of the message so as to be able to interpret it. This brings us back to the idea that the cell has "consciousness"—in the sense of a "memory"—even if it is an elementary one.*

LMV: I totally agree with this viewpoint. I have published an article that shows how the concept of information supports the discovery of what Paul Chauchard calls bio-consciousness, that is, an elementary consciousness that is inseparable from life. Numerous studies have proved the existence of a transfer of information between cells, even at a distance. An analysis of the complicated mechanisms involved shows that messages are transmitted by different molecules and sometimes by electrical impulses, on a relay basis. Ultimately, what is preserved is the meaning, the intention of the message, which can only be explained by the existence of a form of intelligence, however rudimentary. If we deny its existence, we are reduced to the dualist concept of a body–machine and a transcendent mind, along with all the difficulty this entails for interpreting the psychosomatic interactions that are witnessed daily.

EEV: *I would like to quote a passage from your article "L'énergie et la pensée" (Energy and Thought), in which you state: "Information cannot exist alone, without a material medium in which to actualize itself."[6] Doesn't this contradict what you just said?*

LMV: No. I think that information, the abstract component of information, needs a material medium, and I come back once more to the theories to which I referred earlier. I repeat that we must agree on the meaning of the word *material*. What we usually mean by material is something visible and tangible. But a radio wave is neither visible nor tangible, unless it is captured and decoded by some device. It is nonetheless material, since it is energy that we know perfectly well how to measure, channel, and so on. Thus, we must be very clear about the meaning of the word *material*. When I say that the abstract component of information needs a material medium, I am thinking of a type of energy found in another space–time—superluminal or otherwise. As for DNA, or molecules that are in the "material" realm of ordinary space–time, I think these are only vehicles that allow a preexisting thought in the receiver's mental system to become actualized in this space–time. It is therefore somewhat like a switch, something that can reveal, or turn on, in a sense, a preexisting element.

EEV: *In one of your papers you wrote: "We can say that information is the second component of the universe, the first being inert energy that is either condensed or not into matter."[7] Does this mean that everything, absolutely everything in the universe is energy, except for information, which is abstract?*

LMV: I wasn't the one who said it, but that's precisely what I think.

RESURRECTION

EEV: *You are the author of a book entitled,* Peut-on croire à la résurrection? (Can We Believe in Resurrection?). *I would like to know if you mean the term* biological resurrection *to be taken in a symbolic or literal sense?*

LMV: I mean it literally, that is, in the sense of a resurrection of the physical body. In order to escape the difficulties raised by this issue, some theologians have indeed interpreted it in the symbolic sense, but in that case, it is not very clear what it is that is being resurrected.

EEV: *Before getting to the heart of the matter—that is, near-death experiences—I would like to come back to your physical/ biological approach to resurrection. According to your theory of information, we can envisage the preservation of memory—the storage of information, in the computer sense—beyond death and without a material medium. You conceive of a form of intelligence with a memory containing all the elements of a lifetime, thus encompassing a human personality, existing without a material medium and independently of the sense organs and brain. Given this assumption, how do you envisage a resurrection in the bodily sense of the term?*

LMV: I have already explained what is meant by *material*. It would be preferable to use the term *physical* or *transphysical*, the latter term being used to designate phenomena occurring faster than the speed of light. This will avoid confusion. My reply is therefore as follows: preservation without a material medium—yes, but preservation without a physical or transphysical medium—no. With respect to the preservation of the personality, it must be recalled that there are two categories of information: (1) that which is transmitted genetically and concerns the formation of the body (morphogenesis) and its functioning; and (2) the information acquired during a lifetime, which constitutes the "experiential memory." But we must not forget that thought does not consist solely of memorization; it also includes what we do with this information—in other words, its processing. We know that two individuals who witness the same event will not react to it in the same manner. We consider this processing to take place at the mental level by what we refer to in mathematics as an "operator." An example of an operator is the sign "×", or "multiplied by," which is placed between two numbers. What the operator's nature is, I don't know. Is it perhaps what philosophers refer to as the "self"? Whatever the case, the personality consists of all this information, taken as a whole, and its processing. According to Christian dogma, the personality is contained after death in a spiritual element called the soul. There is nothing to prevent us from interpreting this element as being precisely the above-mentioned transphysical medium, for example, the quantum field attached to superluminal particles.

EEV: *How can the survival of the soul explain resurrection?*

LMV: It's very simple. As I have shown, we often wrongly confuse the body with matter. Very precise experiments have shown that the substances of our bodies are constantly renewed, including our DNA. This can be illustrated by simple arithmetic: at the rate of two kilos of food a day for seventy years, an adult consumes and eliminates fifty tons of matter. What remains unchanged, or practically unchanged during this time, is *our form*. It is as if a current of matter were constantly passing through an invisible form.

EEV: *And what is a form?*

LMV: It is a 1-, 2-, 3-,... n-dimensional portion of space. In our case, it is a volume inside which the chemical components of the food we ingest are transformed into our own substance. Stated differently, it is inside this volume that the matter we ingest is informed as to how to become our own substance, to change from matter into the living state. Of course, this is not unrelated to the notion of the subtle or etheric body of some traditions. But here, more so than in other areas, we must remain prudent and guard against hasty conclusions. Getting back to the scientific domain, mathematicians define a *field* as a portion of space in which forces of any kind are exerted. Magnetic or electrical forces, for example. Or information. Therefore, in order for bodily resurrection to be possible, "it is sufficient" for the nonmaterial principle that preserves our information (call it the *soul* or the *quantum field*—the name is unimportant) to preserve somatic information, and in particular information that "codes" with respect to space. Resurrection will occur when matter is reinformed in such a field. But what will cause this to happen is another story altogether!

NEAR-DEATH EXPERIENCES

EEV: *Let us now get to the heart of the matter and talk about the problem of NDEs. We have already attempted to understand how the "nonmaterial self" might survive without a body. But some experiencers talk about having had a "subtle" body during their NDE. What do you think about this?*

LMV: I would not go so far as to speak of "experimental proof," but I would say that it nevertheless seems to support our ideas.

EEV: *Kenneth Ring is probably the researcher who has questioned the most experiencers. On the basis of what he has learned from their accounts, he suggests that the "subtle body" could be some sort of "crutch" that enables experiencers to keep their bearings in the disembodied state. As he explains, it is very difficult for us to think of ourselves as pure consciousness. But once they have assimilated this new condition, experiencers no longer need this artifice. Would the idea of a material body, even a subtle one, seem preposterous to you in this dimension, which appears to be essentially spiritual in nature?*

LMV: Not in the least, but I would not exactly describe it as a "crutch." This is how I see things: The field (I prefer this term to that of the subtle body, which is too esoteric for my taste) subsists with the information it carries. I think the experiencer needs some time to get used to the absence of spatial dimensions, in the usual earthly sense. I'll illustrate my point with an example. Let's say I draw a circle on a piece of paper and form a mental image of this figure. Now, I'm going to represent the same circle by its well-known equation: $x^2 + y^2 = r^2$ (where r is the radius of the circle). I need more time to form a mental image of the equation than of the geometric figure. And yet, they are the same; the same information is contained in the figure and in the equation.

EEV: *Experiencers relate their memories of the images, sensations, and conversations—in short, their interaction with an exterior "environment"—they experienced during their NDE. I would now like to discuss the sensory manifestations this presupposes. Of the five senses, only those of sight and hearing seem to persist, and they do so in an extremely enhanced form. The three other senses, those of smell, touch, and taste, seem to play no role during the NDE, except in the case where an experiencer tries to grab the arm of a living person and simply passes through it. Can you suggest an explanation for this?*

LMV: What strikes me, first of all, is that light and sound are conveyed by waves, whereas smell and taste are conveyed by molecules requiring matter for their transmission. The same goes for the sense of touch. If the field is wave-related, it seems logical that it can be affected by another wave-related phenomenon, but not by molecules. This, of course, remains very intuitive and is not an explanation; it's just a starting point for further investigation. Many issues need to be clarified.

EEV: *NDE accounts concur by and large, in that experiencers felt themselves to be weightless and perceived themselves as either disembodied or possessing an extremely lightweight form. This feeling of weightlessness is often accompanied by an impression of speed. In the words of one of Kenneth Ring's respondents in* Heading Toward Omega, *"Then, after that, I realized that I was able to float quite easily, even though I had no intention of doing that.... Then I very quickly discovered also that not only was I floating and hence free from gravity but free also from any of the other constrictions that inhibit flight.... I could also fly at a terrific rate of speed with a kind of freedom that one normally doesn't experience in normal flight, in airplanes, but perhaps experiences a little more in hang-gliding and things like that.... But I noticed that I could fly at a phenomenal rate of speed and it seemed to produce a feeling of great joy and sense of actually flying in this total fashion."*[8]

LMV: It seems to me that this weightlessness confirms, as do all out-of-body experiences, that our true selves are indeed "invisible forms," to which consciousness and information—but not matter—are joined.

EEV: *The notion of time is greatly altered during a near-death experience. NDE accounts suggest the existence of an atemporal dimension.*

LMV: This also seems to be consistent with our hypothesis. As we saw at the beginning of our conversation, the theory of relativity holds that space and time are closely related to matter or to mass, that is, to extraordinarily condensed energy. In fact, they are created by it. On the other hand, the notion of an atemporal dimension seems indeed to confirm the location of the experiencer's consciousness in other dimensions in which time no longer flows.

EEV: *May we now turn to the most important points, those concerning sight and hearing?*

LMV: If you don't mind, I would prefer to begin with hearing.

EEV: *As far as hearing is concerned, I am not sure that it really continues functioning during the NDE, since experiencers seem to "hear" with their consciousness rather than with their ears, and to read the thoughts of others rather than to actually hear sounds. There are two types of accounts with regard to this point. The first has to do with subjects in a near-death state who hear living persons. Experiencers often hear a member of the medical staff pronounce them dead, for example. They then try to communicate with those around them but find it impossible to make themselves heard. The second type of account concerning hearing has to do with the two-way communication established between the experiencer and deceased persons or the being of light. This type of communication seems to take place directly, from consciousness to consciousness, circumventing the senses. Understanding appears to be instantaneous, with no possibility of misinterpretation.*

LMV: I think you have answered your own question! According to my information theory, if meaning exists only at the level of the cognitive systems of the transmitters and receivers, or, if you prefer, at the level of their consciousness, then it is clear that these two consciousnesses, that of the experiencer and of the deceased person or other entity, will have no need for a material medium in order to communicate, since they are located in the same space–time. Since time does not flow, communication will obviously be instantaneous. However, except in the case of mediums, living persons cannot communicate directly from consciousness to consciousness, but only by means of material messages. We are currently working on a biological space–time model that should allow us to explain this phenomenon. It is therefore clear that although the experiencer's consciousness can have direct access to that of a living person, for example, a member of the medical team assisting the person in a near-death state, the reverse is not true.

EEV: *Let us now talk about sight. Experiencers recount viewing their bodies from an external vantage point, generally located above the physical body. Here is a quotation from one of Kenneth Ring's respondents in* Heading Toward Omega: *"[Could you see your body?] Oh, yes, quite clearly. I was floating in the air above the body ... and viewing it down sort of a diagonal angle."*[9]

An experiencer interviewed in Life after Life *by Raymond Moody recalls, "I became very seriously ill, and the doctor put me in the hospital. This one morning a solid gray mist gathered around me, and I left my body. I had a floating sensation as I felt myself get out of my body, and I looked back and I could see myself on the bed below and there was no fear. It was quiet— very peaceful and serene."*[10]

LMV: This is certainly the most difficult aspect to explain. With what "eyes" does the consciousness of the experiencer see this scene unfold? For it is no longer a matter of communicating with humans, whether living or not, but of images, of scenes with inanimate objects, of pure matter.

EEV: *Indeed, I'm not sure if we can say that sight persists as a sensory perception; otherwise, how could we explain the case of blind persons or individuals with very poor eyesight who are nevertheless able to see during their NDE? Once again, I will quote from an account of one of Kenneth Ring's respondents: "I'm very nearsighted, too, by the way, which was another one of the startling things that happened when I left my body. I see at fifteen feet what most people see at four hundred.... They were hooking me up to a machine that was behind my head. And my very first thought was, "Jesus, I can see! I can't believe it, I can see!" I could read the numbers on the machine behind my head and I was just so thrilled. And I thought, "They gave me back my glasses." [You could see all of this clearly, then, judging from how well you could see the numbers?] "Yes, at that time I could still remember them.... Things were enormously clear and bright."[11] Wouldn't this mean that sight can also take other paths besides the sensory one?*

LMV: This totally confirms my feeling that there must be something else. I must admit that I currently have no satisfactory response. Perhaps the images of material objects are linked to abstract elements, just as meaning is linked to words in language. We should turn to Plato and to the world of ideals and universals. Perhaps physicists could propose something, but I think we still don't have enough data regarding this point. No doubt new analyses of experiencer accounts are needed. It is also possible that we don't know how to ask the right questions of them. Yet it seems probable to me that what we should investigate are the properties of light. The work of Fritz A. Popp of the University of Kaiserlautern on the biology of light is an important contribution in this regard.

EEV: *A great number of experiencers report having seen a brilliant light radiating beauty and love—a light more intense than any earthly light could be, but still not blinding. It seemed to be infused with very powerful symbolic meaning. Here are quotes from three of Kenneth Ring's experiencers in* Heading Toward Omega:

"*It's something which becomes you and you become it. I could say, "I was peace, I was love." I was the brightness, it was part of me.*"[12]

"*An intensity of feeling rushed through me, as if the light that surrounded that Being was bathing me, penetrating every part of me. As I absorbed the energy, I sensed what I can only describe as bliss.*"[13]

"*I mentioned the golden light. It should be* Golden *light and you ask me if it burned my eyes. No, it did not. Fact being, I gained strength gazing upon it. It's as if by gazing upon this beautiful light the power that it was was revitalizing something within the depths of me. There was a transmission of a higher power, knowledge, understanding, and the 'oneness of everything' through gazing upon the light.*"[14]

What do you think about this?

LMV: These accounts confirm my feeling that our research should indeed focus on light. It's still too early to speak about it, but the recent findings of several physicists lead me to think that this light could very well be—excuse the incongruousness of the term—"superluminal" in nature. It could be the medium, or one of the physical media of consciousness, postulated by my theory of information. But, naturally, all of this is still very hazy and remains, I repeat, at the intuitive level.

EEV: *When experiencers encounter deceased loved ones during their near-death experience, recognition arises on the part of the deceased beings and, most of the time, on the part of the experi-*

encers. Does this mean that there is necessarily a body or a visible form? Or can we assume that this recognition takes place exclusively at the level of pure consciousness?

LMV: I don't think that sight comes into play here. Perhaps the experiencer's consciousness is capable of decoding the "spatial information" of the deceased person, that which defines his or her body in a virtual fashion, just as when one reads $x^2 + y^2 = 100$, one might say: "Hey, that's a circle with a diameter of 10 centimeters." But the answer perhaps also lies in the content of this consciousness, in the same way that one can recognize a writer or a musician by his or her style, or a person by his or her way of walking.

EEV: *Our knowledge of all phenomena, whether natural or psychic, is the same, in that originally we did not possess it! Knowledge is acquired in phases. I would like to propose a classification: In the beginning, knowledge is akin to intuition; this is the "religious" phase, which falls into the category of belief and requires an act of faith. Next comes the "philosophical" phase, in which there is some tangible, rational foundation, but nothing very solid. Last, there is the "scientific" phase, in which the phenomenon is proved experimentally and becomes a fact. Whether one likes it or not, believes it or not, the evidence is there. In which of these three categories would you place NDEs?*

LMV: Like Janus, truth has two faces. There are the facts, and there are the interpretations of the facts. Scientific facts arrived at by sound research are never called into question, regardless of what the uninformed public may think. What is called into question is their interpretation, since this is a function of the paradigms in effect at a given point in time. I am therefore completely in agreement with your classification. The work of the theorist is similar to that of the artist. (This is not an original idea; it belongs to

Albert Einstein.) A new theory is born of intuition. Then, over the course of time, experiments either validate or invalidate the theory. But one never—and this is still Einstein speaking—ever goes from experimentation to theory! The results of experiments are like bricks, but a blueprint is needed to build a house. Poincaré, by the way, said that an accumulation of facts no more constitutes science than a pile of stones constitutes a dwelling. There are therefore degrees in the interpretation of a fact, which is gradually supported by the accumulation of other facts. For my part, I would propose the following classification: the possible; the probable; and the certain, or the impossible. Hence, many religions claim that the universe was created by God. This is an intuitive interpretation of what we see. Physicists have discovered that the universe had a beginning in time—the Big Bang. This does not prove that God created the universe; it only shows that this is a possibility. The more our knowledge increases in all fields, in cosmology as well as in the origin of life, the less likely it is that chance alone prevailed. This makes the hypothesis of creation more probable. To answer your question— and this will be my conclusion—the fact that the data concerning NDEs are consistent with the different ideas or hypotheses of quantum physics or of information, causes me to consider as probable the interpretation of NDEs as testimonies of the afterlife.

Chapter Seven

Dialogue with Régis Dutheil, M.D. and Brigitte Dutheil[1]

THE SUPERLUMINAL HYPOTHESIS

EEV: *Professor, you have developed a hypothesis based on* super-luminal *consciousness. What does this mysterious adjective mean?*

RD: My hypothesis is based on a model in which consciousness is a field of tachyonic or superluminal matter belonging to the true fundamental universe, of which our world is merely a subluminal holographic projection.

EEV: The Oxford English Dictionary[2] *gives the following definition of tachyons: "a hypothetical subatomic particle that travels faster than light and has imaginary mass." Your hypothesis of superluminal consciousness is essentially based on tachyons. What can you tell us about these elusive particles?*

RD: Late Professor of Physics and Biophysics, Poitiers School of Medicine; BD: Professor of Classical Literature

RD: We know that according to Einstein's theory of relativity, or more precisely, the special theory of relativity, no material body or particle can reach or, *a fortiori*, exceed the speed of light in a vacuum, which is 300,000 km/sec. This follows quite simply from the mathematical formulation of the equations of special relativity (Lorentz group). The doctrine that it was not possible to exceed the speed of light went unchallenged until the 1960s. At that time, researchers in aeronautics began talking about the possibility of "breaking the sound barrier." This was what gave some physicists the idea that there might possibly be particles on the other side of the light barrier (by analogy to the sound barrier) that always traveled faster than the speed of light. In the 1960s, two American physicists, G. Feinberg and S. Sudarshan, preceded by the Russian J.P. Terletskii, applied a mathematical "device" to the relativistic expression of energy as a function of speed, and showed that a particle traveling faster than the speed of light, and never slower, had real energy and momentum. It was Feinberg who named these particles "tachyons," from the Greek *tachus*, meaning fast. He grouped particles into three categories. The first ones were called "bradyons," from the Greek *bradus*, meaning slow (at one time they were referred to as "tardyons"). These are the particles that make up our universe. They include electrons, protons, quarks, and the many particles detected in accelerators and they always travel slower than light. The second category of particles were called "luxons" (from *lux*, meaning light); these are particles that always travel at the speed of light, such as photons. We know that the speed of light is a constant, which means that if an observer measures the speed of light, he will always obtain a measurement of 300,000 km/sec in a vacuum, regardless of his own movement. This is one of the basic principles of relativity and has been verified by experiment. Thus, luxons always travel at the speed of light. Obviously, this includes light which, when behaving as a particle, is formed of photons. It was once believed that neutrinos fell into the category of particles that travel at the speed of light, but a few years ago it was discovered that they have a very small mass, perhaps 100,000 times smaller than that of electrons, and if they have a mass, they cannot travel at the speed of light. Other particles, such as gravitons, also travel at the speed of light. This brings us to the third category, which consists of hypothetical particles called tachyons that are believed to travel always faster than the speed of light—never slower. Feinberg pointed out that this posed problems of causality, or rather of macro-causality. We know that in our universe, any effect or event has a cause, and that the cause always precedes the effect. We never see the opposite happening. This is what is known as the principle of macrocausality, and although no one has ever been able to prove it, it is accepted as a tenet of physics. Feinberg postulated that the process was different for tachyons. Suppose that tachyons are created and then, in the following instant, from our perspective as subluminal observers, these tachyons are annihilated. If we could position ourselves as observers in the super-luminal universe, we would experience a phenomenon of temporal inversion in that we would observe the ta-chyon's destruction before its creation. In other words, we would observe the effect before the cause. This temporal inversion phenomenon was very disturbing to physicists! The location of tachyons poses a number of problems that, thus far, have not been resolved. Many experiments have been carried out over the past several years, but their results have always been negative. This is what led Fein-berg to say—and I think they are words of wisdom—that either tachyons do not exist, or else they exist, but we are not looking for them in the right place!

EEV: *Have other researchers also attempted to locate tachyons?*

RD: In 1984–1985 a Belgian physicist by the name of Jacques Steyaert purportedly demonstrated the existence of tachyons at the Nuclear Physics Institute of the University of Louvain-la-Neuve. Steyaert used the Institute's large cyclotron to produce high-energy gamma rays and with the help of an experimental device, which I will not take the time to describe here, studied the different ways in which these gamma rays were absorbed by matter. The observation was not made in a space–time system, but rather in an energy–momentum system. The analysis of the data gathered in this fashion required lengthy calculations and tedious manipulations. The result was the appearance of a pair of particles, whose speed was estimated by Steyaert to be 1.2 times the speed of light in a vacuum. These must have been tachyons, since they traveled faster than light. Steyaert was also able to determine the mass of these particles. We usually estimate mass in electron volts because of the equivalence of mass and energy. The mass of an electron, for example, is 500,000 electron volts, whereas the mass of a tachyon is 230,000 electron volts, thus, approximately half that of an electron. These particles also had the characteristic of behaving like magnetic monopoles. Steyaert had demonstrated that a stream of these particles could produce an electrical current by induction. Unfortunately, he was only able to observe these magnetic monopoles once. Thus, Steyaert accumulated scandals, so to speak. For one thing, he claimed to have located tachyons, and for another, he declared these tachyons to be magnetic monopoles. Of course, these experiments would have to be repeated in order to determine if his interpretation was correct. If it turns out to be valid, the existence of tachyons will have been proved experimentally.

EEV: *Does quantum reasoning concur with the tachyonic hypothesis?*

RD: Yes, there are a number of assumptions derived from quantum mechanics that suggest that superluminal speeds must exist. In 1924, Louis de Broglie associated a wave with each particle. Depending upon circumstances, a particle will behave either like a corpuscle or a wave, that is, either like something with a definite position in space, or like something spread out. According to his calculations, this wave always propagates faster than the speed of light. This is known as its "phase velocity." This fact disturbed physicists, convinced as they were that nothing could exceed the speed of light. They got around this by saying that a phase wave could not be observed experimentally and that two of similar frequency would have to be observed while an interference, or a beat, was produced. This beat, which propagates more slowly than the speed of light, is what would need to be observed. It is what carries energy. Nevertheless, the fact remains that there are waves that propagate faster than light. The proof is that they have been made to interfere and recently, even molecules have been made to interfere, demonstrating that this is a general phenomenon. In quantum mechanics, most physicists agree that consciousness affects measurement. There is an interaction between the observer and what is being observed, or to be more precise, between the consciousness, or the will of the observer taking the measurement, and the object being observed. It is as if quantum systems were waves, and the very fact of observing a measurement caused the values corresponding to an object's physical size to appear. These values are interpreted as an entity we call a "particle," which, in reality, is a creation of the observer—or rather of his consciousness. But great care is taken not to specify what consciousness is! Yet, everything can be explained if we assume consciousness to be a field of particles that interacts with the quantum object being observed. If this particle field were composed of subluminal particles, we obviously would already have been observing them for quite some time, and this is what leads us to think that consciousness may be formed of tachyons.

EEV: *You state that* consciousness is matter—*a very distinct kind of matter, endowed with specific properties, but matter nonetheless.*

RD: Yes, absolutely. We can define mathematically the possibility of the existence of a form of matter—of a reference system constituted of this matter—that would last forever. In other words, this matter could not be destroyed. We would find ourselves in a kind of time that does not flow, space itself would have changed in ways we cannot imagine, and even the notion of speed, which we perceive as a sensation linked to linear time, would be different.

EEV: *I think it would be useful for you to describe what is meant by the term* psi collapse.

RD: We know that in quantum mechanics, measurements are linked to the reduction of the wave, or psi collapse, of the quantum object being observed. There is a close interaction between the result of the measurement and the observer himself, or to be more precise, the observer's consciousness. It is as if a large spectrum of possible values existed for each physical dimension. We only know the probabilities for the appearance of one of these values, and we can only be certain of a result once the measurement is taken, that is, at the moment of the psi collapse,

which results from the interaction between the entity being observed and the observer. Thus, the psi collapse
causes the psi wave to break down and a particle to
appear; this is referred to as "wave reduction." During
observation and measurement, we might think that, at the
appearance of the "particle" entity—which is characterized by a certain number of physical dimensions whose
probabilities of appearance were calculated previously
(on the basis of standardized characteristic functions)—
the wave disappears. Yet, we know (thanks to Louis de
Broglie) that there is a phase wave associated with the
particle, whose velocity (phase velocity) is always greater
than the speed of light in a vacuum. Recent experiments
(in 1991) were carried out in the United States in order to
determine if there was a "guide wave" that directed the
particle in some way. Although the findings of these experiments seem to discredit the guide-wave theory, they
are nonetheless quite surprising. American researchers
used a device resembling an interferometer, which contained a source that could produce photons one by one.
They then split a beam into two. We know that an individual, particlelike entity carrying energy and momentum—
the photon—will be propagated in one of the beams. But
does anything happen in the second beam? The answer is
"yes." Traveling the path of the second beam is what is
referred to as an "empty wave," because it carries no
energy, although it does produce physical effects. Thus,
the empty wave can rightly be likened to the phase wave.
Louis de Broglie had examined this problem from a theoretical standpoint and supported the idea that the phase
wave carried a very small amount of energy. These findings on the photon may obviously be extended to particles
of matter, such as the electron. In these conditions, and in
the case of "matter" particles, we see that following the

psi collapse and the appearance of the particle, there would exist a phase wave—the empty wave—which travels faster than light and is able to produce effects, since, despite being devoid of energy, it would convey information. Of course, the psi collapse also applies to superluminal tachyons. But, in this case, the velocity of the phase wave, or empty wave, would be slower than the speed of light.

PARALLELS WITH EARLIER AND CURRENT RESEARCH

EEV: *I assume that your model of superluminal consciousness draws upon* previous research. *Which scientists have inspired you?*

RD: Between 1955 and 1960, the Australian neurophysiologist Sir John Eccles, who in 1963 would receive the Nobel Prize in medicine for his work on synaptic junctions in the cortex, put forth the idea that the brain is nothing more than a simple computer that transmits information. The software, or the programming, was to be found elsewhere. On the basis of a set of arguments borrowed from neurophysiology, neurosurgery and the neurosciences, Eccles advanced the hypothesis that there exists a field of particles as yet undetected by the instruments of physics that would correspond to just this programming or software of the computer–brain. The cortex transmits and coordinates information originating in the mind's field of matter. It filters this information for the brain, which actually perceives only a small part. This is in fact the first model of material consciousness.

EEV: *German physicists have very recently made some interesting discoveries in this area. What exactly do these have to do with?*

RD: The German physicists Enders and Nintz of the Physics Institute of Cologne recently (in 1992) published the findings of experiments carried out with waveguides, along which centimetric radio waves are propagated. Their experiments were confirmed by the American researchers of the CHIAO Team in 1993. In these experiments "wave packets" were observed to propagate perpendicular to the wave of the waveguide, to convey energy and to possess a group velocity several times greater than that of light in a vacuum. If we assume that the photon is composed of one bradyon and one tachyon, as is the case in the photon model that I have published, we can say that in certain conditions the photon decomposes and releases a tachyon. This is what Enders and Nintz may have observed.

EEV: *Can you briefly define Sheldrake's theory of morphic fields and tell us if you see any link between morphic fields and tachyonic fields?*

RD: Rupert Sheldrake developed the idea that each type of cell, tissue, organ, and organism has its own field. These fields shape and organize developing plant and animal microorganisms, and stabilize the forms of adult organisms. He proposed to call these "morphic fields," preferring the term *morphic* over *morphogenetic*, because its definition is more general and includes other types of organizer fields. According to Sheldrake, the organizer fields of animal and human behavior, of social and cultural systems, and of mental activity may be considered morphic fields with an inherent memory. In his view, these morphic fields are actually fields of information, for they contain an innate memory supported by morphic resonance, which is based on similarity. This memory is cumulative. The more a particular pattern of activity is repeated, the more it tends to become habitual. This may very well be the origin of the "genetic program"; we think it is, in fact, the software that makes this program run. However, we feel that the programmer is to be found elsewhere—at the level of superluminal consciousness.

THE IMPLICATIONS OF THE SUPERLUMINAL MODEL

EEV: *According to your hypothesis, superluminal consciousness is located in what you refer to as the* fundamental universe— *which I suppose one might also define as the universe of death.*

RD: Yes, consciousness, or the mind, is composed of a field of tachyons or superluminal matter, located on the other side of the light barrier in superluminal space–time. To draw upon the ideas of Pribram and of Bohm, we make of the superluminal universe what Pribram calls the "frequency domain," or the fundamental universe. Our subluminal universe is merely a holographic projection of the fundamental universe, where information and meaning are located. This projection is made through the cortex, which acts as a filter to let in no more than a very limited amount of information and meaning, which is arranged according to causal sequences in entropic, linear time.

EEV: *This would mean that there are* two universes—*the subluminal universe, with which we are familiar, and a superluminal one, in which particles travel faster than the speed of light.*

RD: Yes, that's correct. There may be two universes, one of which is our own familiar subluminal universe. The existence of another universe, another superluminal space–time—and only one—is, mathematically speaking, a definite possibility. There is, of course, what one might call an interface between the two universes. We are familiar with this interface—it is what relativists refer to as the light cone on whose surface light, photons, and other particles that travel at the speed of light are propagated. The boundary between these two universes is a common area, probably composed of photons. I have developed a model in which photons are presumed to consist of one subluminal and one superluminal component. They have, so to speak, one foot in the subluminal universe and the other in the superluminal universe.

EEV: *One might think of it as the front and the back, or the visible and the invisible,* with the boundary between the two universes being the light barrier. *How do NDEs fit into this view?*

BD: According to our hypothesis, the NDE would, in effect, be the human, or living being's passage from the subluminal to the superluminal world. Near-death experiencers report having traversed a passage, which would correspond to the preliminary entry into the superluminal world. Several phases characterize this passage. There is, in particular, a loss of ability to communicate with the subluminal world, although the senses of sight and hearing remain. Next, there is an out-of-body experience, followed by a passage through a dark space, often described as a tunnel, at the end of which a majority of experiencers report having seen a brilliant light. It is this tunnel phase that may be referred to as the passage. When traversing this dark space, experiencers have the impression that there is a genuine boundary between the subluminal world—the world of our physical existence—and the superluminal world, which would be the world of death. What is the meaning of this dark passage or tunnel (which, incidentally has been depicted in art, by Hieronymous Bosch, for example). Why this impression of a dark space? We maintain that this is unquestionably the crossing of the light barrier. In other words, at the precise moment of passage, the partial consciousness of the person in the process of dying and having the experience passes through the light barrier and is filled with particles traveling at the speed of light—hence, with photons. The experiencer him- or herself becomes light and perceives everything around as darkness, which explains the impression of a tunnel and a dark space. It is true that NDEs offer only a preliminary explanation of the superluminal world, since the accounts of those who have had the experience are quite brief, given that they come back to the world of the living. These persons have undergone only the beginning of the experience.

EEV: *For most people, death signifies the unknown, and the unknown, as most would agree, engenders fear.* Couldn't we think of death as actually a return to our origins? *As a reunion with the fundamental universe, where time no longer flows and where past, present, and future no longer exist? As a place where consciousness is absolute and where all events exist simultaneously? Our emergence in the subluminal world would thus be only a brief and isolated actualization of an existence rooted in the superluminal world. Existence after death should therefore be interpreted as a return to our origins.*

BD: Exactly. One might say that the question summarizes the answer. It's true that we consider the fundamental world—the source of consciousness—to be the superluminal world. Consciousness is partially incarnated in bodies living in the subluminal world. At the time of death, consciousness simply returns to its original environment. This notion coincides with the Platonic theory, which holds that the soul is imprisoned in the body, and that upon death, it is released and returns to its origins, or birthplace. Plato also developed an entire theory of knowledge, in which knowledge was considered to be reminiscence, meaning that at birth, the soul already possessed total knowledge. We could indeed say that consciousness potentially possesses total knowledge, and that over the course of a lifetime and through the accumulation of experiences, it partially rediscovers certain elements of this total knowledge.

EEV: *Let us now turn to a somewhat philosophical aspect of your hypothesis. It seems to me that everyone would like to believe that the world is more than it appears to be, and perhaps even completely different! Who has never been disturbed at the thought that life might be nothing more than a somewhat happy existence, followed by death, and perhaps a void? Who has never held out hope that there must be something else, a hidden side,* an unknown and better world, one more "luminous" *than this one?*

BD: Indeed, all philosophers have wrestled with this question. We have already mentioned Plato, who argued that our universe is merely an illusion—the reflection of something located on the other side. This is the cave myth, where all we can see is the reflected light of the sun shining on the real world outside. Philosophers have always been divided between those who believe in the existence of another reality, which may be experienced after death, and those who consider everything to be limited to this life, as do the materialists, the Marxists, or the existentialists. We have attempted to reconcile all philosophies in our hypothesis. There is indeed a somewhat materialistic element in the idea that consciousness is formed of particle matter, but it is clear that our hypothesis is nevertheless mainly spiritual in nature, since the matter that makes up the particles of consciousness is endowed with spiritual properties (e.g., the instantaneousness of time, ever-increasing order, harmony, and the lack of the causality that is associated with passing time). We are definitely persuaded that there is something else—a more beautiful, more intense reality—on the other side.

RD: I come back to the term *materialism*. I think we are restricted by words—it is a question of semantics. When we say *materialism*, it is always in terms of a nine-teenth-century view of matter. What is matter to today's physicist? Is it waves? Is it a creation of his or her mind? There is no longer any such thing as materialism, or spiritualism.

EEV: *One of the most fascinating aspects of your hypothesis is undoubtedly the inversion of reality. We naturally have a tendency to assume that reality is what we see. Yet, quantum mechanics has already helped us to recognize the huge flaw in our manner of perceiving reality.*

RD: I think we should indeed start from the perspective of quantum mechanics, which has shattered our former ideas of reality. What is a particle at the quantum level? It is nothing more than a figment of the observer's mind! Yet, most people imagine that we are made of particles, which they think of as small objects stacked on top of each other in the form of atoms and molecules. This seems very real, but it isn't anything like this! A particle is not an object. Then what is reality? Today's physicists accept the wave as the predominant aspect, unlike Louis de Broglie, who opted for the particle aspect. It is believed that there are quantum systems, which are stationary waves, and that the intervention of the observer, or rather of his or her consciousness, transforms these quantum systems into certain sizes, giving the impression that they are particles. This alone delivers quite a blow to our notion of reality. Continuing with this reasoning, if we assume that consciousness is a field of tachyonic matter, then tachyons may also be considered to be waves. If this is true, then it would be the fundamental universe—the one possessing information—that would be projected in the form of sub-luminal holograms. This interpretation is coherent with the ideas of Eccles, Pribram, and Bohm. We have extended these ideas by saying that the frequency domain corresponds to the tachyonic domain, or the superluminal domain. But the basic idea is the same: There is an inversion. We have mistaken the back for the front, and vice versa. We only know the back; the front is on the other side of the light barrier.

EEV: *In order to fully understand this new way of perceiving reality, I would like to ask you to clarify the concept of* holograms.

RD: In order to clarify it, we can generalize Karl Pribram's holographic model. Originally a neurosurgeon, now a brain specialist and holographic expert, Pribram thinks that what we refer to as reality is nothing more than a holographic projection of the fundamental universe—the frequency domain where time and space are collapsed, and where only waves exist—which he places in another dimension. In this frequency domain, all elements exist without temporal or spatial connotation. The interface between consciousness and the cortex is capable of making a Fourier analysis and of projecting, in a system of arbitrary coordinates that we call time and space, all the interference patterns of the frequency domain in the form of holograms. Accordingly, stars, galaxies, particles, and living beings are merely holograms, as is the entire visible universe. The ideas of David Bohm, which he expresses in different terms—the implicate order and the explicate order—are virtually identical to those of Pribram.

EEV: *How does* holography *work?*

RD: Holography is a photographic technique. One method consists of bouncing light off the object to be photographed. The object reflects the light, in keeping with the laws of optics, and its image is projected onto a sensitive film with the help of a lens. This is the usual method. According to a second method, all points of the object receive light and each point reemits it, thus behaving as secondary sources of light. These multiple sources then create interferences. The holographic procedure consists of photographing them. It is important to note that not just any kind of light will do; the light must be coherent, that is, produced by atoms that vibrate in unison, which, in turn, produce photons that are in phase, as is the case with laser light. An object is illuminated with a laser beam, and the interferences produced by the reflected light are photographed. This produces what is called an "interference pattern"—a kind of vortex that doesn't look like anything. However, when this interference pattern is lit once more with a coherent light, such as a laser beam, a three-dimensional image of the object appears in space. It is quite astounding, really. Furthermore, if we divide the interference pattern into various parts, we find that each part possesses the same properties as the initial pattern; in other words, we can reproduce the whole object. This is an approximate description of the holographic method. Since the mathematical theory is quite complex, it's sufficient to remember that it requires Fourier transformations, without going into any more detail than that. At its base, quantum mechanics also requires Fourier transformations. This is a very important point. According to Pribram's theory, the cortex plays a role similar to that of the laser beam, or the coherent light; I would say that it is the interface between the cortex and consciousness that plays this role. I think consciousness, in particular, can produce this effect, since the cortex is itself material, and therefore a hologram. This interface will play the role of coherent light, but what will the interference pattern be? Still keeping to Pribram's theory, it will be the frequency domain. The cortex, like the laser beam, will use Fourier transformations to project frequencies, and these frequencies will form the hologram. It will do this within a system of perfectly arbitrary coordinates created by the brain or by consciousness. As it turns out, this system of coordinates corresponds to ordinary space–time, where particles travel slower than light. We have used this theory as a basis for claiming that the frequency domain is the tachyonic domain, and that the projection is subluminal.

EEV: *I can conceive of the idea of the tachyonic dimension and its implications, but it is very difficult for me to imagine myself as a hologram. To what extent are these two concepts inseparable?*

RD: We must come back to Plato's cave image: The cave dwellers cannot see themselves as they are "in reality," but identify themselves with their shadows projected onto the cave walls. This is how it is with the hologram, which is a projection of our superluminal higher self. We see only the hologram (our body) and we identify this holographic shadow—the only thing accessible to our perception—with our superluminal self. The two cannot be separated, since the shadow (or the hologram) "exists" only as a function of higher consciousness, which is also the "laser beam" that "creates" this hologram.

EEV: *I would like for you to talk about the function of the cortex,* about the origin of a sensation *generated by electrical impulses sent to the cortex, and especially about consciousness, which intervenes at the miraculous moment when a simple electric impulse becomes a sensation.*

RD: You are entirely right. The issue of sensations has never been resolved by psychophysiologists. And for good reason. Let us take the case of the eye, for example. Light stimulates the retina, the cones, or the rods; this is the photochemical stage. Next, the message is coded along the axons of the optic nerve with the various synapses and, last, this message, which has been coded several times, is transmitted electrically and arrives at the cortex, where a local stimulation of the cortex occurs. At this instant, a new element comes into the picture, as this electrical stimulation is not the sensation itself. The sensation occurs when we perceive, say, a color. What mechanism is it that transforms the electrical stimulation of the cortex into a sensation? We suggest that the sensation already belongs to superluminal space–time, that the cause of the sensation is not the physical stimulus—that is, the light—but that there is a simple correlation. The idea that sensations belong to the superluminal world is reinforced by what happens during the near-death experience. Subjects report having had sensations during their NDE that were much stronger and more intense than usual, especially with respect to colors and light. They perceive colors they've never seen before, of unimaginable intensity. Their senses are greatly heightened. In fact, we could say that what we see, the sensations we receive, are sensations that have been weakened by the fact of having passed through the cortex. This would mean that the sense organs are like filters that diminish sensations.

EEV: *Speaking of sensations, it would be interesting for you to describe your view of the sensation as a form of information.*

RD: Yes, I think if we assume that sensations are truly an element of tachyonic space–time, then they would constitute the information of the superluminal universe. The heightened, or total, sensation would be the information.

EEV: *You postulate that the superluminal universe is the site of absolute information in its pure state.* Entropy *(disorder) diminishes constantly, and* negentropy *(information) increases constantly. Can you clarify this idea for us?*

RD: There is a very important principle in our subluminal universe—one that is well-known to physicists—which is that entropy increases constantly in a closed system. Ultimately, we could say that the universe is a closed system. Thus, the principle of increasing entropy applies to the entire universe. In the subluminal universe, linear time corresponds to a constant increase in entropy; in other words, we are always moving from a situation of order to one of disorder. We cannot oppose this increasing disorder except by means of information. In a closed system of tachyonic matter, on the other hand, entropy is constantly decreasing, which means that information and meaning are continually increasing. This becomes evident if we look at a living being. At birth, we notice a highly elaborate order at the molecular level. We can see very well that over time and as it ages, the organism deteriorates, and disorder gradually increases. There is only one way to fight disorder, and that is through information. I am referring here to living beings, but this applies to matter in general. In order to illustrate, I will take the case of a human being's temperature, which is normally 37 degrees Celsius. If the weather is too hot, the body temperature will rise. The sense receptors will immediately capture this information, send orders to activate the thermostat, and bring the temperature back down to normal. Had the temperature continued to rise, the subsequent increase in disorder would inevitably have resulted in death. But, thanks to information, the situation was returned to normal. This is negative entropy, and is referred to as negentropy. This works for some time, the span of a lifetime, then entropy begins to increase. We can think of human beings as negentropy pumps: They absorb negentropy in order to fight against entropy, but at a certain point, the pump stops working and entropy gains the upper hand. In the superluminal universe, on the other hand— and incidentally, this is not guesswork, but has been calculated mathematically—entropy diminishes constantly. This means that negentropy, or information, increases constantly. We are heading toward greater and greater states of order, information and, consequently, of harmony.

EEV: *I would now like to hear some of your thoughts on the critical issue of free will. Human beings have always wanted to be master of their destiny, free to lead their lives according to their wishes. What is your position with respect to the issue of determinism versus free will?*

BD: According to our hypothesis, determinism is linked to causality and to the flow of time; it is a characteristic of our subluminal world. In the superluminal universe, on the other hand, since time no longer flows, causality ceases, since it depends on the passing of time. There is, however, a law of affinity that links events to one another known as synchronicity—a term invented by Carl Jung in the 1930s. Jung, together with physicist and Nobel laureate Wolfgang Pauli, developed an entire theory on the subject in 1950. Synchronicity refers to the simultaneous occurrence of two events that are linked not by cause, but by meaning. We experience instances of synchronicity in our everyday lives. From time to time, such instances may override the law governing the superluminal world. We believe that at the tachyonic level, where causality no longer exists and time no longer flows, it is possible to simultaneously know the past, present, and future of an individual, or even of all individuals, and therefore to act instantaneously upon future events. Consequently, individuals living at the superluminal level are presented with an array of possibilities for their future, allowing them to alter their destiny, or their world line, atemporally and at the subluminal level—hence, at the level of their hologram. Since the change is made instantly, this adaptation will not be noticed; it will appear to be something that should have happened, that was predetermined. Thus, at the level of consciousness there is free will, or the possibility of altering a sequence of events, whereas at the subluminal level, there is determinism.

EEV: *I don't see how we can have access to the superluminal world during our lifetime, and consequently, how we can alter our destiny at the superluminal level, unless you assume that we can have partial and momentary access—without even knowing it—to this tachyonic dimension.*

RD: The alteration of destiny would take place only at the level of superluminal consciousness. It would not require a means of access at the subluminal level experienced by subjects at their level of reality. The alteration of the sequence of events on their subluminal world line takes place "without their knowing it," and is carried out solely by the higher self, which modifies a causal sequence of events atemporally.

NDEs IN THE LIGHT OF THE SUPERLUMINAL HYPOTHESIS

EEV: *In your superluminal model, you associate tachyons with spatial time. What do you mean by this?*

RD: Tachyons are associated with a different space–time than our usual, subluminal space–time. In superluminal, or tachyonic space–time, the properties of time and space are no longer the same. Time itself, that is, the experience of time, becomes spatial and no longer flows, which corresponds to the concept of infinite velocity. From the standpoint of the tachyonic observer, the past, present, and future no longer exist; rather, all events exist instantaneously yet lastingly. Such a field of matter has total perpetuity.

EEV: *You postulate that there is* instantaneousness of all events *in the tachyonic dimension. Causality no longer exists, since an event can occur before its cause. Indeed many experiencer accounts seem to confirm this hypothesis, particularly as regards the life review.*

BD: Yes, absolutely. Experiencers frequently report having had the impression of seeing their entire life pass before them. This life panorama takes place at an incredible speed the moment they enter into the world of light. Very often, in this life panorama, past events are intermingled with future events. Some experiencers have witnessed important events in their future. I am reminded, in particular, of a woman who viewed herself in the company of her son, at a time in her life when she did not have any children. Others were able to see more or less what their future lives would be like. This seems to indicate that once the light barrier has been crossed, one has total mastery over time and can access a future event as easily as a past one. In our opinion, the main characteristic of the superluminal universe is the total instantaneousness of events, given that time no longer flows. Time merges with space, and since one can travel at infinite velocities, it is logical that in moving through space, one also moves through time. Apparently, one can also access the past and future events of other persons, but reports of this kind are much less frequent.

RD: There is a case reported by Raymond Moody of a man who, during an NDE at the age of fifteen, I believe, witnessed himself as a married man twenty years into the future and found himself sitting in a room with his wife and children. According to him, this was not a vision; he *lived* it during his NDE. He was thus literally transported into the future.

EEV: *One interesting aspect of this account was that he sensed an object behind him that he was not able to identify.*

RD: You're absolutely right, Evelyn, it was something that did not yet exist at the time of his NDE.

EEV: *I remember now—it was some type of heater that did not yet exist at the time of his NDE, when he was fifteen.*

RD: Yes, there was something about a heater. I think this provides a good illustration of the foregoing point.

EEV: *Wherever we look, we find the notion of "light," which* seems to be of primary importance in understanding the mystery of life. *The Bible says that in the beginning there was light and the light was good. The* Bardo Thödol, *or* Tibetan Book of the Dead, *talks about how, for three and a half days after death, deceased persons are surrounded by a bright light, and how they must recognize this light in order to be released from the cycle of rebirth. Those who have had a near-death experience lack the words to describe the warmth, the brilliance, and the infinite beauty of the light, or being of light, they encounter during their experience, and which seems to leave them with an ever-present longing. Light also occupies a primordial, key position in your hypothesis. What connection do you make between all of these testimonies?*

RD: Light indeed plays an essential role in all religions. It is also a fundamental aspect of NDEs. It should be noted that in the superluminal universe, light plays a very different role than in our usual universe, and I am speaking simply from the physical perspective. First of all, light would have the slowest possible speed; it would truly travel at a snail's pace in the superluminal world. We can assume that this would imply differences in the laws governing the interaction of photons and tachyons; the laws of reflection would not be the same. In another connection, let us imagine a tachyonic body, that is, one formed of tachyonic matter. According to a phenomenon called the "Kerenkov effect," if an electrically charged subluminal particle—an electron, for example—is traveling at a constant speed, it will not emit light. In order for it to emit light, it would have to be slowed down, implying a loss of energy. At that precise moment, it will emit a photon. Inversely, if this charged particle—either an electron or some other particle—is found in an environment other than air or a vacuum—in a crystal, for example— then even at a constant speed this charged particle *will* emit a photon, and thus light. This is what is known as the Kerenkov effect. Now, we can show mathematically that a charged tachyon traveling at a constant speed in a vacuum will emit light. We can deduce from this that a tachyonic body will be luminous; it will emit light constantly as a result of the Kerenkov effect. All tachyonic bodies are therefore luminous. This observation may be compared to what experiencers report about NDEs, as well as to the descriptions found in religious traditions of bodies being surrounded by light. I agree with you—light plays an absolutely capital role.

EEV: *Those who have had an NDE unanimously emphasize* the importance of knowledge and of love *in its broadest sense. It seems to me that there is a connection to be made between these testimonies and your hypothesis, which postulates that there is absolute knowledge in the superluminal world, but only partial knowledge in the subluminal one.*

BD: Indeed, from our point of view, the world of death is indistinguishable from the world of knowledge. Since we say that the superluminal world is characterized by a constant increase in information, order, and harmony, it seems plausible that persons who have crossed the light barrier during an NDE are able to perceive this knowledge, and harmony, which characterize the world of death. It is true that a large number of experiencers claim to have had access during their experience to absolute knowledge and feel a deep need for learning following their NDE. As for the connection between love and knowledge, it would seem to be rather logical, since in the superluminal world there is an increase in harmony due to knowledge. Sensations exist in a pure, unfiltered state, and without constraint. They are amplified and come across as an impression of love. This simply brings us back to the teachings of the mystics, who have always associated love and knowledge.

RD: I am reminded of an acquaintance who had an NDE. She states very clearly that when she was beyond this tunnel and found herself in the presence of the being of light, she could see other entities, which, by the way, were of a luminous nature. She was at once herself and these other beings. How could one possibly not love others when these others are also oneself? That would be equivalent to not loving oneself. I think this reveals the full meaning of the gospel admonition to "love your neighbor as yourself."

EEV: *According to the reports of some experiencers, at a given point they had the choice of either entering the superluminal world definitively—thus dying physically—or of returning to*

life in the subluminal world. I wonder if everyone has this
choice when crossing the light barrier. *We can think of those
who die as not having been able to resist the attraction of the
superluminal world, and view each death as a choice. On the
other hand, there are obviously physical constraints, and it is
difficult to imagine that a body that had run its course, whose
metabolism had collapsed, could become functional again if its
"owner" so decided. Where do you draw the line between
consciousness—to which one can associate will, I think—and
physical constraints?*

BD: It's true that experiencers tell us that the return to life
was the last stage of their NDE. The notion of a choice
does not, however, seem to me to be as clear-cut as you
suggest. Some experiencers found themselves confronted
with an actual barrier—often manifested physically as the
vision of a river, a mountain, or a hedge, and almost
instantly thereafter found themselves back in their physical body. These experiencers did not really have a choice.
Others, however, were given a choice by a deceased friend
or relative, who came in order to advise them and told
them, for example, that their life was not over, that they
had some unfinished business to attend to, and so on.
Some of them bargained of their own accord—this is the
case of a mother who begged the being of light to allow
her to raise her children. In fact, nearly all possible situations are represented: the imposed return to life, being
given the choice by either the being of light or a deceased
friend or relative, and bargaining at the experiencer's
initiative. Not to mention the fact that we have only the
testimonies of those who came back! Can we deduce that
those who died also had this choice? We have no way of
knowing. Just as those who found themselves instantaneously back in their body after having been confronted
with a barrier were given no choice, perhaps those who

were taken to the other side of the barrier and never returned were given no choice either. Consequently, the question of physical constraints and consciousness loses its relevance to the extent that, in my opinion, the people whose physical bodies are truly worn, who have finished their time on earth, do not really have a choice. The question may be relevant for young people, some of whom come back and some of whom do not. In this case, we can perhaps allow that there may be a choice, and that this choice originates in consciousness. Why does consciousness seem to be the determining factor? Surely because it is consciousness that imprints its form on the physical body and consciousness to which life traces its origin. We believe superluminal consciousness to be at the origin of the material form of the body and at the origin of the birth of life.

EEV: *Can we take a closer look at the problems experiencers encounter in attempting to communicate their experience? One young woman complains about having at her disposal only three-dimensional words to describe her NDE, whereas the world she experienced had more. Is it our brain that creates our three-dimensional reality out of nothing?*

RD: Definitely. I think we can imagine only what we see in our three-dimensional space and linear time—in other words, in subluminal space–time. All our concepts, all our imagination, is limited to this three-dimensional space, and it is difficult for us to even conceive of time as a fourth dimension, as is held by the theory of relativity. If we assume that experiencers have been to the threshold of this superluminal world with its own space–time, there will obviously be a semantic barrier, for they have experienced things that are impossible to put into words. Our language can only describe objects and images in three dimensions. Mystics also say that they are unable to verbalize their experience, that their feelings go beyond the range of words.

EEV: *Does this inability to communicate perhaps also come from the fact that the intensity of the feelings they experienced in the superluminal universe is attenuated by the cortical filter once they are back in the subluminal world?*

RD: Yes, I think this is a very clever observation. This filter affects everything, and as soon as it is removed, there is a kind of release, and an intensity and expansion of both the senses and the emotions of such proportions that the mind is overwhelmed.

EEV: *Sensations, we have seen, are altered and intensified in the superluminal universe. Let us take, for example, the extraordinarily beautiful colors described in the NDE narratives. What is the physical explanation for this phenomenon?*

RD: The effect of the filter definitely comes into play. Also, I think that if experiencers are truly in tachyonic space–time, then the laws governing the propagation of light, reflection, and all other optical phenomena, will be altered. Tachyonic optics will be completely different, and it is very likely that other colors will be perceived with an intensity and tonality we cannot even imagine. This is due to the physical structure of this matter, which is very different from ours.

EEV: *A number of scientists today consider our world to be a black hole. Is there a parallel to be drawn with the famous "passage through a dark tunnel" described by so many experiencers?*

RD: Yes, that is one interpretation. There are, in fact, theories (which, incidentally, I have helped to develop) that consider the electron—in terms of its behavior as a particle, of course, and not as a wave—to be a very small particle, measuring 10^{-53} cm. That is very small indeed! The inside of this electron—and this can be shown mathematically—is thought to be a superluminal, micro-black hole. The electron itself may be made up of even smaller particles called preons, which may also be micro-black holes. It is possible to interpret death, or the return to the fundamental state, as passing through a micro-black hole, from the subluminal world to the superluminal world found inside the particle or inside all particles. This is one hypothesis.

EEV: *Let us now consider a fundamental and at the same time fascinating aspect of* The Tibetan Book of the Dead. *I am referring to one of its essential teachings: that the thoughts of the deceased person are what create his or her environment after death.*

RD: Yes, that's true. This tenet is found in *The Tibetan Book of the Dead* and in Far Eastern religions in general. In fact, it is linked very closely to the idea that the world in which we live is an illusion. If our world is an illusion, if reality is to be found elsewhere, this elsewhere is necessarily spiritual in nature and thus closely linked to consciousness. Indeed, in *The Tibetan Book of the Dead*, the deceased person is warned about images that might terrify him, that might lead him astray. It is very tempting to classify these images as holograms. In our opinion, some aspects of NDE accounts may be interpreted in terms of holograms and, precisely, in terms of the creation of holograms by thought. Many experiencers report having been greeted by deceased loved ones who often took on the appearance they had during their lives, or even during their youth. There are other visions of magnificent landscapes, of rivers, prairies, multicolored flowers, and so on. We think these images are holograms created by the thoughts of the deceased person. We have designated them as holograms of the second kind to distinguish them from the holograms that we ourselves are in the living world, which are the basic holograms, or holograms of the first kind. Holograms of the second kind would be images whose purpose is to acclimate the experiencer, the deceased person, to the new mode of existence in the world of death, in the superluminal world, and to avoid too brutal a transition between the world of images—the world of holograms he or she has known until then—and the world of pure abstraction that the world of death must be. These holograms of the second kind would be a means of transition that is quite characteristic of the NDE and of what must happen immediately following the NDE, before the consciousness of the deceased person penetrates further into the superluminal world.

EEV: *I think we should come back to these holograms of the second kind. I am aware of the fact that the superluminal universe is difficult to imagine, given our sense of reality. But I would like for you to clarify whether the being of light, the deceased friends and relatives, and all of these apparitions really exist, if they really are located in the superluminal world, or if they only exist in the thoughts, and therefore in the imagination of the experiencers. Is it a lure or is it reality? If we are holograms, reflections so to speak, and if the superluminal world is absolute abstraction, where is the real being?*

RD: In fact, everything exists and nothing is imaginary. It is our concept of reality that is false. The superluminal universe of information is not an abstraction, but rather another level of reality where time and space do not have the same meaning. Holograms of the second kind "exist" in the same way that we exist as holograms of the first kind. Beginning with the level of reality of "superluminal consciousness," we can create other levels of reality, which are just as real as a reflection, whose existence no one would dream of denying.

UNEXPLAINED PHENOMENA VIEWED FROM THE PERSPECTIVE OF THE SUPERLUMINAL MODEL

EEV: *I think it would be interesting to draw some parallels between your hypothesis of superluminal consciousness and* psychic phenomena. *There certainly has been a great deal of fraud in this widely publicized area, which has been exploited in every possible way. Nevertheless, some of these are unexplainable and disturbing phenomena.*

RD: I think that, as you quite correctly say, 99 percent of the "phenomena" are fraudulent, but there is a small part that is real and quite extraordinary in the sense that most of them go against currently accepted concepts of physics. In parapsychology, the phenomenon of premonition is found not only in gifted subjects, but in all of us. Everyone has, at one time or another, had a premonition or a precognitive dream. Unquestionably, telepathic phenomena also exist. As for other psychic phenomena, such as telekinesis, these have been analyzed under extremely serious conditions, both in the United States and in Russia. I think an interpretation might be found for all these parapsychological phenomena if we accepted the hypothesis of a material superluminal consciousness composed of tachyons. The explanation would always be found in the filter problem and in the intrusion of a piece of information, an additional energy, which, depending upon circumstances, could provide access to information not normally actualized concerning the future, or else an energy capable of moving an object. This would allow for a very clear interpretation of parapsychological phenomena, which would then become part of the framework of general physics.

EEV: *The phenomenon of* premonition *is indeed very strange and remains disconcerting so long as we cannot explain it.*

RD: Yes, absolutely. It is extremely disconcerting. Incidentally, it has been included in the classical theory of relativity. According to the theory of relativity in Einstein's and Minkowski's space–time, matter is expanding not only in space, but also in the thickness of time, which means that future events are already here and that past events still remain. According to the famous statement of Sir Arthur Edington, events do not occur, they are there and we find them along our way. But what way is that? It is the world line. But what is it that moves along the world line? This is something the theory of relativity was not capable of explaining. Of course, we were able to say that consciousness extended along the world line, and that at a certain point it became aware of future events. This was a somewhat abstract explanation. On the other hand, if we were to accept the existence of superluminal consciousness, we would accept that the latter has properties enabling it to know all of the events in the life of an individual. We could thus assume that at a certain point, the cortical filter would allow a tiny bit more information than usual to pass through, such as, for example, the vision of future events. This is what may be happening in precognitive dreams or in the flashes of certain mediums, in which they unquestionably see the future. This is where I think an analogy can be drawn with NDEs, since, if we assume that the experiencer has entered superluminal consciousness, precognitive phenomena can occur during this experience. But precognitive phenomena are not exclusive to NDEs, they are also found at our level and constitute a momentary and partial access to superluminal consciousness.

EEV: *According to various belief systems, there is a "subtle" or "astral" body that separates from our physical body at the time of death. This idea seems to be confirmed by near-death experiencers. Not realizing that they were "dead," many experiencers were startled to find that they could pass through objects and even people, but that despite their best efforts, no one could either see or hear them. Yet, they were conscious of their identity, of being themselves, and even of possessing a body, albeit a different, lighter one. How does this notion of "subtle" body fit into your hypothesis?*

RD: At this point, I think we should talk about the electromagnetic field of Harold Burr, Professor of Anatomy at Yale University. Surrounded by a team of physicists and biophysicists, Burr conducted research lasting thirty years, until his death in 1972, that indisputably demonstrated the existence of an electric field surrounding the body of every living being. Its shape can be charted by moving electrodes around the body from a distance of a few centimeters away from the skin. Burr discovered that this electric field varies constantly, in response to emotions and to a set of internal and external factors. He concluded from this that the human body is surrounded by an electromagnetic field. We should note that according to quantum mechanics, the particles associated with an electromagnetic field are photons. Hence, we can speak of a veritable photonic body, which would be part of what may be referred to as the electric body of the human body. I think that the intermediate stage at the time of death, during the transition to the tachyonic universe, would correspond to an electromagnetic, or photonic body. We could liken the subtle body to this photonic body, which would have roughly the same form as the physical body, but which could pass through objects, since a luxonic body can pass through objects without encountering any resistance. When I say photonic body, this may refer, incidentally, to other particles traveling at the speed of light, or perhaps to neutrinos, which pass through anything. Consequently, I think that this concept is not at all incompatible with the existence of the subtle body reported by esotericists or by Orientals.

EEV: *I would like for us to discuss the problem of the collective unconscious. According to your hypothesis, each of us carries within him- or herself a portion of universal knowledge. Our consciousness, although partial, is a component of total consciousness. Could this idea contribute anything new to our understanding of the phenomenon of the collective unconscious, which has never been very clearly defined?*

RD: Yes, I think so. Ultimately, we always come back to the principle of inseparability. What is the self? It is very difficult to say. Our usual self is a very fragile thing, and even classical psychology and psychoanalysis have only managed to explore it superficially. The fact that experiencers describe being at once themselves and others during their NDE reinforces the hypothesis of the collective unconscious. The collective unconscious could be a manifestation of the superluminal world, of all the superluminal consciousnesses that are at once unique and multiple, at once unique entities and other superluminal consciousnesses. I think that this goes a little beyond our usual framework; it places us in a kind of non-Aristotelian logic that we have already encountered in the area of particles, where certain types of particles are indiscernible. Yet, a given number of such particles do exist, but we aren't able to catalog them because they aren't discernable. This gives some idea of what Jung's collective unconscious might be.

EEV: *Let us now turn our attention to those children who, as soon as they are able to express it, emphatically claim to be the reincarnation of such and such a person. They usually provide lots of details, accurately describing the house they lived in and the people they knew. Upon verification, it turns out that the person described so minutely did indeed exist, but died a relatively short time ago. Several researchers have investigated this problem; the most well known of these is professor Ian Stevenson. He undertook an in-depth study over the course of several years in order to shed some light on the phenomenon of reincarnation. Do your studies concerning superluminal consciousness enable you to put forward a hypothesis on this subject?*

RD: Yes, there is one hypothesis that comes to mind. This superluminal consciousness has total knowledge and total information. It has information, in particular, on the lives of subluminal human beings belonging to the past, the present, and the future. Hence, it would be sufficient for the filter to function in some subjects in the manner discussed previously and to capture this information concerning the life of a human being in the past, or even in the future, in order for the subject to think he has had a past life. In fact, there would not have been a reincarnation at all, but simply awareness of information originating in the superluminal universe concerning someone else's life. This is one hypothesis.

EEV: *Would the same type of interpretation be valid for people under hypnosis who remember past lives and suddenly begin speaking in Coptic or in Latin?*

BD: Yes, exactly. We believe that when subjects are in a hypnotic state, their consciousness has momentary access to superluminal knowledge. Indeed, subjects may very well gain access at that particular moment to the consciousness of other individuals who lived in the past as a result of simultaneity, or else truly find themselves at a level of superluminal consciousness in which they may simultaneously experience several lives, giving them instant access to this information. In terms of what the person experiences, I think it is the same. Either consciousness truly projects itself in the form of different holograms, or else it has access to the consciousness of other persons.

EEV: *I would like to have your opinion on an intriguing phenomenon, that of gifted children, or child prodigies. There is no doubt that there are children with mysterious talents in both the artistic and intellectual domains. These children possess aptitudes and knowledge, which logically they should not possess, given their youth.*

BD: I think this ties back in with Plato's theory of reminiscence, which we spoke of earlier. It would seem that human beings cannot ever attain total knowledge so long as they are imprisoned in the subluminal world of holograms, because the cortical filter prevents them from having the totality of this knowledge. In certain individuals, the filter has a larger opening, which allows for much greater access to knowledge. This could explain the case of child prodigies, who have a quicker and broader access to knowledge.

EEV: *Are children more likely to have access to this type of knowledge because they are still* closer to the superluminal consciousness from which they originate?

RD: I think this is a good observation, Evelyn. We had not thought of this particular aspect, but I think you have a very good idea there.

Chapter Eight

Dialogue with Paul Chauchard

THE BRAIN

EEV: *Professor, allow me to get right to the point by quoting a passage from your book* Le cerveau et la conscience *(The Brain and Consciousness): "Consciousness and will originate in the cortex. The mind cannot function unless the cerebral cortex is in good condition. It is the essential human organ."[1] How then can we explain the phenomenon of NDEs, which, in most cases, occur in a state of cerebral death?*

PC: You have proceeded straight to the main issue. If I were to let down my guard, I would say that it is indeed impossible. Of course, I do not at all deny the existence of these phenomena, which are very interesting, but I would find it extremely difficult to explain them at this point in time. In fact, everything the near-death experiencers describe corresponds to cerebral imagery. Because it is based

Professor of Neurophysiology; Former director, Ecole Pratique des Hautes Études, Paris on what is derived from the senses, cerebral imagery is completely body-related. If it's true that the brain is no longer in working order, one might ask how this phenomenon is possible. For the time being, I really don't see any explanation. I would perhaps ask this: Are we sure that the brain has absolutely ceased to function? In reflecting upon consciousness, a particular notion occurred to me. When philosophers speak of consciousness, they mean reflective human consciousness. Some go so far as to deny the existence of consciousness in higher animals, which is ridiculous. What interests me in this debate is the fact that we have "unconscious" levels of consciousness. Our higher consciousness corresponds to verbal, left-brain consciousness, but there is also the nonverbal, animal-type consciousness of the right brain, as well as a level of consciousness at the base of the brain that may be considered a veritable bioconsciousness. When we refer to a flat electroencephalogram (EEG), we might question to what extent the centers at the base of the brain responsible for bodily unity have in fact ceased to function. Ultimately though, this is not the real issue. The real issue concerns the fact that the brain, regardless of what state it is in, is located in the body. Therefore, what interests me perhaps even more than NDEs are out-of-body experiences. These out-of-body phenomena are, for the time being, totally unexplainable, as are, for example, instances of bilocation on the part of certain mystics.

EEV: *In your opinion, is the near-death experience the result of a physiological upheaval at the time of death, caused by the collapse of the vital functions, or do you think that these experiences belong to a nonmaterial dimension?*

PC: My professional orientation obviously leads me to think about all the disruptions and shocks produced by the lack of oxygen to the brain, as well as disturbances in the transmitter substances. Scientists tend not to want to talk about the nonmaterial, but being a believer, I am faced with the problem that the nonmaterial exists, the spiritual exists. But isn't the spiritual merely a material property, a property of the brain? Or is it something else? My faith leads me to believe in the possibility of a nonmaterial dimension, and consequently, I think we will manage to prove it scientifically one day.

EEV: *Do you think that there is some mechanism in the brain capable of activating an NDE, such as the secretion of a chemical substance, for example?*

PC: Certainly, and this is the problem with all cerebral hallucinations. Hallucinogens can cause such phenomena. Unfortunately, the word *hallucination* has a negative, pathological connotation, whereas our brain is a machine for producing images. It doesn't bother me at all, for example, to say that Saint Bernadette Soubirous had a cerebral hallucination at Lourdes. This simply means that she formed an image in her brain. There is nothing pathological about that. We cannot declare it pathological without a corroborating psychological analysis. If the subject is not mentally ill, there is no reason to say that his or her hallucination is pathological.

EEV: *Have neurophysiological experiments been undertaken to analyze the phenomenon of the NDE?*

PC: Based on what I've read, I think that all they've managed to do is register flat EEGs, which doesn't mean anything, since the EEG has to be flat for a long time, and upon repeated readings, in order to conclude death. In reality—and this still has to do with the complexity of death—there are very special cases, such as barbiturate intoxication or hibernation, in which the subject's brain is not functioning at all, yet he or she is not dead, since vital functions can be resumed at some later point. In order to perform neurophysiological experiments on NDEs, it would be necessary, first of all, to find out if the phenomenon occurs in animals, but this is something we know very little about. We would have to determine if any signs could be detected in the higher order primates.

EEV: *As Raymond Moody said at a conference in Bruxelles, which I attended: Morally speaking, it is very difficult to perform such research. If a person suddenly had a heart attack, the emphasis would obviously be on trying to revive the heart, rather than to analyze what was happening in the brain at that particular moment.*

PC: Obviously. Research on human beings is always problematic. Fortunately, we can place electrodes in the brain in order to remove tumors or check the condition of the brain without detriment to the subject, but we are clearly not going to place electrodes in the brains of mystics in order to see what happens during their illumination! We have to remain outside the skull, which is less enlightening.

EEV: *In their book,* Closer to the Light, *Melvin Morse and Paul Perry describe research carried out by neurosurgeon Wilder Penfield in 1955 that may possibly explain the phenomenon of the NDE. Penfield found that electrical stimulation of the "fissure of Sylvius," located in the right temporal lobe just below the right ear, can produce an out-of-body experience, an encounter with deceased loved ones, and even a life review—hence, the main elements of a typical NDE.[2] With this in mind, I would like to quote a passage from your book,* Le cerveau et la conscience (The Brain and Consciousness): *"Electrical stimulation of the region located between the occipital and temporal lobes elicits the recollection of real memories. The*

subject is convinced, for example, that someone is playing a
record for him when he hears the lullaby his mother used to sing
for him when he was little. What happens is that the electrical
current in the brain creates a certain pattern of excitations and
inhibitions—not just any pattern, but one that corresponds to a
pre-existing cerebral possibility, i.e., a memory."[3] *Is what we*
have here a material explanation for the "life review" that occurs
during an NDE?

PC: I was not aware of this discovery on the part of Penfield, but as you know, he was a great explorer of the active and functioning human brain. To me, the basis of consciousness is the image of the body. It is the synthesis of all that comes from the skin and, especially, of the muscular tension that forms the image of our body in childhood. You know that there can be a gap, from the pathological viewpoint—take for example, the phantom limbs of amputees. Individuals who are missing a limb can sense the limb's position and feel pain in it because the cerebral image of the limb remains after amputation. There is an even better example, the phenomenon we refer to in French as *héautoscopie*, or "seeing oneself," and especially negative *héautoscopie*—the great pathology from which the writer Maupassant suffered. His short story "Le Horla" explains this extraordinary phenomenon in which the subject loses the ability to see himself in the mirror.[4] The disappearance of the image of oneself in the mirror is closely linked to these disturbed states of consciousness in which the cerebral image becomes dissociated from reality. It's something to add to the file, although it remains to be seen how all of this can be reconciled.

EEV: *During an NDE, brain activity is often observed by medical*
staff to be nonexistent. The subject is in a state of clinical death.
However, this state is reversible, since the individual in question

comes back to life and is able to relate his or her experiences. Does this mean that brain activity in such cases had not actually ceased?

PC: I would take it to mean that the cessation of brain activity does not equal death. The only way to find out if a seed that shows no biological activity is alive is to place it in water and see if it sprouts. Seeds that sprout are alive; seeds that do not sprout are dead. There is currently no way of knowing if a cell, whether a nerve cell or some other kind, is dead or alive. Contrary to the notion that life is essentially an activity, life can be defined merely as the ability to come back to life, without any activity whatsoever. Researchers have been able to block the thermoregulation of a monkey by chilling the animal to a temperature below freezing and causing everything in its brain to appear dead, although it was merely stopped. When the monkey was heated back up, everything began to function again. We could do the same thing with man, but we would, of course, have to be careful, because he might not start back up again! Nothing says that one day we won't be able to start back up a life that had been stopped for quite some time.

EEV: *NDEs occur both in a state of apparent death and in a coma. Yet, during a near-death state, brain activity is nonexistent (flat EEG), whereas during a coma, the brain is functioning. It's strange how such resolutely different physiological states can produce the same effects.*

PC: As always, these phenomena are quite complicated to explain. Basically, the differences are in degree, rather than in nature.

EEV: *Is there some aspect of the NDE that would allow us to say that what is experienced during the NDE could extend beyond physical death?*

PC: What allows us to know about these experiences is precisely the fact that the subjects in question have returned to life and to consciousness. If this were not the case, there would be no possibility of knowing more about them.

EEV: *Do you think, then, that there is no evidence to suggest that these experiences occur in another dimension?*

PC: No. The individual who has this extraordinary experience is convinced that everything does not stop at death—but this is not proof. Incidentally, all the fancy, rational proofs of the existence of God have never converted anyone. The experience of God is a private experience.

EEV: *One experiencer tells us (in Morse and Perry's* Closer to the Light*): "The mind is one thing, the brain another. The brain cannot do what the mind does."[5] Extrapolating from this, we can hypothesize that the mind is more powerful than matter, that it possesses a higher energy than that contained in matter. We could even go so far as to say that this energy could be atemporal and capable of surviving the destruction of matter. In this connection, I would like to know your opinion regarding the classic dichotomy of mind and matter—the basic notions that pit materialists against those with a more spiritual understanding of existence. Life is more functional than material, since the cells that make up our bodies are constantly being renewed. Life is therefore to be found in the impressive collaboration between these billions of cells, in this extraordinarily complex machinery, and not in matter, which transmutes constantly. Wouldn't it be more reasonable to oppose the* functioning *of matter and the mind?*

PC: What gets in our way here is this dualist terminology of mind and matter. In the current scientific context, we know that everything is energy. We can stretch things and say that matter consists of elementary particles. Thus, what counts is the organization of matter, and the mind manifests itself by informing matter. We often compare the animal brain to the human brain. Clearly, the animal brain is more simple. But if I say that human spirituality is an electrochemical property of the brain, every philosopher will protest and say that this is impossible, though as a physiologist, I would say that it is entirely correct. This raises the question of how the human brain can have spiritual qualities that the animal brain does not, if, precisely, the spiritual does not exist, or is not truly something of another order. When, in the name of atheism—whether scientific, Marxist, or other—one claims that everything is in the brain and that, consequently, everything disappears at death, one goes completely beyond the scope of science. I think that the dichotomy between mind and matter no longer exists; we have arrived at a much more unified understanding. As a believer and a neurologist, I was forced to examine the question of the relationship between mind and matter in regard to the brain and, having discovered Platonic and Cartesian spiritualists who separated them and deemed it impossible for one to act upon the other, I was fortunate to come across the philosophy of St. Thomas Aquinas (through Father Sertillanges), who showed that the soul is the form of the body. The human soul is simply more complex, because it is spiritual, than the animal soul. Incidentally, this was Aristotle's position, which was handed down to us in the Middle Ages by his successors, Averroës of Islam and the Jew Maimonides.

EEV: *Current scientific thought tends to be heading away from the material and toward the transcendental. You seem to take the opposite tack in this passage from your book,* Le cerveau et la conscience *(The Brain and Consciousness): "These human assets of consciousness and freedom have long seemed to belong to a purely spiritual order. Physiology was expected to define only their limits, with the result that, faced with the magnitude of the determinisms imposing such limits on us, some reached the point of viewing freedom as an illusion. Today, on the contrary, we are beginning to understand the cerebral conditions of the free act. The characteristic of the normal human brain, thanks to its complexity, is to be the organ that permits freedom. It is the inadequacy of the brain in animals that prevents them from rising sufficiently above determinisms to be able to control these deliberately."[6]*

PC: Contrary to many scientists who, in the name of neurophysiology, come close to denying all consciousness and freedom, I rediscover them in the brain. It's true that this seems to be completely paradoxical, especially if there is not something of another order. A scientist would not use the terms *immanent* or *transcendent*, but there is a word that is dear to their hearts and which, incidentally, is found in Engels's *Dialectics of Nature*,[7] and that is the word *emergence*. We see emergences. We explain them scientifically, but that does not mean that the philosopher has nothing to say. On the contrary, this is the point at which the philosopher must intervene—not to contest, but rather to provide another level of explanation.

EEV: *Has your great knowledge of the human brain led you to a more immanent or a more transcendent conception of the mind?*

PC: I absolutely refuse to separate the soul from the body. We always have a tendency to separate them. There are immanentists who become pantheists, and then there are transcendentalists. I completely agree with the Church in its condemnation of pantheism. The Church is right: A god who doesn't have a transcendental dimension cannot be the true God. But I would also have liked—though this did not happen—for it to condemn transcendentalism. Of course, God is transcendent, but also immanent; the two should not be divided. If you say that God is purely transcendent, then we don't know where to place Him anymore. As Father Von Balthasar said, truth is in panentheism, God is in everything, so to speak. As a scientist, I see the emergences, and these emergences imply a call from transcendence. As Teilhard de Chardin said, we do not only go forward or up, we go up and forward, we rise ... and it is also possible that we go backwards!

EEV: *How far does this freedom, made possible by the human brain, go? As far as a comatose state, a near-death state? Does it end the moment the brain stops, or does it continue beyond this?*

PC: I do not separate the material and the spiritual. At one time, many years ago, I attempted to find the spiritual in the functioning of the brain, and I entertained all sorts of ideas. I was considered scandalous by the old mechanistic materialists of times past, who said that I distorted science in order to force them to change. Then, there were the new materialists, with some Marxists among them, who were not at all scandalized, and who thanked me for compelling them to recognize the spiritual in the brain's functioning. Nowadays, we can say that everyone qualifies as a spiritualist—in other words, man is definitely a spiritual being. The issue dividing us, and the one responsible for the fact that materialists do not dare call themselves spiritualists, is the fact that the full dimension of spiritualism implies knowing whether everything stops at death or not. But this is not a scientific issue and, consequently, calls for another order of reflection.

CONSCIOUSNESS

EEV: *Do you believe consciousness to be located in the neurons of the cortex, or do you think that it is atemporal and aphysical, and located only temporarily in the brain during earthly existence? In other words, is the brain the seat of consciousness or only a mechanism to decode it?*

PC: I do indeed agree that consciousness is spiritual, but it manifests itself materially to science as a cerebral integration. The soul is the form of the body. We keep coming back to the immanence of the transcendent.

EEV: *Is consciousness necessarily linked to a material medium, or can you envision the survival of consciousness without a material medium once the body, and thus the brain, is destroyed?*

PC: I have no scientific means of proving that everything is destroyed upon death. If the soul is the form of the body, as held by the philosophy of St. Thomas Aquinas, then science sees the body only as alive and informed by the soul, but I don't have any means of knowing scientifically if there is a difference in nature between the soul of an animal, which supposedly disappears at death, and the human soul, which supposedly survives. Generally speaking, the objective difference between man and animal is more coherent with the possibility of survival. Take for example the science of aging. Old age is normally accompanied by diminishment, but this diminishment goes hand in hand with maturity. Therefore, we can ask ourselves if it is logical for individuals to continue improving themselves only to disappear one day. On the contrary, it would be much more logical to think that we are heading toward a veritable change in state, but that is something that science cannot prove.

EEV: *In your writings, you speak of bioconsciousness, which you define as follows: "Degree of consciousness of lower beings; term coined by Paul Chauchard to mark both the difference from and resemblance to human consciousness."[8] I would like to know if you also recognize a form of consciousness at the level of the human cell, and if this would have any implications for NDEs.*

PC: This is a certainty, and it allows me to pay homage to my teacher Louis Lapicque, who was a great neurophysicist. It is interesting to note that Lapicque was a materialist, freemason, and atheist. In 1951, when one of the first cybernetic conferences was held, physicists were saying that one day we would produce a conscious robot. Lapicque protested, declaring that it was absolutely impossible, because consciousness is a property of life; without life, and regardless of how complex the contraption, such efforts were doomed to failure. In some of his last publications, sent to the Académie des Sciences on March 10 and April 7, 1952, he concluded that cellular consciousness must exist. He said that human consciousness is the sum total of our cellular consciousnesses or souls. He added, going far beyond his field, that the soul is nonmaterial but not immortal. He had no scientific argument to prove it. It was at that particular moment, when reflecting upon this question, that I invented the word *bioconsciousness*, to show that consciousness has a biological basis, while at the same time obviously belonging to another dimension.

EEV: *Dreams are unconscious. They do not enter into consciousness unless we remember them upon waking. Could the mechanism responsible for NDEs be similar?*

PC: There is certainly a similarity between the two. What actually happens in the brain when we dream? We don't know—and it is nearly impossible to distinguish between what really happened in a dream and what we report about it afterwards. Dreams, in general, are completely nonverbal. One of the greatest discoveries in neurophysiology has to do, precisely, with dreaming. Jouvet, in particular, has done a lot of research in this area. Before this research, neurophysiologists could tell us their own dreams, but that was it! Psychoanalysts talked about dreams, but we were convinced that either we were conscious and awake, or else we were asleep, and that while we were asleep, we might perchance dream. Now we know that there are three states: the wakeful state, the sleep state (deep sleep, quiet sleep) and the paradoxical state, which is characterized by the rapid waves associated with dreaming. This discovery introduced neurophysiology to the concept of states of consciousness, which was the start of a veritable revolution. It was then that many neurophysiologists started taking an interest in mystical states and the various phenomena related to these other states of consciousness. This gives you an illustration of the complexity of consciousness. Take for example the case of hypnosis. At one time, it was considered to be a sleep state, that is, a state of induced sleep. Then, it was realized that this was totally false. Researchers tried desperately to find in hypnotized subjects the slower waves associated with sleep, but the brain under hypnosis remains awake. Therefore, the best way to define *hypnosis* would be to speak of hypnotic wakefulness—in other words, an overconcentration of the wakeful state in one's relations with the hypnotist. The mystic states, for example, once appeared to spring from some mysterious source, whereas now we see that persons in these states of consciousness are more alert than most of us, given our normal, everyday, stressed condition.

EEV: *Dr. Anthony Marcel of the University of Cambridge, who has studied the functioning of intellectual activity, developed a test that consists of flashing words onto a screen too rapidly for students participating in the experiment to see them. When the students were asked to repeat the words, he was astonished to discover that 90 percent of them were able to correctly recite the words that had been flashed on the screen. Dr. Marcel's conclusion is that we register the meaning of words without the intervention of consciousness. He shares the opinion of philosophers who consider consciousness to be, to a certain extent, a social construct. What do you think of this?*

PC: Problems arise when you oppose the biological and the social. I may speak of bioconsciousness, but I stress the fact that everything is biosociological. The human being is a social being and, consequently, we do not really become fully human until we learn how to speak a language and verbalize our body image. Deaf persons who don't hear themselves will be mute, even though they are perfectly capable of speaking. In order for me to be truly conscious, there must be an association between my self-image, my body image, and every other phenomenon that occurs in my brain. Sensations are initially unconscious in the brain, and a certain amount of time is required before there is true awareness, which illustrates the complexity of all these phenomena.

EEV: *Therefore, Dr. Marcel's experiment did indeed occur without the intervention of consciousness?*

PC: Words are registered before we become aware of them; that much is certain. Here we come across Freud again, who, though not a neurophysiologist, said that all brain functioning is by definition unconscious, that awareness is simply an additional phenomenon—an essential one, of course—but that everything happens first without conscious awareness.

ALTERED STATES OF CONSCIOUSNESS

EEV: *In the West, materialists have defined four, and only four, states of consciousness. These are: wakefulness, sleep, coma, and death. Fortunately, the current trend is toward a broader range and one that is undoubtedly closer to reality. What is your position on this?*

PC: This list omits an important state—the dream state. Dreaming is an entirely different state, which gives you an idea of the variety of levels of consciousness. Furthermore, there is a reflective wakefulness, which is more human in nature, and an affective and intuitive wakefulness, which is more animal-like in nature. If you are wondering what animal-like human consciousness is, it is quite simply the nonverbal consciousness of the human right brain, which is definitely more advanced than the animal brain, because it is more highly evolved. It is nevertheless completely animal-like. Thus, we can say that man is an advanced animal. With respect to the coma and especially death, the conclusion has been that consciousness is absent in these states. Herein lies the entire problem.

EEV: *During altered states of consciousness, such as meditation, for example, what is occurring at the neurophysiological level?*

PC: Studies of subjects practicing yoga or Zen clearly indicate that this is indeed a state of relaxation, an alpha wave state, thus a perfectly normal brain state, which has nothing to do with psychopathology. Unfortunately, electroencephalography is still too rudimentary to be able to give us very precise information, but the findings available today refute the notion once held by materialist psychiatrists that meditation is a mental pathology.

EEV: *In meditation, is the brain in a completely normal, ordinary state, or is it in a more alert state?*

PC: According to the Japanese Zen neurophysiologists I met through Deshimaru, with whom I published *Zen et cerveau (Zen and the Brain),*[9] the brain is in a more normal state during meditation than it is in people like you and me—that is, your average not-so-normal persons. The brain is in a calm and lucid state, including, by the way, a state of emotional peace, whereas we are often perturbed, as is amply demonstrated by lie detectors. This reminds me of the story of a German named Herrigel who went to Japan to learn archery. In proper Western fashion, he overly tensed his muscles and tried desperately to succeed but instead failed. The teacher said to him, "The day you no longer wish to succeed, you will be calm inside and you will succeed." This seems to be the opposite of will, but instead, it is the secret of genuine will—a state of optimum alertness.

EEV: *Numerous experiencers claim to have possessed a heightened sense of perception as well as absolute lucidity during their NDE. They had the impression of having access to universal knowledge, of truly understanding the connection between all things, and of knowing the meaning of life. It is as if the fact of being imprisoned in matter blinds us, and prevents us from seeing and understanding that only separation from our physical body can permit us to achieve our real potential.*

PC: If I tend to agree with this idea, even though I cannot prove it, it is because I see it from another level. In fact, we are greatly hindered in seeing true reality, because quite often we use our brains poorly—we are intellectuals lost in a world of ideas, who fail to see reality. You know that Jean-Paul Sartre, in his memoirs, *Les mots (The Words),*[10] tells how in his childhood he hated the outdoors, preferring to close himself up in a library in order to read and think, thus completely removing himself from reality. Our thinking is verbal and conceptual, whereas current knowledge of the right brain indicates that it is intuitive thinking that puts us into touch with reality. Stated differently, we are part of reality, we are the culmination of the evolutionary complexification of reality, which is what allows us to understand it. I always like to say that if you want to find the rule of all balance, understanding, and morality, don't forget your *corpus callosum*! You know, the *corpus callosum* is the slab of white nerve fibers that connects the two cerebral hemispheres. These discoveries were made by Sperry when the *corpus callosum* was cut; they allowed the right brain to be rehabilitated. The two brains must be interconnected. It is not a matter of denying the superiority of the intellectual brain, but the role of the more human part, that is, the frontal brain, is precisely to link the two. Thus, when we see what the proper functioning of the brain is—as opposed to everything modern education leads to—we see the reality of good cerebral functioning. That's a word I use all the time, and it's normal for a neurophysiologist to use the word *cerebral*, but I often say that those we refer to as "cerebral" in the usual sense are intellectuals who are lost in thought, and thus persons who don't know how to use their brain. This is the point at which women enter the male–female dialogue. At one point, women nearly fell into a trap when men, in a burst of generosity, recognized that women were not inferior, but equal, and able to be like them. Today, fortunately, women seem to have understood that they are women, that it is they who are much closer to reality, and that it is up to them to wrest men from their abstractions and help them rediscover their feelings.

MEMORY

EEV: *Memory is an essential field of NDE research. Before addressing the questions that refer to it directly, I would like to know if the seat of memory is in the conscious or the unconscious?*

PC: As with all brain mechanisms, everything registered by consciousness is basically an unconscious phenomenon—the awareness of memory comes later. As psychoanalysis has shown, the proof is that before our consciousness was developed in the first years of life, everything was already inscribed in us. Naturally, when hypnotists say that a subject screamed because he was the egg in his mother's body that was penetrated by his father's sperm, I am skeptical. But it is true that there is a prenatal memory, even if the recollection of it is limited. The memory's potential is enormous. However, certain emotional shocks—and psychoanalysis has fully demonstrated this—cannot ever spontaneously enter consciousness. It is the role of psychoanalysis to bring these to awareness, particularly by working with dreams.

EEV: *In your opinion, what is the purpose of this data bank that lies buried in our unconscious, is only partially accessible during our lifetime, and that during an NDE releases what probably represents only a fraction of the information actually recorded?*

PC: Yes, these are the memories of a lifetime. It has always been said that some people see their life pass before their eyes at the time of death. Our memory, what is recorded in us, indeed surpasses by far what we remember. Consequently, in circumstances such as those present at the time of death, it is entirely possible that everything recorded in us is manifested. The truth is that the neurophysiology of memory is still in its infancy. Particularly in the aged, or in certain cases of alcoholism, recent memories are not retained and only older memories remain. But what is the material basis of memories? Research has been carried out on the assumption that various chemical substances are involved, but nothing has been proved. This phenomenon is necessarily linked to a cerebral mechanism, although there are nonetheless cases in which monkeys, for example, are put into hibernation and their brains completely stopped, but once revived, remember very well that pressing the red button doesn't give them any reward and that the green button gives them a banana. Thus, the memory is there. How then is this possible, how is it retained? There are a lot of hypotheses, but basically, we know very little about this.

EEV: *And what, in your opinion, is the meaning of this database, which, ultimately, we utilize very little in our lifetime, and of which we perhaps use only a small part during the NDE?*

PC: Memory, you see, is a sort of cerebral restructuring. It is therefore a cerebral phenomenon that has occurred and that returns. You ask whether memory is material or spiritual—I think it is both at the same time. Memory is a cerebral organization, but if the soul is the form of the body, then the spiritual aspect behind this organization works in such a way that if the material disappears, the spiritual is able to continue.

EEV: *During the NDE life review, an enormous amount of information is released. Experiencers remember events from the distant past, details they had long since forgotten. Our conscious memory seems therefore to be extremely poor in comparison to this unconscious memory, which unceasingly stores all the information of our daily lives, and is activated during an NDE. Is it possible to quantify the conscious memory with respect to the unconscious memory?*

PC: We can identify three typical cases: that which we remember easily, that which is blocked (as demonstrated by psychoanalysis), and the intermediate cases. One such intermediate case is that referred to in Penfield's experiments, in which the active brain was stimulated to produce memories. The subject had not remembered these and was astonished to be able to recall certain events at this time. No doubt these recollections would one day have reentered his memory in connection with a particular place or situation. Hence, some memories are retained and some are not, but these are very complex mechanisms.

EEV: *But our unconscious memory contains much more than what we remember.*

PC: Yes, that's right. Basically, consciousness does not attain its fully human level until the child begins to speak. Everything in his previous experience, everything since conception, has been recorded in him. This concept was applied in a very scientific context by Françoise Dolto, who conducted experiments in which she spoke adult language to newborns and was able to obtain absolutely extraordinary results. As far as consciousness is concerned, we once had a tendency to consider the fetus as something purely material, or biological, for we had forgotten this hierarchy of consciousness and the fact that the centers at the base of the brain, the centers of emotion—unlike the cerebral cortex—develop long before birth.

EEV: *We know today that only 30 percent of those experiencing a near-death crisis remember having had an NDE. It is possible that the remaining 70 percent did not have one, but it is also possible that everyone in a near-death state has an NDE, but that only 30 percent of them remember it. What is your opinion on this subject?*

PC: Obviously, we have no way of knowing, but I think that such a hypothesis is entirely plausible. Everything depends upon the personality of the individual. We are all different. It would be interesting to know the percentage of NDEs considered to be pleasant, as some are apparently negative. Perhaps between these two types of NDE may be found a much more neutral experience—one that has much less of an impact on the individual, and is therefore more likely to be forgotten.

EEV: *The ability to remember is greatly enhanced when one finds oneself in the same state of consciousness as when the event in question occurred, or more generally, when a given item of information was registered by an individual. Can the fact of having left the particular state of consciousness associated with the near-death experience explain why 70 percent of those who were on the verge of death have no recollection of a near-death experience?*

PC: The current view of ordinary memory might perhaps explain that. As psychoanalysts have discovered, it is possible for unpleasant emotional shocks to be repressed, and this phenomenon may play a role in these situations as well.

EEV: *The recollection of an item of information seems to be strongly linked to the emotions associated with it. Could we say that the ability to remember is not only linked to a specific state of consciousness, but also to a particular emotional state?*

PC: Absolutely. Intellectualism and rationalism have vastly underrated emotional states, which, on the contrary, are the essential phenomena. In conditioned reflexes in animals, we know that if we don't present the animal with something of interest to it, it will not react, and the experiment will fail. It is the emotional attribute that reasserts the value of the right brain, and this is something that hasn't been understood well enough. The heart or the head, which one will prevail? The answer lies in the combination of the two, though the pinnacle of the human being is certainly the heart, or the "conscious heart" to borrow Bettelheim's expression, which signifies the synthesis of the heart and the head, yet is so difficult to achieve.

EEV: *Is it possible that appropriate psychological conditioning might allow the other 70 percent of persons who were on the verge of death to remember an NDE that they perhaps experienced but forgot, and do you think this would be desirable?*

PC: Whether it is desirable, I can't say. For those who have experienced their NDE as positive, it is obviously very good. In fact, everything that is cerebral is essentially education, and thus, educates the memory. It is very possible that those who are well-trained will find it easier to remember. You are pointing the way to some very interesting research.

EEV: *Prenatal memories emerge only in special circumstances, when induced by specific techniques. In their book,* Les étonnants pouvoirs de la mémoire, *Sheila Ostrander and Lynn Schroeder tell the story of a French scientist named Alfred Tomatis,[11] who devoted his life to exploring human memory, in order to restore its role in health, happiness, and creativity. One day Tomatis was faced with a particularly baffling case, which eventually led him to demonstrate that prenatal hearing and memory are capable of shaping later existence. An autistic four-year-old girl named Odile was brought to the Tomatis Clinic in Paris. She was completely mute and didn't seem to hear anything. As her treatment (based on exposure to high-frequency sounds) progressed, she slowly began to emerge from her long silence. In one month's time, she was listening and speaking. Her family was overjoyed and astounded. After four years of silence, Odile could finally speak. Yet, to their great surprise, she spoke in English, rather than French. Where had Odile learned English? Dr. Tomatis decided to research the mother's background and discovered that during her pregnancy, Odile's mother had worked in Paris for an import–export company where only English was spoken. Odile had therefore heard English in* utero *until her birth. I think there are some parallels to be drawn between this particular case and NDEs, since, in both instances and at both extremities of life, memories come from quite far away!*

PC: Tomatis's interpretation would not have been accepted in the past. Now, this type of thinking tends to be totally acceptable. There have indeed been many experiments involving prenatal hearing and babies who, having heard a particular melody during intrauterine life, later showed joyful recognition when the melody was played back to them.

EEV: *Do you see any parallel with the recollection of an NDE, which also comes from quite far away, but which occurs at the other extremity of life?*

PC: It's hard to say, but it is definitely something to look into.

EEV: *But the mechanisms are not the same since the fetus exists, whereas we don't quite know where to place someone in a near-death state.*

PC: The problem has to do with the relationship between what happens in the brain and that which is no longer part of the brain. When we say that an experiencer saw such and such a thing during his NDE, he did not see it with his eyes, whereas the fetus obviously hears with its ears, since these develop quite early. The whole problem with NDEs lies in the fact that they seem to imply that there can be psychological activity without a functioning brain, but that such activity is nevertheless recorded in the brain. This would be like a temporary separation of the body and the soul, as opposed to psychosomatic unity.

EEV: *In other words, what happens with the fetus is more material than what happens with the experiencer?*

PC: Yes, definitely.

EEV: *The automatic or reflex memory continues to work when the intellectual or semantic memory is not functioning, as in the case of amnesia, for example. Yet, the recollections of experiencers do not seem to arise from this type of memory, given their significantly sharper clarity than those of ordinary consciousness. What type of memory is operating during the near-death experience?*

PC: The emotional aspect always prevails over the intellectual. Therefore, it is no doubt the emotional and sensory memories that operate during these experiences, more so than the intellectual memory.

EEV: *Many experiencers report having had access, during their NDE, to a kind of absolute knowledge that could be compared to a universal memory. In this context, I would like to hear your opinion on multiple personalities. There are pathological cases of individuals who harbor up to ten or twelve personalities, one of whom often plays the role of "teacher," and is endowed with an almost omniscient intelligence and memory. Do you see any correlation between this phenomenon and that of NDEs?*

PC: Multiple personalities are the domain of psychiatry. But there are also mystical experiences, such as out-of-body phenomena, in which individuals leave their bodies, go visit others, and give them advice. We often suspect trickery in such cases, and it is true that these are merely testimonies, but ultimately we don't have a very clear idea of what is happening.

EEV: *What interests me about this particular point is the total knowledge to which experiencers claim to have access. In the case of multiple personalities, we find this same notion of universal knowledge.*

PC: We tend too often to cut ourselves off from the world; yet we are born of the world and consequently are connected to a cosmic consciousness, which we ordinarily do not perceive.

EEV: *Is this Jung's collective unconscious?*

PC: Yes, I was just thinking of Jung. We have too great a tendency to separate individual consciousness from what is universal—not only from the social, but also from the cosmic perspective. Basically, the world expresses its conscious awareness through us. If we are capable of understanding the world, it is precisely because our brain is made of the same matter, and the same energy as the world. If this were not the case, the brain would not be capable of understanding it.

EEV: *And some states, such as the near-death state, provide us easier access to it than others.*

PC: That's right. In these kinds of states our higher, intellectual, verbal consciousness disappears, and we are much closer to affective consciousness, hence, to right-brain, or animal-type consciousness.

EEV: *Closer to instinct than to intellect.*

PC: Yes, that's it.

DEATH

EEV: *In your book entitled* La mort *(Death), you say that "... death in these conditions is a prognosis that has every chance of coming true. If, therefore, by means of some known or yet-to-be-discovered procedure we can manage to revive this supposed cadaver, we should not, as we often do, call it resurrection. Science does not resurrect, and never will resurrect the dead. But it can stop the process of death, and will increasingly do so in the future, by preventing the death of cells that would normally die, but are still alive. Yet, it does this merely through reactivation or resuscitation techniques."[12] I suppose that you conclude from this that experiencers did not really die during the experience, even if they were declared clinically dead, since they came back to life?*

PC: Yes, that's correct; these persons were not dead and there was no resurrection. Regardless of whether one believes it or not, it is only in the Gospel that I see what might have been a genuine resurrection—that of Lazarus. This is something entirely different than resuscitation.

EEV: *Thus, the term* clinically dead *doesn't mean anything; it doesn't mean that the person is dead?*

PC: You might look at it as a transition from life to death that does not reach completion. But we might ask ourselves the following question: In approaching this postmortem state, to what extent can we perceive something and remember it?

EEV: *What do you think of the testimony of this experiencer in Kenneth Ring's* Heading Toward Omega: *"The next thing I knew, I was in—I was standing in a mist and I knew immediately that I had died but I was still alive. And I cannot tell you how I felt. It was, 'Oh, God, I'm dead, but I'm here! I'm me!' And I started pouring out these enormous feelings of gratitude"?*[13]

PC: We all have some anxiety about what happens after death, because in the end, we don't know anything about it. Believers are not sure; they may have arguments, but they don't have any certainty. Experiencers, on the other hand, have a sense of certainty that everything does not come to an end. It's quite remarkable how you can try to show them that this isn't true, but they are so firmly convinced that you cannot change their minds. It's very interesting.

EEV: *To them, it's no longer a question of faith; it's a fact.*

PC: Yes, that's right.

EEV: *It's more than a belief; it requires less effort but has more force.*

PC: Yes, it is curious to use this term, but it is something that has been experienced. The accounts I have read are ambiguous in some ways: When, for example, during a near-death experience, a subject is deciding with the help of others around him whether or not to return to life, he often chooses to return because he has some unfinished business to take care of on earth. The contradiction has to do with the fact that the doctor will sometimes say: "He's not the one who decided to come back, it was I who successfully brought him back to life!"

EEV: *It's true that experiencers are sometimes very irritated at the doctor who resuscitated them.*

PC: Yes, so I've heard.

EEV: *In your writings, you have defined three stages of death: apparent death, clinical death, and absolute death. Do you see any reason for placing the NDE in one or the other of these categories, or do you think this question is inappropriate since these experiences fall into "another dimension," one that is not physical?*

PC: This experience seems to be situated at the far end of clinical death. You know, we can come up with great classifications, but as usual, they are theoretical. When one is faced with the problem of resuscitation, the big question is when to stop trying. We have no idea as to when we should stop! People sometimes complain, with good reason, about therapeutic insistence, but you never hear a word about it when it works! There was once a case involving a Russian physicist, whom doctors were able to resuscitate at the end of a long period. He was truly clinically dead; there were no signs of life, and this had gone on for months. But since he was not just the local plumber, they wanted to revive him at any cost, and they ended up succeeding! Ultimately, it isn't clear to us when we should stop. Thus, we keep coming back to this idea that we cannot distinguish between what is stopped and what is dead. The same phenomenon may be observed in poliomyelitis. At the beginning, the subject is completely paralyzed, the bone marrow cells are dead, and we think the patient will never walk again. The dead cells are indeed dead, but some cells may still be alive and are just suffering from shock—these simply have stopped, but may be reactivated by massage or other means.

EEV: *Our knowledge of all phenomena, whether natural or psychic, is the same in that originally we did not possess it! Knowledge is acquired in phases. I would like to propose the following classification: In the beginning, knowledge is akin to intuition; this is the "religious" phase, which falls into the category of belief and requires an act of faith. Next comes the "philosophical" phase, in which there is some tangible, rational foundation, but nothing very solid. Last, there is the "scientific" phase, in which the phenomenon is proved experimentally and becomes a fact. Whether one likes it or not, whether one believes it or not, the evidence is there. In which of these three categories would you place the NDE?*

PC: First of all, I don't think we can isolate it. It is true that scientific research is rational, yet imagination has an extraordinary role to play in it too. The scientist imagines something, develops a hypothesis and then verifies it … either it works or it doesn't work. Currently there is a lot of talk about the chemical transmission of nerve impulses in the brain. Did you know that these theories are traceable to the Austrian Otto Loewy, and that the discovery that earned him a Nobel prize was the result of a dream? It's true that not just anybody would have dreamed his dream; it was something he possessed within himself, but he nevertheless did dream the experiment—only the next morning he couldn't remember it! He was desperate! The following night, when he had the same dream again, he jumped out of bed, got some paper and wrote down all the details of the experiment, and this led to a very important discovery. In the beginning, it was pure intuition, but it eventually led to all the necessary experimental research. As far as NDEs are concerned, the problem has basically to do with the fact that these are testimonies. Obviously, this phenomenon should be studied scientifically and, to the extent possible, this is what is being done. NDEs also pose philosophical problems. Consequently, the three phases must be considered simultaneously.

Chapter Nine

Dialogue with Monsignor Jean Vernette

EEV: *Monsignor, do you think the testimonies of near-death experiencers can provide us with an insight into "life after death"? Or do you think the fact that experiencers return to life diminishes the importance of their revelations, given that they were "not really dead"?*

JV: It is true that all accounts of near-death experiences have aroused passionate debate. This reflects an enduring interest in metaphysical issues concerning the hereafter. But ultimately we must ask ourselves what to make of it all. Are NDEs purely physiological reactions, are they psychic phenomena to be explored, or are they experiences that prove the existence of an afterlife? In my opinion, an account of what is experienced during a coma

Delegate of the French Episcopate for questions concerning sects and new religious phenomena, Advisor to the Vatican, and writer cannot be taken as a description of the hereafter. It is the farthest point to which human beings can go, but since they come back, there is no "death" involved. What these accounts describe are specific states of consciousness, not experiences of the afterlife. Raymond Moody's use of the term *temporary death*, and especially *clinical death*, to refer to the state of apparent death, creates some confusion. His criteria of cardiac arrest, absence of breathing, and drop in blood pressure are not sufficient indicators. If a patient were given intensive care at this point, it would not be impossible for him or her to "come out of it." Hence, the expression "near-death experience" is preferable to that of "life after life," as it does not connote a journey to the hereafter, but simply the feelings experienced during a dramatic life event that is retold with all the power of emotion inherent in the recording of that which is symbolic, imaginary, and affective. Consequently, I am not surprised to note that two out of three apparitions reported by experiencers are of deceased persons with whom they once had close emotional ties. Or that the religious figures who appear to them are surrounded by light, since light is an archetype in religious iconography. In Christianity, we speak of the "glorious body." I am not surprised either by the profusion of emotional terms used to describe the feelings that accompany the entry into the other world, such as peace, joy, and harmony, especially during the last stage of the journey, where the accounts burst into myriad descriptions of celestial bodies, of fusing with the light, and of absolute and unconditional love. These words reveal that what has occurred is an intensely emotional and ineffable experience. But inevitably, the question arises as to whether, strictly speaking, we may refer to it as a "spiritual" experience.

EEV: *I think that at this point it would be interesting if you could state for us the official position of the Catholic Church as concerns NDEs.*

JV: There is no "official position of the Catholic Church," but there is a set of reference points that may help to clarify the issue. At the initial level, such clarification falls within the province of theology and research. For example, let us go back to what I have just said: That which is spiritual is not to be confused with that which is emotional. I hasten to add that the positive effects of the NDE seem to derive from this level. According to Patrice Van Eersel, it creates a total upheaval in the value system of the individual concerned. The wish to make a good impression, the desire for fame, the fear of being ridiculed by others—all of these disappear like a childhood disease. So does an excessive attachment to material things. Conversely, certain values show a decidedly vertical shift, such as the enjoyment of life, attention to others, and a complex mixture of patience, tolerance, consideration, understanding, and compassion. In other words, some sort of spiritual life has been awakened. And the traveler discovers that death, which once filled him with a dreaded fear, masks a clarity of dazzling beauty that is full of life—"the black source," as it is described with wonder by Van Eersel in his book by the same name (*La source noire*[1]). But in order for death to become a source of inspiration and meaning in one's life, one must use *discernment* in considering these experiences. And this is where we should refer to the teachings of the great spiritual masters. They all say that we should judge the tree by its fruits. If the NDE brings peace and joy, there is a chance that it is genuinely spiritual, because it is the fruit of a good spirit.

If it is a source of anxiety, sadness, and depression, if it leads to religious confusion between eternal life and an altered state of consciousness, between resurrection and reincarnation, between spiritual theology and parapsychology, it may be the fruit of an evil spirit, a close companion of the *diabolos*, the "devil" (meaning "the confuser"). The paranormal has nothing to do with the supernatural, nor does spiritism have anything to do with the Communion of Saints. And to the Christian, the desire for immortality that is expressed in the NDE still does not equal faith in the resurrected Christ. The discovery that there is a spirit in man that, in certain circumstances, can live a life detached from the body, confirms what most men think of human nature. But it does not give us any direct information as to what the next world is like, because that knowledge comes from faith, which is based on Divine Revelation. This is what Catholic theology has to say concerning near-death experiences.

EEV: *Monsignor, what would you say to skeptics who claim that NDEs are hallucinations caused by intense fear at the prospect of imminent death, medications given to a patient, or a lack of oxygen in the blood?*

JV: It is difficult to answer this question because these states and "trips" may also occur as a result of an extended fast or the ingestion of certain drugs. Are visions at the moment of death then simply hallucinations caused by chemical changes within the brain, a lack of oxygen to the brain, or an excess of carbon dioxide? The question must be asked. However, my first impression is that these are not hallucinations, because hallucinations are projections of internal visions, worries, or needs. Yet, NDEs do not resemble fantasies that project the hopes and fears of the dying person. They appear to be ordered accounts with their own consistency and a certain objective weight.

For example, they contain entities that are often foreign to the subject's environment; therefore, they are not projections. An experiencer's religion rarely affects his or her NDE, which is not an expression of desires. At most, the being of light appears to some Christians to have the face or body in which Jesus Christ is traditionally represented. Yet, it has often been observed that a dying person's encephalogram is very similar to that of a person in a deeply meditative state (i.e., rapid beta waves alternating with slower alpha waves). This seems to indicate that the approach of death induces an altered, euphoric state of consciousness, conveying feelings of peace and happiness in much the same way as does meditation, hypnosis or, for that matter, the ingestion of certain drugs. The images that appear during psychotropic "trips" are sometimes similar to those reported during NDEs. But here again, I repeat, one intense emotional experience is not in itself spiritual, even if it may subsequently become so.

EEV: *The fact that there are people who "come back from the realm of the dead" and who remember what happened while in this near-death state, is, historically speaking, completely new, apart from the accounts of some miraculous recoveries in the past. Can we consider this to be the most important revelation in the history of humanity?*

JV: In the eyes of Christians, no. The most important revelation in the history of humanity is the resurrection of Jesus Christ and the testimony of the apostles. This revelation tells us that someone has returned from the other shore, from the other side of the mirror. The risen Christ is the prototype, the model of what our own resurrection will be like, sometimes at the end of a period of suffering and passion. The accounts of witnesses are clear on this point. Scarcely thirty-five years after the death of Christ, the apostle Paul wrote to one of the communities he had founded on the shores of the Mediterranean: "I handed on to you first of all what I myself received, that Christ died for our sins in accordance with the Scriptures; that he was buried and, in accordance with the Scriptures, rose on the third day; that he was seen by Cephas, then by the Twelve. After that he was seen by five hundred brothers at once, most of whom are still alive, although some have fallen asleep. Next he was seen by James; then by all the apostles. Last of all he was seen by me, as one born out of the normal course" (1 Corinthians 15:3–8). Paul wrote this letter for a specific reason: to strengthen the faith of the Corinthians in the face of their doubts about the hereafter and their own resurrection. This is what interests us. For Paul does it by calling upon a belief shared by all: the resurrection of Jesus, which is the anticipation and the ransom for our own resurrection. It is therefore a historical event, in the sense that it took place at a particular time in history. This does not mean that history, as a science, can prove the resurrection of Jesus, but it can register the testimony of reliable witnesses. As for the faith of the apostles, in the eyes of historians, there is no room for doubt—it is fully historical. Numerous accounts illustrate this: the Gospel according to Matthew (28:1–8), Mark (16:1–8), Luke (24:13–35), and John (20:19–29; 21:12). But there is a big difference between the accounts of experiencers "returning from the realm of the dead" and the revelation contained in the Scripture concerning the resurrection of Jesus.

EEV: *I think that if we knew how to listen to the accounts of experiencers, not only with our reason, but also with our heart, it would change the world, and true solidarity and brotherhood could at last prevail. I feel the importance of the near-death experience is such that it may be capable of leading humanity to evolve toward a higher level of consciousness.*

JV: That is why proponents of the New Age see these accounts as evidence that we have entered into a new era in human history. And certainly, new awareness is dawning. But there are also instances of regression. In any case, it demonstrates a fundamental aspiration to peace and universal understanding, which lies hidden in the hearts of all men and women, but is obscured by sin.

EEV: *The NDE transforms the person who has undergone it in a radical and lasting fashion. The Bible teachings, which say that we are all brothers and that we share a common destiny, are viewed as an absolute truth and reality by these experiencers. We could almost say that if everyone were to have the "good fortune of experiencing an NDE," the world would look quite different. How is it that such a fundamental Bible teaching has never been truly understood? Are we to think that the testimonies of experiencers have more of an impact on people than the words of the Bible?*

JV: In one of his parables, Jesus anticipates this question. In it, the evil rich man suffering the torments of hell asks Abraham to send Lazarus to warn his brothers: " 'I ask you, then,' the rich man said, 'send him to my father's house where I have five brothers. Let him be a warning to them so that they may not end in this place of torment.' Abraham answered, 'They have Moses and the prophets.... If they do not listen to Moses and the prophets, they will not be convinced even if one should rise from the dead.' " (Luke 16:27–31).

EEV: *I think it would be interesting to draw some parallels between the testimonies of experiencers and the passages of the Bible that describe these same phenomena. To my knowledge, such a comparative study has never been undertaken.*

JV: To answer your question, I will take the example of the "ethereal body" or "subtle body" described in NDEs, and the "glorious body" mentioned in the Bible, to show the parallels and the differences. The notion of ethereal body, or of the ethereal double of the body, is based on the idea that, beyond the groups of molecules and cells that make up the physical body, which undergo periodic renewal and ultimately decomposition, there circulates an accumulated energy charge, called the "ethereal double" by theosophists, since it is described by visionaries as a luminous body, or aura, that extends beyond the body. Some then extrapolate from this and point out its similarity to the "glorious body," or the spiritual body we will have in the next life. This supply of energy is supposedly received at birth in sufficient quantity to allow for the gradual development of the individual up to adulthood, at which point it begins to disperse and is ultimately exhausted in old age. The normal relations between the astral body and the personality may be altered through the use of drugs. This would explain drug takers' "trips" to another plane, as well as the bodily "splits" experienced during NDEs. Some particularly gifted individuals can actually induce these "splits" while in the normal state, thus traveling to other, higher planes. Death would correspond to the breaking away of the astral body from the physical body, or the rupture of the "fluidical" cord. This precise moment marks the passage to the world beyond. But this takes us into the area of spiritism.... This is not, however, a neutral doctrine. The birth chart, for example, is a diagram that attempts to explain in an exhaustive manner many phenomena of this world and the world beyond. But it should also be noted that there is a little of everything in this vision of things—some relevant notions, and others based on more questionable belief systems, such as that of spiritism, which was mentioned previously, or occultism. The mystical tradition throws a somewhat different light on this subject. Spiritual persons speak of the "spiritual body" after the example of St. Paul. Admittedly. But this is another, metaphysical, order of reality. Moslem mystics speak of a world where images are real and lasting. This, in the words of Henry Corbin, is the "imaginal world," where bodily realities become spiritualized and spiritual realities take on bodies, in a different space–time than ours. The difficulty of identifying the underlying doctrinal theory has to do with the vagueness of the terms used in the accounts, particularly those of NDEs, which make reference to an "ethereal," "subtle," "glorious," or "spiritual" body. There seems to be some vacillation between the occult theory of the astral body and a more spiritual vision of things. The Christian must be able to exercise discernment. The same applies to knowing whether such a body is perceptible from our earthly perspective. People then become aligned into two different camps—one more materialistic, and the other more spiritual in nature. Allow me to clarify this. Some feel the "ethereal" body is manifested by a radiation known as the "aura," which may be detected by mediums and which, supposedly, has been photographed by the Kirlian couple. This would be its physical manifestation. Scientists, by the way, contest this interpretation. But others quickly add that the color of a person's aura depends upon his or her level of spirituality. Ultimately, it would take the shape of a white halo with golden reflections, like the sun. This is how it is pictured by icon painters. Such halos surround the heads of saints, whose wide-open eyes seem transfixed by the ineffable beyond. This brings us to the more spiritual notion of the "glorious body." The apostles, for example, who witnessed the transfiguration of Jesus at Mount Tabor (Mark 9:3) were said to have had, during their lifetimes, the privilege of seeing the Eternal Glory that Christ has always radiated: "His face became as dazzling as the sun" (Matthew 17:2). This glorious, luminous body is the one we will have in the next life, in the Light of God. During the Eucharistic Prayer II of the Catholic Mass, the intercession for the departed implores, "Bring them and all the departed into the light of Your presence!" From this perspective, the glorious body would already have begun to take shape here on earth. It is thanks to it that the apostles, in passing to another plane, were able to perceive the glorious body of Jesus, and thanks to it that mystics like Francis of Assisi, Teresa of Avila, Joseph Cupertino, or Bernadette of Lourdes were able to perceive the light of glory of those who appeared to them. As the Bible says, "In Your light we see light" (Psalms 36:10). And according to some Fathers of the Church, the glorious body progresses in stages toward increasing perfection into the next life. The surprising manifestations of this body, which, to facilitate matters I shall refer to as "subtle," are thus an undifferentiated element that may be found in most civilizations and religions. Their value is derived, first of all, from their presumed origin (the power of occult forces in black magic, or the power of the Spirit of God in mysticism); second, from the use one makes of them (the proud domination of others through the exercise of "powers" on the part of occultists—the fakir, or the elevation and edification of disciples on the part of the spiritual masters); and last, from the doctrinal body on which they are founded, all of which are not of equal value. The validity of the testimonies may also be determined by the general tone of the messages, on the basis of their mental and spiritual wholesomeness. What is marvelous is not always authentic; what is emotional is not always spiritual; and what is abstruse is not always mystical. Once more, it is a question of discernment.

EEV: *I read with great interest your book,* Jésus dans la nouvelle religiosité *(Jesus in the New Religiosity),*[2] *in which you talk about how many of the marginal spiritual groups and sects enjoying great success today have abandoned the traditional image of Jesus, replacing it with a cosmic and depersonalized Christ. I see a general tendency in the accounts of experiencers to consider the "being of light," which they sometimes refer to as "Jesus," as a universal, cosmic being. However, the being of light seen by experiencers is not at all depersonalized, but rather impresses them as being the kindest friend they have ever had.*

JV: It is a matter of repositioning the role of Jesus and of Christ, respectively, in esotericism and in Christianity. In esotericism, Jesus of Nazareth is simply an avatar of the universal cosmic Christ, who is also "descended" in such exceptional persons as Buddha, Krishna, Zarathustra, Mohammed, and so on. In the Christian tradition, Jesus of Nazareth is the Only Son of the Father, the Word, that is, the visible transcription of the Ultimate Word of God. He is the Son of God and God himself. And this is why He is at once Jesus and Christ, in one. He is the Only Son of God. This is one of the main tenets of the Christian faith.

EEV: *A key element of many NDE accounts is light, which has a highly symbolic meaning. Experiencer accounts are consistent in regard to it, and a composite statement might read as follows: "I could call it a 'light' or 'love,' and it would mean the same thing." Light also enjoys a special place in the Bible.*

JV: Once again we see the notions of "glory" and "light" used as attributes of God, in addition to that of the "glorious body."

EEV: *A "profound" NDE, that is, an NDE that includes most of the typical features, seems to provide direct access to the source of faith. Experiencers no longer "believe," they "know." Here are two accounts on this subject: "It [the NDE] didn't make me go to church, but I feel close to God, much closer, since. Now I*

*know that he exists." And, "I know there is a God now. I don't
question it anymore."*

JV: When you say "they know," you emphasize the "testi-
monial" aspect of NDEs. While they do not provide the
observer with any objective proof of an afterlife, one must
recognize that those who have had these experiences view
them as personal proof, as obvious facts and irrefutable
testimony. To their way of thinking: "After having seen
what I've seen, I can no longer deny that there is something in the next life." The unanimity of the testimonies
gives weight to their authenticity, even if it is a subjective
authenticity. What strikes me most is that this unanimity
in our contemporaries suggests an enormous aspiration to
hope and an irrepressible desire for eternal life. From the
standpoint of the religious historian, the fact that all experiencers claim that their fear of death has given way to
great serenity is a reminder that one of the traditional roles
of myths—which are a founding element of life in
society—is precisely to calm fears and facilitate the important "passages" of life. Seen in this way, NDE accounts
would be a contemporary collective formulation of this. In
short, this need to believe in and hope for something else,
even if it is in some cases a projection of the personal and
collective unconscious, points to the existence of an irre-
ducible religious dimension in man. In my opinion, it
would be careless and unscientific to fail to take this into
account.

EEV: *I suppose that more and more people will have NDEs in the
coming years, thanks to advances in medicine, particularly in
the area of resuscitation technology. The media have provided
widespread coverage of experiencer accounts and will probably
do so increasingly in the future. The United States is a case in
point. This leads me to wonder if the churches might not lose
their status as intermediaries between the people and God, once*

more "direct" sources of information from experiencers become available, and if their role might not be fundamentally altered as a result. In the words of one woman who had an NDE: "Now, I no longer need the ritual of Church." She is apparently in direct contact with God.

JV: This raises the deeper question as to whether we need Christianity to believe in a life after death, and in the ability to communicate with the next world and those who dwell there. Let us turn to the Bible to see what it has to say about Christian faith. The Bible is particularly stern with regard to those who "apply to the dead" and practice mediumship, trances, or possession: "Should anyone turn to mediums and fortune-tellers and follow their wanton ways, I will turn against such a one and cut him off from his people." "A man or a woman who acts as a medium or fortune-teller shall be put to death by stoning; they shall have no one but themselves to blame for their death" (Leviticus 20:6, 27; cf. 19:26). These practices are equivalent to the "abominations" of the idolatrous, among whom the chosen people lived. The prophet Isaiah renewed the interdiction: "And when they say to you, 'Inquire of mediums and fortune-tellers (who chirp and mutter!); should not a people inquire of their gods, apply to the dead on behalf of the living?'—then this document will furnish its instruction" (Isaiah 8:19–20). Yet King Saul, after having formally prohibited spiritism, went in secret to consult the famous witch of Endor. He was instantly punished severely for his disobedience: "'Why do you disturb me by conjuring me up?'" protested Samuel's ghost violently. "'Because you disobeyed the Lord's directive ... the Lord has done this to you today. Moreover, the Lord will deliver Israel, and you as well, into the clutches of the Philistines.'" (1 Samuel 15:18–19). In the eyes of the Apostle Paul too, it is very clear: Those who practice "magic" "will not inherit the kingdom of God!" (Galatians 5:20–21). As for the book of Revelation, concerning "sorcerers" of every kind, "their lot is the fiery pool of burning sulphur, the second death!" (Revelation 21:8). This does not, however, mean that communication with the next world, with the dead, is not possible. This possibility exists because our departed ones are still present with us, for they are still alive in God. But their presence is a spiritual one, and so communication with them is basically spiritual, as is taught by the Catholic tradition, in particular. Such communication is not accomplished through the techniques of spiritism or through near-death experiences. What then does this mean? It means that true communication may be established with the next world, and that it goes both ways. Hence, our departed brothers and sisters are still present, but not the same way that a piece of furniture in the middle of a room is present and occupies a particular space. We could grasp this better if we think of a speaker whose presence is felt by thousands of people thanks to radio or television waves. And especially by evoking this communication through thought, and through our feelings of love, which allow us to remain present in the hearts of those who have just left us standing on the train-station platform, for example. Spiritual realities, therefore, are not located in space. Our spirit is not separated into as many compartments as there are cells in our bodies. Hence, spiritual realities can make themselves present anywhere in space. Just as we are present through knowledge and affection in the minds and hearts of those who have gone far away. Likewise, our departed ones now close to God are present with us. They see, for example, the happy or sad events of our lives. According to the medieval theologian St. Thomas Aquinas, the souls of the Saints who see in God are aware of all the events that take place here below. Therefore, in order to communicate with them, we have no need for mediums, seances, or NDEs. We merely have to become aware of an unceasing presence. In the language of Christians, this type of communication, marked by particular sensitivity, is called the "Communion of Saints."

EEV: *I think we can say that up to this point, believing in the soul's survival was an act of faith. Now, thanks to the NDE, it appears to be obvious. This represents a fundamental shift in thinking.*

JV: That belief is not based on mathematical facts supported by reason, but on the strength of testimony, supported by what is known in the heart. Allow me to explain. Personal testimony is not on the same order as a proven experiment that may be repeated at will. Nor is artistic inspiration repeatable according to the procedures of natural science, but it exists just the same. The love relationship is not reproducible in the laboratory, yet it nevertheless exists. Thus, testimonies concerning the hereafter are primarily valuable to those who believe in them. This is the kind of testimony experiencers are likely to give us: "I saw what appeared to be an opening in the wall of darkness that had surrounded me until then." The recounting of this experience, which is as personal as telling about the beginning of a romance, arises from its own order of understanding. The description of a chemical experiment or the demonstration of a theorem arises from another order. Hence, things are knowable either through the intellect, or through the heart. Both paths are of equal value, provided that they remain within their respective domains.

EEV: *At every period in history and in every civilization, man has wrestled with the basic question of what happens after death.*

The accounts of near-death experiencers raise the question anew and seem to provide an inkling of an answer.

JV: The prospect of death does indeed haunt many people. For some it is due to their fear of divine judgment, terrorized as they are at the idea of standing before an irate and vindictive God, who throughout their lives has silently mulled over their offenses, just waiting for the chance to spread them out before them, "settle accounts," and perhaps banish them until the end of time. But God is not this sadistic and vengeful being. Do not such images come rather from within ourselves, as we project upon Him all of our own desires for vengeance, as well as our cruelty? The first face-to-face encounter between two friends who have been waiting for such a long time to see each other cannot possibly be likened to such an atrocious settlement of accounts.... According to near-death experiencers, the "being of light" comments upon and explains all their good and bad deeds, and helps them to understand the impact of these upon others. The same idea may be found in the Catholic tradition. In the first encounter at the time of our death, we will indeed find ourselves in the presence of the Lord, but we will be dazzled by the Light of His Love. And it is in this light that we will become aware of what we are: defenseless sinners bearing the weight of all our imperfections. It is not so much God, the dispenser of justice, who will accuse us with an icy stare; it is we who will judge ourselves, after evaluating our lives as a whole in the Light of God—our life in its truth, with the glass of water, the piece of bread, and the alms offered to our brothers, as well as with the burden of our selfishness and unkindness. The Word of God is clear on this point: "If anyone hears my words and does not keep them, I am not the one to condemn him, for I did not come to condemn the world but to save it" (John 12:47). God does not answer violence with violence. His light merely reveals us to ourselves the way we are as we stand before Him, in the truth of our relationship with Him throughout our lives. Then the choice is up to us: Either we continue to refuse Him—and He respects our freedom, our desire to be separate from Him always—in which case we would speak of "hell," or else we turn toward Him, asking Him to wash away our sins and take us with Him. For He is always ready to forgive us. And the door to His house is always open. In this case, we would speak of "heaven" and of "eternal life," once purification has been obtained. For the weight of our sins prevents our immediate entry into life with God. It is true that Jesus took all our sins upon himself and "saved" us, thereby opening the door to divine life. Unlike the doctrine of transmigration, it is not solely up to me to "pay my debts," to liberate myself from my karma. Jesus has done this for me, once and for all. Yet it is still necessary for me to join together with Christ through my active participation in this work of liberation. In my life on earth, I would do this through the sacraments, through a life lived as closely as possible to the Gospel, but also beyond death, by completing the purification begun in this life through repentance. For not one ounce of selfishness or unkindness can enter into our life with God. In Catholic theology, this process of final cleansing is known as the stage of "purgatory." It is a process in which we ourselves achieve paschal maturity—the completion of our identification with Jesus that began at baptism. It is not a matter of a physical place, like a temporary hell, nor of a period of time marked out on our calendars, like so many years of prison. Yet, we always have the possibility of refusing to enter into eternal life. Hell's only reality is that it is the refusal of God—a deliberate and obstinate refusal. Thus, it is not something reserved until the end of time; it exists right now: in the refusal to open the door to another, creating insurmountable barriers; and in giving free reign to hatred, violence, and inhumanity. Some of the feelings conveyed by experiencers reflect this vision of "hell".... But in Christianity there is an even stronger affirmation, which is that love will have the last word, provided it is not definitely refused. The Christian credo is not "I believe in sin," but rather "I believe in forgiveness." The Christian does not say, "I believe in hell," but rather, "I believe in eternal life." The Apostle John summarizes this whole intuition from the very heart of the Lord Jesus when he writes, "Yes, God so loved the world that he gave his only Son, that whoever believes in him may not die but may have eternal life. God did not send the Son into the world to condemn the world, but that the world might be saved through him" (John 3:16–17). This "good news" of happiness culminates in the revelation of "heaven," or "paradise," when we will know Him as He is. This too has already begun in this life: "Anyone who loves me will be true to my word, and my Father will love him; we will come to him and make our dwelling place with him" (John 14:23). These are the similarities and differences with respect to the accounts of near-death experiencers.

EEV: *Some experiencers are particularly gifted with psychic abilities. Is it conceivable for them to use these exceptional gifts to serve humanity?*

JV: According to the view of man proposed by the Indian tradition, the life force is depicted as a coiled serpent at the base of the spinal column and is referred to as the *kundalini*. When stimulated by appropriate techniques, *kundalini* energy surges gradually upward, streaming into little known channels that make up a network comparable to the web of energy activated during acupuncture. By rising from the base of the spine to the top of the skull, this energy arouses the "seven" force centers, or *chakras*, which are energy plexii. According to experienced yogis, when the sixth and seventh *chakras* (those of the head and skull) are aroused, the subject has access to out-of-body experiences, profound feelings of peace, and visions of light very similar to those encountered during the NDE and other parapsychological phenomena. The only difference is that this awareness is the result of an intense inner discipline acquired over a long period of yogic training, whereas the NDE occurs without any prior learning. This leads us to the hypothesis you spoke of: Is it possible that experiencers are the forerunners of a new type of person? Some say yes, we are entering a new age—the Age of Aquarius—as we approach the year 2000; it is characterized by the profound transformations in consciousness taking place on the planet. The plethora of NDEs and out-of-body experiences could be the sign that a race of "mutants" is emerging, perhaps to make the transition between the closing Age of Pisces and the new age to come. They might be included among the so-called "Aquarian children," the precursors of humanity's vast transformation. But this takes us once more out of the field of objective reality and into the sphere of analogy and symbolism, as well as syncretism. It allows us to float in a very pleasant cosmic reverie—one that stimulates the imagination, but in my opinion, has no confirmed validity.

EEV: *One experiencer tells us: "Yes, there is another life after death. More beautiful than anything we can imagine! Once you have understood it, nothing else can equal this certainty. You simply know!" The existence of a life after death is obvious to this experiencer. But what will it be like?*

JV: Christianity is loath to give figurative representations of the afterlife. The Sacred Congregation for the Doctrine of Faith, which expresses the tradition of the Catholic

Church, declares that neither the Scriptures nor theology provide us with sufficient clarification to obtain an image of the hereafter. But this does not mean that Christianity is devoid of indicators. First among them would be this: After death, there is both continuity and rupture. According to the above-mentioned authority, Christians must take into account two essential points: They must believe, on the one hand, in the fundamental continuity that exists, by virtue of the Holy Spirit, between our present life in Christ and our future life—indeed, charity is the law of God's kingdom and our charity on earth is the measure of our participation in the glory of heaven—and on the other hand, they must recognize the radical break between the present and the future that occurs when the order of faith (i.e., that of our earthly condition, in which we do not see the end of the journey) is replaced by that of the full light when we will be with Christ and we will "see" God (cf. I John 3:2–3). The notion of the soul's immortality is useful, declares the same Catholic authority, as it signifies the survival and subsistence following death of a spiritual element endowed with consciousness and will, thus permitting the human self to remain. But this immortality must not be understood in terms of Cartesian or Platonic dualism. For it is man in his wholeness who will live again: The Church believes in the resurrection of the body, that is, the resurrection of the whole man. To the chosen ones, this resurrection is nothing other than the extension of Christ's own resurrection to humanity. This raises a new question concerning the subsequent states through which humankind will pass following death. Indeed, the Church, which in accordance with Scripture awaits the glorious manifestation of our Lord Jesus Christ, nevertheless considers this to be different from the state in which we will find ourselves immediately following death. Hence, there is an intermediate state between death and the final resurrection. What does this state consist of? There are numerous accounts in the New Testament that attest to one's life with Christ out of the body. When Jesus was dying on the cross, He said to the two criminals hanging beside him, "I assure you: this day you will be with me in paradise" (Luke 23:43). And the Apostle Paul exclaimed, "I repeat, we are full of confidence and would much rather be away from the body and at home with the Lord" (II Corinthians 5:8). But how are we to conceive of this intermediate stage? The Spirit (*pneuma* in Greek) is present in human beings and is what instills new life in the Christian at baptism. It therefore remains essentially bound to the resurrected body of Jesus beyond the death of the flesh. But we do not know what type of new life awaits those who, having died with Christ, wait outside their body for the resurrection of the last day. Along the same lines, the bodily glorification of the Virgin, which Catholics call the "Assumption of Mary," is the anticipation of the glorification awaiting all God's chosen ones: the "glorious body" state.

EEV: *Many experiencers report having had encounters with deceased relatives or friends during their NDE. The Bible warns us about attempting to enter into contact with the dead. How can we reconcile this?*

JV: I would like to summarize my remarks by listing the major points of the Catholic faith concerning the hereafter. This faith is based on the Word of God.

(1) Our departed ones are present with us; their presence is both real and spiritual. They are invisible, yet alive, and are also waiting for the moment when they will be reunited with us.

(2) The closer we come to God, the closer we are to them. And the closer they are to Him, the closer they are to us, for then they are living through His life.

(3) According to the Catholic faith, they are intercessors; we can talk to them and they can hear us. We can also help them, particularly through prayer, if they are in the process of becoming purified. For we all belong to the same Body in which each member serves the others. This is known as the "mystical body of Christ." And they are ready to lend us their real and effective help if we ask them for it. For example, Saint Therese, The Little Flower, made a promise to spend her time in Heaven doing good on earth.

(4) They retain the integrity of their personality and character, along with all their affection and tenderness; nothing is lost. They continue to love us with all their heart. They are not submerged in an immense cosmic ocean where all personal traits are lost, nor in an impersonal nirvana, for each of us is a unique individual in the eyes of God. They are not condemned to an infernal cycle of reincarnations from one body to the next. They are not wandering spirits seeking a medium in order to make themselves heard. For we will be reunited with them one day. And we believe in the "resurrection of the body" during the great final encounter "under new skies and on a new earth" as described in the Bible.

(5) The moment of the greatest proximity in the encounter is the Eucharist. For our intimate communication is ensured by the very life of God to which we are all connected like offshoots of the main vine. We enter into a special place—the "Communion" of Saints—when we partake of the resurrected Christ, who gathers to himself "the living and the dead," as well as when we engage in daily prayer, where the Spirit of Jesus binds us to one another. The main message is the one contained in the Bible: "Do not be like those who have no hope!"; "Hope does not disappoint."

EEV: Many people have visions shortly before their death. Do you think these visions are real, that they actually provide access to the other world, and that they may be viewed somewhat as precursors to the NDE?

JV: These visions are part of a much larger issue; that is, what does the Christian think of signs from "the other side"? Materializations, dreams, apparitions, inner voices, NDEs—we find ourselves confronted with a set of occurrences that seem to reveal the existence of places and times in which communication between our world and the next is possible. It would be quite unscientific to deny these on the pretext that they do not enter into accepted categories. Even if they are inexplicable, and therefore suspect from the perspective of the strict rationalist, they nevertheless *are*. The only thing that remains is to understand them. The believer—not to be confused with the gullible person—has in his or her faith a number of solid elements to assist in understanding their meaning and discerning their value. Indeed, the Christian Creed affirms the existence of "all that is, seen and unseen." Actually these two worlds are but one, since in the beginning they emerged from the same hand of the Creator and, in the end, are destined to come back together in these "new heavens" and on this "new earth" of which the Bible speaks. The boundary separating one from the other is not an insurmountable barrier, like the former Berlin Wall. Jesus himself, according to the circumstantial testimony of several of his friends (at one point there were "more than five hundred" of them, according to the New Testament), came back from the land beyond death. Not in the same way as a ghost or an ectoplasm, but with His own personality—His face, His body, and His mannerisms. "We ate and drank with Him after His death!" unfalteringly claimed these witnesses of two thousand years ago. After this came a long string of mystics, who related a set of authentic experiences of communication with the inhabitants of the other world that are difficult to reject out of hand. They range all the way from Catherine Emmerich to Jean-Marie Vianney, the *Curé d'Ars*.

A quick look at history will furthermore reveal that the reported "signs of life" the departed attempt to send us are universal and common to all religious traditions. We cannot dismiss them with a shrug of the shoulders, saying that "we'll only believe it when we see it." As mentioned previously, these experiences are based on knowledge acquired through the heart. For they are signs, and signs are always destined for those to whom they are addressed. They are personal, in the same way that a poem or a song is meaningful for one person but not for another. This also applies to "signs of life" from the next world, including those contained in NDEs. They are like comets streaking across the night sky; they come from beyond our world and cannot be summoned at will. These signs or testimonies may be accepted or not depending upon the personality and openness of heart of the person receiving them. Unlike communication through mediums, they are not received in a trance. And one cannot force them to come, as in the case of someone who would like to have an NDE in order to see what the other side is like. For the believer, they are even considered to be a free gift, like grace from on high. For one does not issue ultimatums to heaven. These signs [I repeat] are founded on the Communion of Saints, that is to say, on the interdependence of our spiritual destinies. And their authenticity may be measured on the basis of their spiritual value. For the tree is judged by its fruits. Thus, the fruits of an authentic message from the next world, as part of an NDE that is truly an approach from the other side, would be: a certain inner radiance, renewed peace and confidence, personal transformation, and a spirit of openness to others. Such signs have often been sent to those not expecting them. This makes them different from spiritualistic procedures, whereby particular techniques are used to entreat those of the next world to manifest themselves.

Signs are like guideposts: They indicate a direction, just like the "signs" Jesus gave to show the truth of his message, that is, his "miracles" (in Greek, the same word is used for both). These miracles were intended to show those who witnessed them the road to the Kingdom of God. They signal the eruption of the invisible world into the visible one. They are a privileged form of communication in this borderland where both coincide. Symbolism and analogy are therefore the royal gateways to this convergence of the earthly and the unearthly orders. If the sign is understood by the one receiving it, it is because it is also a response to a personal, and more or less conscious, question. Are such persons exceptional or marginal? This does not appear to be the case. Some individuals do in fact have a fine inner sensibility that places them more readily in harmony with the interface between the visible and the invisible. But like those survivors of the next world, who have found expression in the books of Dr. Moody, persons who have experienced communication with the dead dare not speak about it for fear of being treated with either scorn or pity. These signs must therefore be greeted, like the near-death experience, not with naivete, but with a positive spirit. This will require that we exploit all means of *discerning* the wheat from the chaff, in accordance with the Word of the Gospel, and that we carefully determine the validity of the experiences reported, by comparing them first of all to those that have already been authenticated. The Christian believer will compare them, in particular, to the experience of the community of believers, to the great Tradition of the Church, and to the teachings of the spiritual masters. Religious persons will compare them to the rules of discernment given by their own faith, while keeping in mind that the mystics of all religions concur in the main lines of their teachings. The Hindu master Patanjali, the students of Buddha, the instructors of the Bardo Thödol, all unanimously say, "Learn first to discern." And whether they speak of "crumbs of miracles," "spiritual scraps," "glimpses of the hereafter," or "heavenly warnings," all converge in the belief that the next world may sometimes attempt to send us a sign. It is up to us to decode these guideposts in our human adventure, doing so not only with great openness, but also with an alert sense of discernment.

Chapter Ten

Dialogue with Michel Lefeuvre

EEV: *In order to provide a context for our discussion, would you please describe your main areas of activity and research?*

ML: I have always been interested in the broad metaphysical questions, but at the same time wary of what Kant called the "transcendental illusion." My research has therefore been characterized by a very concrete approach to these questions, avoiding the pitfalls of language (the pure abstractions), of the unconscious (desire), and, in general, those inherent in the mind's innate tendency to search for the absolute. I consequently developed a great interest in science, because of its more pragmatic and down-to-earth approach, and became a professor of logic and the epistemology of science, without, however, losing sight of my fundamental interest in metaphysical issues. In order to address these—not in the abstract, but rather in concrete terms—I turned in my youth to the study of perception. For although perceiving is an act of conscious-

Professor of the Philosophy of Science, University of Dakar

ness, it is an act that relies upon very definite physiological and neurophysiological mechanisms. The same may be said of language. My doctoral thesis dealt with these questions, and my subsequent work has continued in this direction. Metaphysics is neither biology nor neurobiology, and any attempt to draw metaphysical lessons from them would be dangerous, for metaphysics is located on another plane of intelligibility. And yet, metaphysics simply cannot continue to distance itself from the science of living organisms and of the brain. Forgive me for taking too long, and at the same time, not long enough, to explain all these interrelations.

EEV: *I would like to quote a passage from your book,* Nature et cerveau (Nature and the Brain)*: "Reality is more vast than thought and its conceptual empire."[1] Indeed, therein lies the whole difficulty of human understanding. We are eminently limited in our perception of reality. Do you think that the study of NDEs opens up new avenues for research, precisely because it seems to provide access to a dimension that is no longer reduced to a purely theoretical concept, but can henceforth be studied on a more empirical level, given the fact that NDEs have been experienced and reported by millions of individuals?*

ML: That's absolutely correct. Our brain is a magnificent instrument for accessing the space–time reality of the universe, but at the same time it prevents us from seeing a much broader reality. It is precisely this reality, or surreality, to which NDEs open the door—that of experience. Our discussion will therefore deal not with theory, but with the much more concrete realm of experience. I think it is very important to find the best angle from which to approach the material provided us by millions and millions of experiencers.

EEV: *Life, as it is currently defined, is governed by time. Vital phenomena are distinguished from nonvital phenomena by the time factor, which is at the very source of their functioning. The study of NDEs compels us, I believe, to consider the possible existence of a consciousness that is reflective, emotional, and hyperpowerful—thus, possessing all the characteristics of a living being—and that evolves in a timeless dimension. Would this render obsolete the law that necessarily associates life with time?*

ML: That is an interesting and fundamental question. The organization of space plays a major role in the long chain of atoms forming a macromolecule or polymer. Many of the synthetic products manufactured by industry are polymers. The carbon, hydrogen, and other atoms of which they consist are not arranged randomly in space. But what does time have to do with these polymers, such as polyethylene, for example? As far as they are concerned, time is only an external factor. They are swept into its current by the arrow of time, as physicists would say, but time is not part of their internal constitution the way space is. The situation is different when it comes to living organisms—even the most rudimentary; they are carried along by time and they age, the same as any inanimate object does. But within this process of aging may be found a phenomenon of reiteration that is constantly recurring up to the point of death. Through it the organism affirms itself to be the same as it ever was, doing so from the time of birth to that of death. Biologists speak of the spontaneity of living things in regard to this reiteration, but it is the philosopher's task to determine all its implications. The living organism binds itself to itself over the course of time. Concretely, this occurs by means of various types of spontaneous metabolism, but what is of interest to us here is the identification of its underlying structure. There is at once aging, disintegration and reiteration, repetition, and recurrence. In other words, a blueprint of eternity—that is, an unending period of time—has already been traced into each living thing. Yet, this blueprint of eternity is thwarted by the weight of materiality, which all living things must bear, and which is part of their being, their form, and the internal spatial organization of their cells, tissues, organs, and limbs. As we progress up the scale of living organisms, and especially when we come to humans, the importance of constant reiteration, of one's life experience, becomes more striking. I am quite fond of impressionist painting, and what fascinates me most about it is the extreme tension involved in transferring to the canvas *the instantaneousness of the moment*—the invisible, secret soul of the entire universe, as it were. It is what the painter encounters through his or her own experience; he or she recapitulates the entire universe—in the fluttering of a butterfly's wings, in the arrangement of its colored spots—by capturing it at its source. Every living organism reiterates its life with each passing moment. Man, in his highest manifestations, seeks within the instant, within the elusive spark of genius, to recapitulate the mystery of the world. The fact remains, however, that Monet, or Renoir, are also incarnate, flesh-and-blood beings subject to the passing of time.

EEV: *All philosophical reflection is governed by the notion of living beings as embodied—never disembodied. After having heard the numerous accounts of experiencers, I wonder if we should not give some consideration to the hypothesis of living beings as liberated from matter and space–time. Experiencers clearly report having been conscious, even hyperconscious, but detached from their physical body during their NDE. In this context, I would like to quote another passage from your book,*

Nature et cerveau (Nature and the Brain): "*Consciousness is not primarily subjectivity, a Sartrian void, a vacuum; it is a particular mode assumed by living matter. Consciousness is only conscious of itself as incarnate consciousness, united as one with living matter, and intrinsically bound to it in one same, indivisible reality.*"[2] How do the testimonies of experiencers fit into your theory?

ML: We are getting closer and closer to the heart of the matter, as well as to my personal difficulty in interpreting it. One of the most important aspects of the NDE is the life review. On the basis of what I have just said regarding instantaneousness, I have no difficulty understanding this aspect. Everything that was experienced during mortal life from the successive, ephemeral perspective is concentrated in a momentary flash and illuminated by an irrefutable light. In my opinion, this seems consistent with the profound nature of the human being as a unique spirit. As long as it lives in the flesh, it cannot help but be subjected to the mode of succession, but that is not its deepest truth. When its ties to the world threaten to dissolve, it is normal for the being to once more assume its true nature. This occurs in a timeless dimension; however, the out-of-body experience does not occur in a spaceless dimension, since experiencers always watch what is happening from a particular location in space. This vantage point is no longer located in their body, but rather somewhere in the operating room where they are undergoing surgery, for example. At first glance, it is difficult for me to think of this as anything other than an imaginary phenomenon. In my dreams, I can imagine that I am in Venice or London; I can see people walking around the Grand Canal or Big Ben, but when I come back to reality, I know that these people existed only in my imagination. The situation is obviously different for experiencers; their testimony is corroborated by those who were at the scene. So for some time now, I have been formulating an idea, but it is still just a vague hypothesis. All bodies are located somewhere, whether an office, a conference room, a museum, and so on. The place changes, but the body is always subject to some type of bond, which imposes limits on consciousness and prevents it, among other things, from flying over space and from having a Sirius-like perspective of itself. I therefore see as a possibility that, as it contracts into a momentary flash during the life review, the experiencer's consciousness must acquire a new relationship to space, which enables it to overcome what it usually experiences as the multiplicity and mutual exclusiveness of parts—if I am here, I cannot at the same time be somewhere else. The experiencer's supratemporal consciousness would progress from a condition in which it was subordinate to space, to one in which it was supraspatial.

EEV: *What intrigues you the most about NDEs?*

ML: I would say, though this is nothing new to you, that NDEs have the features of altered states of consciousness. You know that better than I do, but it is from this quite general perspective that I see them. You provide a very detailed breakdown of these alterations of ordinary consciousness; you list, for example, the out-of-body experience, and describe the way in which consciousness extracts itself, so to speak, from the body, and views from an external vantage point what is happening around it. This is not how things ordinarily happen. It is usually from within my body, my location in space, that I see the world. Turning from space to time, and in reference to the life review, you say that a genuine compression of time often takes place during the NDE. Instead of flowing, as it usually does, time contracts and gathers itself together— in the flash of an instant, one's entire life passes in review.

EEV: *You just used the term* altered states of consciousness *in referring to NDEs. Do you mean to imply that these are mere illusions of consciousness?*

ML: That is a very interesting question, and it will allow me to delve a little deeper into the matter. Jean-Paul Sartre was, for many years, interested in imaginal consciousness, that is, the image-producing aspect of consciousness. He chose to use himself as a subject of experiment, injecting himself with mescaline. In her memoirs, Simone de Beauvoir tells of strolling through Venice with Sartre and listening to him describe the distorted way in which things appeared to him. Everything seemed to be elongated and to have an appendage resembling a lobster's tail. Sartre was seeing lobsters everywhere in Venice, perhaps even in the paintings of Titian. This was definitely a case of an altered state of consciousness, although Sartre was not entirely taken in. Under this first layer of consciousness, which is delusional, lies a deeper consciousness consisting of reflective thought that is able to maintain its grip on reality. This one is capable of holding out. There are other, much more serious cases, in which consciousness is literally submerged—trapped, one might say—by the images produced by the brain. Psychiatric literature can provide us with all too many examples of these hallucinatory states.

EEV: *Do you mean to imply that NDEs are merely hallucinations?*

ML: No, on the contrary. But I need to continue with my line of reasoning and draw some distinctions. It must be recognized that without images there would be no consciousness. In the animal world, consciousness exists with certainty only in those species capable of dreaming. Dogs and cats definitely dream, but does an oyster dream? It's very doubtful. An oyster is alive, but can we speak of psychology in reference to it? Mammals, on the other hand—at least the most evolved of them, such as dogs and cats, for example—play with [and make a game out of] a stick or a ball of yarn. The image, in the form of a dream or a game, is like a component of psychological existence: In the form of a dream, it seems to imprison the individual, whether man or animal, in phantasmagoria; in the form of a game, it expands the universe and opens it up to possibilities and choices. Art is a massive enlargement of the material world, but without images, whether auditory or visual, there could be no artistic creation. Take, for example, any famous painting by a great artist: It is not raw reality—not merely quanta, waves, rays, energy, or matter—but rather the representation on canvas of an interior image of the world—a portrait, a landscape, a scene proper to the painter.

EEV: *Everything you say is undoubtedly very interesting, but I wonder if we aren't straying too far from our subject.*

ML: I'll grant you that that's the way it looks, but allow me to continue. Even if I still seem to be getting away from our subject, what I want to emphasize is that the image is part of a blueprint in the history of evolution whose ultimate purpose is to obtain knowledge of reality. The image appears at its designated time along the path. We should not see nature as something static, something that holds still under our gaze, that we merely look at in the form of continents, mountains, oceans, plants, animals, human beings, and so on. Nature is active; it contains a dynamic and creative principle, and is at one with it. In nature, time is not only an expenditure of energy, it also functions as an organizer. Over the course of time we have evolved, through the complexification of matter, from inert to animate matter—in other words, to life. And much closer to us in the arrow of time, we have evolved from animate, living matter to thinking matter, to the human species. You might say that nature was being blockheaded— excuse the anthropomorphism—in her drive to create.

EEV: *But to create what?*

ML: To create, first of all, life—living cells, microorganisms; then, much later, multicellular organisms, both vegetable and animal, that is, those of a sentient nature; to culminate in human beings, that is, those of a conceptual nature. We're talking about a real adventure here.

EEV: *I am beginning to understand that you want to place NDEs within a very large framework!*

ML: Exactly. To my mind, it is a matter of giving them an ontological status—a status of truth—within a general theory of consciousness.

EEV: *What do you mean?*

ML: At the beginning of our discussion, I began by telling you that I considered NDEs to be altered states of consciousness. Perhaps it would be useful for the purposes of our discussion to specify what is meant by "consciousness."

EEV: *All right, please tell us what you mean by "consciousness."*

ML: I will begin by saying that consciousness is closely linked to life. In every living thing there is a subjectivity, a "nearly someone," however minute. But this is absent in rocks, crystals, and everything belonging to the world of inanimate matter. Bacteria and yeasts, on the other hand, are living things, because they do have subjectivity. They are not merely sophisticated machines; they have an interiority, they have spontaneity, they interact with their environment, they mate and reproduce, and so on. Yet, I do not claim that they have consciousness: subjectivity, yes; consciousness, no. Consciousness can only make its timid appearance in the living world through the birth of a very special type of cell: the neuron. And even then, in order to truly be able to speak of consciousness, that is, of subjectivities that experience themselves as such—which is the case with evolved mammals—these neurons must be organized into centralized systems with a sufficiently developed brain.

EEV: *In your opinion, consciousness is therefore not only linked to life, but also to a particular organ of the living being, that is, the brain. Can we therefore say that consciousness is simply a product of the brain?*

ML: If you mean to imply by that that consciousness is simply a product of matter, my reply would be "no." But the issue is more complex than that. In one sense, it doesn't bother me to say that the human brain creates thoughts, but I would like to specify what I mean by "brain." Every living organism has a certain material organization, which biologists can explore with the help of microscopes, radioactive dyes, and so on. They can then put together a detailed description. But once they have done all this, they still have not said everything there is to say about living organisms. Living organisms *assume* their materiality; they are one with it by *being it*. What I'm saying is perhaps complicated, but important nonetheless. The subjectivity that characterizes living organisms neither adds nor takes away anything from organic materiality; it is a different dimension of animate matter—one that is not quantifiable or measurable—but nevertheless an essential component of its reality. Let's not make subjectivity into something distinct or separate; it is simply living matter's *mode of being*; its particular, distinguishing characteristic; that which ensures that it remains identical to itself from birth to death and retains its form despite the torrent of matter and energy that stream through it, and despite the constant molecular and cellular renewal for which it—the living organism—is headquarters. Although immersed in time, there is something in it that defies time, that withstands it in order to remain the same from birth to death. I am speaking of living organisms in general, but as we gradually progress up the scale of life, this existential, informing aspect of living matter becomes transformed. And it does so thanks to the appearance of neurons and to their organization into centralized systems, in brains, as I mentioned previously.

EEV: *I understand that matter has evolved in living things, that the first ones to appear did not have brains, and that much later, they acquired brains—big ones, even—as in the case of higher mammals. Yet, does this really change the questions we are asking? Perhaps it is the billions and billions of neural interconnections in the human brain that produce thought by functioning.*

ML: Of course, but not all alone—which would suggest that the brain were a complex, independent machine—but rather by being joined to our subjectivity to the point of together constituting a single entity, a human being like you and me—a hybrid being that is at once sentient and material, on the one hand, and nonmaterial and spiritual on the other, as witnessed by our ideals of justice and goodness, and by our search for truth and beauty, if we are the least bit philosophical, scientific, or artistic—or quite simply, human.

EEV: *You are speaking about subjectivity again, but if I understand you correctly, there is an enormous difference between the subjectivity of animals and that of humans, that is, between their experiences and their feelings.*

ML: Precisely. In the case of the animal, or the bacterium, or the blue algae, subjectivity is entirely invested in the organism's physicochemical reactions; it is also subordinate to the environment. Now, as I mentioned previously, with the appearance of adequately developed brains, the image made its debut in the world. The environment is less ponderous, less constraining for the dog than for the slug; the dog's behavior is less stereotyped as well. There is a much bigger difference between the attitudes of two dogs of the same breed toward life and their surroundings, than there is between those of two slugs. Simple biological life has already begun to assume the characteristics of a psychological existence. The latter obviously relies upon the former, but has already begun to differentiate from it. In order to manifest itself, it needs to become rooted in all of the cellular and neural mechanisms that support it; nevertheless, a new dimension has emerged.

EEV: *I understand, but this dimension is very dependent upon its physiological, neurobiological foundations. It is perhaps merely its reflection and its epiphenomenon.*

ML: That is what a materialist would say, but I do not agree. Let us examine, if you will, what happens to this dimension in humans, since it is they who interest us here. This dimension undergoes an enormous transformation, not only of degree, but also of essence. Dogs and cats have an affective, emotional life with respect to others of their kind, their masters, other species, mice, rats, and so on, but they are not aware that they possess this psychological life—they merely live it. Man, on the other hand, by reflecting upon his environment, himself, his actions, knows that he is an animal endowed with a psychological life. Obviously, this leap from animal to human nature required profound cerebral reorganization, including a larger brain, tighter folding, considerable development of the frontal lobe, functional asymmetry of the hemispheres, and so forth. This complexification of the brain entailed an increase and diversification of the web of neurons, whose reciprocal exchanges allow for the fine processing of sensory information—the data of experience. But herein lies the crux of the problem: This ballet of exchanges between the neurons and the brain graphs, this passing game between its different parts to help each other process the information needed to produce a thought, or a reflective, comparative judgment, *cannot achieve its purpose without the emergence of a unifying consciousness*, whose simplicity contrasts with the multiplicity of the neurons and the complexity of the brain. Keep in mind what we said earlier: In all living things, even the most simple, there is an incredible material and organic complexity, as well as an act, unique to living things, that confronts this diversity and forges out of it one single and unique existence from birth to death. The history of evolution is not merely the history of the growing complexification of animate matter. It is that, of course, but it is also the development, the growth, the transformation of this original, revolutionary act, which we find already in the earliest living organisms— an act that makes of their life not merely a sequence of impersonal events, but an existence.

EEV: *What life are you referring to here? Biological life or psychological life?*

ML: This act by which living things unendingly bind themselves to themselves, from one end of their life to the other, exists at even the lowest echelon of biological life. It is involved in physiological processes, but if these are vital processes, vital functions, such as breathing, for example, *it is thanks to the fact that they possess this existential property, this ability to be spontaneous*—in other words, to originate within the living organism, and not to be determined by some external source, as is the case with inert matter. This spontaneity already exists at the bacterial level, but it is not the same as in the human being. *We cannot speak of motivation in regard to a bacterium*; its spontaneity is one that is governed by nature, and its interiority is in a state of potentiality. It is this interiority that will continue to develop over the course of evolution, obtain independence with respect to the external environment, and ultimately result in the freedom characteristic of man. This increase in independence with respect to the environment should also be recognized as an increase in independence with respect to the body. Even in the most evolved animals, behavior is dictated by instincts whose roots are in the body, whether considered from the individual perspective—the soma—or from the perspective of a member of a particular species—the germen. In man, however, behavior may be dictated by values.

EEV: *I like your comprehensive approach to the NDE phenomenon, which, I am convinced, we cannot begin to explain unless we place it in a broader context. Yet, I wonder how this will ultimately tie in with our subject.*

ML: It is not my intention to go all the way back to the Flood, but I have no choice but to take stock of the nature of human beings, who are at once animals of flesh and blood, as well as spirits. As far as each of us is concerned, to exist means to exist in a body, and our ties to the body are extremely close. Our psychology is not derived solely from our genes, though it does depend upon them to a large extent. The genes we inherited from our parents do not govern solely our physical appearance—whether our eyes are blue or black, our noses hooked or straight—but also our psychological makeup—whether we are impulsive or deliberate, calm or violent, and so on, with the help of chemical substances, and the neurotransmitters and neuromodulators they synthesize. It is by affecting the metabolism of these chemical substances that psychotropic drugs are able to induce hallucinatory phenomena. This is one side of human reality; the other is that human existence transcends this fleshly incarnation. Earlier, I spoke of Sartre who, under the influence of mescaline, saw lobster tails everywhere along his stroll through Venice. I will give another example that is well known in literature—the story of Proust and the madeleine. As he brought to his lips a spoonful of tea in which were floating a few crumbs of a madeleine, Proust was overcome with a feeling of delight. As he explains it, there was no reason or cause for the feeling of pleasure that filled his entire being. His view of external reality was not distorted, as was the case with Sartre, and his brain was even at rest on that "dreary morning," totally lacking in promise, when this internal phenomenon, which was at once so calming and so exalting, occurred. Had we been able to film what was happening in his brain with a positron camera, we would most likely have discovered nothing out of the ordinary. Yet, something marvelous was presenting itself to him, something that expanded his sense of himself, and gave him a feeling of absoluteness, eternity, and fullness. Immediately thereafter, Proust set about trying to understand what had happened. In the actuality of the moment, in the taste and smell of the drenched madeleine he had brought to his lips, he managed to produce some images from his past, to tie them in with what he was experiencing at that particular moment, and to formulate a thoughtful judgment. He recognized in his memories of Combray, of Aunt Léonie's house at Mass time on Sunday morning, what was in the back of his mind when that delightful feeling overcame him. What interests me here is not so much the explicit judgment—which is nevertheless the mark of a mind, for only a mind can compare, discern, and judge—but rather the fact that the brain has so little importance at the moment consciousness comes into full contact with itself, its spirituality, its internal essence. For what usually separates consciousness from itself—the materiality of things, the density of events, the space–time of the world—is somehow abolished. It is even as if the brain's suspended activity allowed consciousness to reach itself in the fullness of its being; this explains the impression of release and expansion during that isolated moment of intense pleasure that Proust describes. I won't go into this any further, but I think you can see the parallels with certain aspects of the NDE.

EEV: *I'm beginning to see what you are driving at, but can you be a little more specific?*

ML: At this level of our discussion, I would like to emphasize what is attained through this illumination of consciousness. It is not an illusion, as in Sartre's case, but a special kind of reality—one that cannot be materialized, of course, or represented, because it lies beyond the material world we inhabit throughout our lives and to which we gain access by means of our brains. I will give you another, more convincing example, that of the great French mathematician, Henri Poincaré, who suddenly had an intuition into one of his greatest discoveries at the very moment he one day routinely lifted his foot to step onto an omnibus in Coutances. This discovery had, of course, been preceded by long hours of preparatory work, but when it occurred, the mathematician's brain was at rest. Suddenly the mathematical world was illuminated; connections were established between fields which until then had been separated. They became luminous, and the unity of Poincaré's consciousness became one with this mathematical unity and was expanded by it. What Poincaré discovered was not mere nothingness; it was not an illusion. It was a mathematical reality, united and complex, rich in developments and applications—a sort of invisible armature of the world. From what I have read of your and of Kenneth Ring's work, this is something at least similar, if not identical, to what happens during an NDE.

EEV: *Would you like to elaborate?*

ML: What I find they have in common is a sense of reality. Sartre—I keep coming back to him—did not have a sense of reality in Venice. Poincaré, on the other hand, had a very definite sense of reality—I would even say sur-reality—in that his consciousness fused with a realm of mathematical truths that demanded recognition because of its obviousness. This almost fusional knowledge expands the mind, but it is not an empty, hallucinatory perception. It is a discovery beyond physical time and space of a world in itself. I compare this experience to that of one of Raymond Moody's experiencers, whom you quote in your interview with Kenneth Ring: During his NDE and immediately following his life review, he suddenly had the impression of being elevated to cosmic, nearly universal, knowledge of all things.

EEV: *Yet, there is perhaps a difference between the states of consciousness described in these two cases.*

ML: Yes, no doubt the consciousness of Poincaré at the instant of his discovery was in an expanded and alert state, which was not the case with Moody's experiencer. His was not a detailed knowledge of the links that exist between the things of the world; *however he did feel absolutely certain that these links exist, and this feeling presented itself as indisputably obvious.*

EEV: *We therefore find ourselves presented with a reality—or a surreality, as you say.*

ML: Yes, to my way of thinking. When experiencers come back to life, they come back to the humdrum routine of everyday life, and their brains process the individual succession of events characteristic of earthly space–time. Yet, lingering in the back of their minds is the memory of a reality that is more real, more true, more inherent, more primitive, more substantial than space–time. This is in contrast to what happens in dreams. We sometimes have a strong feeling that our dreams are real, but this feeling fades immediately upon waking. It does not stand up to the fact that we are rooted in space–time. The same, however, cannot be said of NDEs; in this case, it is rather space–time that is a degraded form of the being perceived by the mind's intuition during the NDE.

EEV: *Can you tie this together with what you said earlier on the subject of living organisms, consciousness, and the human being?*

ML: I will try. My philosophy is a philosophy of existence, not in Sartre's sense of the term, but rather in the Thomistic sense. A living organism is not merely a set of physical and chemical data, of observable and measurable physiological functions. It is also an existence, an existence that takes the form of subjectivity—that is, a being that interacts with the external world: food, habitat, and the environment of light, oxygen, mineral salts, and so forth—by *binding itself to itself* through the constant renewal of metabolism. You can see clearly from this that the living organism as an existence, or a subjectivity, is inseparable from its body. Let us turn our attention to the human being. In humans, that which is specific to them no longer depends directly upon the body. Indeed, in the name of certain moral ideals, such as justice, solidarity, love, or good, human beings may even choose to die, to sacrifice the life of their bodies. Humans exist in their bodies, but not in the same way as animals, which do so in a completely dependent fashion. So, what is their status? The act by which man spontaneously binds himself to himself as an individual in relation to his physical and social environment has distanced itself somewhat from the body and from biological materiality. Yet, can he separate himself from it? This is where NDEs begin to raise questions for me. I, in turn, raise questions whenever specialists on the issue, like Kenneth Ring, speak of out-of-body experiences and life outside the body. Are these illusions or are they reality? What I would like to know exactly is if, through extrasensory perception—since it can only be a matter of that—experiencers on the threshold of death really see in detail what is happening around them.

EEV: *I would like to ask you to be more specific, as I'm wondering if there isn't some contradiction here. On the one hand, you seem to believe in an out-of-body reality, but on the other hand, you hesitate. You seem to question whether, in the context of a near-death experience, this reality can come between the body and the mind and take the place of ordinary space–time.*

ML: Yes, that's exactly it. I'm not too sure how to interpret the phenomenon of the out-of-body experience you often speak of with those interested in NDEs. Sometimes I wonder if it isn't an imaginary phenomenon. But let us look at things a little more concretely. My body is alive, and all sorts of metabolic processes are occurring in it. My brain is also active: Through the hypothalamus, for example, it registers what is happening in the body and monitors blood pressure, heartbeat, and so on. Let's say that suddenly I have an important decision to make. Suppose I am Captain Vladimir Orekhov of the KGB and I decide to risk my life to warn some dissidents of their impending fate. Some new zones, particularly in the frontal lobe, switch on in my brain. My decision is produced by my brain, but how? In its capacity as a network of neuronic connections? Not so. In my capacity as an individual who exists, I relate to the external world, to my sociocultural environment. I mature along with my brain in this universe. My individual existence extends beyond my brain; it uses the brain as it would a machine, to which it is joined, but it is itself more than that. It is a spirit bound to a body, with everything that this entails in the way of affectivity, sensitivity, emotionality—everything that escapes the brain's function as an interconnected web of neurons. This underground, unconscious life in me is assumed by my being, which remains identical to itself from birth to death, and which, thanks to my brain's complexity, can produce acts of freedom that it could not produce with a monkey's brain. If a piece of information that barely enters the brain comes back out again, because the brain contains only a relatively limited number of networks, that information cannot be processed properly and broken down to produce mental categories as dematerialized as general concepts or universal ideas. It is because the brain is sufficiently complex that beings—that is, the human mind—who have such a brain can become aware of themselves by producing thoughts and voluntary, free decisions. Otherwise, this would not be possible. You can see quite well how over the course of evolution, organisms that were originally indistinguishable from their biological mechanisms were able, after hundreds of thousands of years, to become free beings with respect to their bodies and to their physical and sociocultural environments.

EEV: *If human beings are at least partially free with respect to their bodies, why do you find out-of-body phenomena to be such a problem?*

ML: As far as I am concerned, this is still the main issue. By means of my thoughts, I can leave the place where my body is located. I can be in Venice or London and I can conjure up images of the Grand Canal or Big Ben, but I am not really there. I cannot see what is happening at this very instant on the Grand Canal or at Big Ben, as we discussed previously. In order for me to see what is actually happening in those places, my body would have to displace itself in such a way that while remaining here, it would also somehow be there. This makes me think of those cases of bilocation that some great mystics have been privileged to experience. All this calls into question our notions of space and time, which serve as the foundation and framework of our mental functioning. In the case of bilocation, it is as if the time required to get to a distant place were suddenly abolished, and as if, in this new dimension that is unimaginable to us, the body could produce a virtual double of itself. This is obviously very difficult to interpret, though it is true that advanced quantum mechanics is equally difficult to interpret. Let us take for example the notion of *inseparability*. What does it tell us exactly? It tells us that elementary particles of matter that have interacted but are no longer in contact with each other because of the distance between them—which common sense tells us are separated—are nevertheless *inseparable*. This seems contradictory, and yet it is one of the key notions of quantum mechanics. Does this mean that Father Pio or Mother Yvonne, who are here and there at the same time, have access to a different dimension than that of microphysics, a dimension of *inseparability*? A dimension in which the real body and the virtual body (the real body's double) appear to be separated by distance, concealing what is, in fact, their inseparability and intrinsic identity? Could this notion of *inseparability* also apply to out-of-body experiences, in which, for example, the physical body is present on the operating table and its virtual double is at another, external vantage point, observing the scene around it—expressing through this apparent separation a hidden reality of inseparability? This would imply that what our imagination and understanding view as separate (i.e., the physical body and its double) would, physically speaking and on another scale of reality, actually be inseparable. Naturally, I stress the fact that we must be very careful when it comes to dealing with these notions, and respect their spheres of application. The foregoing is perhaps merely an analogy. But I would like to point out to those who are shocked at my going from the microlevel (elementary particles) to the macrolevel (the human body), that there are macroscopic quantum phenomena in nature. We listen to the radio on metric waves, yet what reaches us is radiation with quantum properties. At any rate, what we perceive as absolute and finite, because our daily experience relies upon it, such as the way space and time appear to us, is not at all absolute or finite, as far as relativity and quantum mechanics are concerned. As Shakespeare's Hamlet said, "There are more things in heaven and earth, Horatio, than are dreamt of in your philosophy."

EEV: *There is something I would like for you to explain. You are now stressing a hypothesis of* inseparability *in an effort to explain the out-of-body experience, whereas at another point in our discussion you were stressing the* separation *of the body and the mind that might occur during an NDE. What exactly do you think?*

ML: I think that we are in a realm in which our usual bearings—the ones that are convenient for anchoring our thoughts—are no longer valid. Think of St. Paul on the road to Damascus, to whom Kenneth Ring refers in discussing NDEs. On the subject of his ecstasy, St. Paul writes that he doesn't know whether it took place in his body or out of his body. We are in a realm in which our spatial and temporal bearings are confused. Yet, if it came down to a choice, I would opt in favor of inseparability. From the instant of our conception, the mind and the body are united as one in forging our individuality. Death is truly a violent rupture of our being, and on that basis, several hypotheses may be formulated: (a) The death of the body is the total death of our individuality; (b) it is the breaking of the bonds that unite the body and the soul, which then becomes free from material constraints; or (c) the unknown, which haunts our minds at the simple thought of death, acquires its true countenance and reveals itself to be a luminous surreality, of which the NDE offers us an initial glimpse. If I reject the second hypothesis, it is because it seems to imply overly physical bonds between the soul and the body; as a philosopher, I have difficulty accepting such a dualism. The third hypothesis seems better to me: This compromise of space that we are by virtue of our body, *and* of interiorized, dominated time that we are by virtue of our mind—one of whose major functions is to remember—is undoubtedly a compromise in which time and space are inseparable. All that was experienced on earth in the body is preserved and enhanced in a supratemporal memory.

EEV: *Still on the subject of space and time, you seem to be very interested in drawing a parallel between NDEs and certain very modern aspects of physics.*

ML: Exactly. Everything that exists around us exists in space. What differentiates a living being from a nonliving thing is that its material expanse, its internal space, is organized differently *due to its distinct relationship to time.* That is because time, instead of passively and gradually wearing away at only the exterior of matter, turns matter into a source, a spontaneous outpouring, a perpetual renewal, in which the metabolic processes that express this are not impersonal processes, but processes attached to an existence, to a spontaneity. It is thanks to this particular dimension of time within the living organism that the latter constitutes subjectivity and is connected to itself. All living organisms already possess the beginnings of consciousness. Humans are much more advanced, in that they possess a higher consciousness, which is capable, thanks to language and thought, of simulating everything that exists around them in space and time, in the laws of mathematics, in the formulas of physical mathematics, and in philosophical notions. An enormous change in consciousness takes place when we progress from the animal to the human being. This is because human consciousness is supported by a brain of such complexity that it is capable of achieving the feats we know it to achieve. But what we must understand is that if it is capable of such feats, it is because it is joined to a principle that is not material, a principle that provides the basis for the existentiality of our being—one we might call the soul, the spirit, etc. In the current state of affairs, it uses the brain as an instrument of its interaction with the world, in the formation of our space–time experience. Getting back to NDEs, let us say that when the body is suddenly threatened with death, it is also the ordinary experience of the world that consciousness may perceive as being threatened. An immense upheaval most likely takes place in it. With the almost total cessation of brain activity, which is its tie to the universe, consciousness undergoes a considerable alteration and joins, in the flash of an instant, the uncreated light, from which everything seems to derive its existence, including the space–time in which we live.

EEV: *You clearly speak of the separation of consciousness from the body in these extreme cases known as NDEs. I would like to ask you once more to explain how you reconcile this separation with the inseparability that we were discussing a few moments ago.*

ML: Separation and inseparability are undoubtedly to be found on two different levels. There is definitely a physical separation from the material body at death. The notion of inseparability is more subtle; it could apply to the acts and events that occurred during mortal life, in the form of a recollection. Nothing that was experienced during the course of a lifetime could be separated, even events separated by a considerable lapse of time, such as that between childhood and old age. In terms of memory, we already have here on earth something that resembles separation and inseparability. Bergson already understood that it was the material nature of the brain that introduced forgetfulness and separation into the psychic flow of consciousness, which, in itself, is a simple and indecomposable duration. In the NDE, the preservation by consciousness of the events and acts that have taken place over the course of our existence in space and time keeps us from dissolving into the void or—what amounts to the same, from the standpoint of our individuality—into a great, pantheistic all. From this perspective, NDEs dramatically emphasize the process of personalization that has developed in the cosmos since its origin and until the appearance of man. But this extreme personalization is accompanied by the fusion of the many—all the acts and events of our life in space–time—with the inseparability of consciousness from the creative principle, the Light from which all flows, and in which all originates.

EEV: *Can you say a few more words about what currently most captures your attention?*

ML: One of the things that has held my attention throughout most of my philosophical career is the relationship between the body and the mind. I believe in psychic causality: Because I have decided to leave tomorrow on a trip, I am going to perform all sorts of movements and gestures, such as packing my bags. These gestures and movements, which can be explained very well by the neuronic structure of my nervous system, are not what produce my decision to take a trip. Rather, the inverse is true. Yet how can a decision that is immaterial make my muscles move materially and make my neurons interact? Must I therefore conclude that this decision is itself material, to the extent that it is inserted into a chain of deterministic events? From this point of view, there would no longer be any free causality. This would be the triumph of Spinoza. Despite the enormous problems raised by this interpretation, I think that it is this solution that classical physics would lead us to adopt. It seems to me that quantum mechanics can help us out of this bind. In living organisms, and more specifically, in the nervous system— I am thinking particularly of the presynaptic vesicular network, in which the size of each vesicle is measured in angstroms—there are elements that enter the field of quantum mechanics. The transition from quantum to classical, to the rules of classical physics, could occur in these elements. The point at which a voluntary decision is applied could be found in these same locations, and the mind could move the neural matter. It is within the context of this line of reasoning that I joyfully accepted to debate NDEs with you. I am well aware of the fact that we have only just scratched the surface of this issue. I hope that others—physicists, neurobiologists, biologists, psychologists, philosophers—will continue the debate in an interdisciplinary spirit. But I think you still wanted to discuss the subject of the unconscious.

EEV: *Yes, precisely. What do you make of the unconscious, used in its psychoanalytical sense, in all these phenomena?*

ML: This is a very broad question since we must, first of all, agree upon what the unconscious is. We have too great a tendency, at least in ordinary language, to treat it like an "open sesame"—a password that opens all doors. I am unfortunately not able to elaborate on the question in the context of our discussion. What I can say is that the unconscious is personal, it belongs to someone, even if that someone is overwhelmed by psychophysiological mechanisms that are beyond his or her understanding. In these cases, as in those in which death approaches quickly—a fall off a cliff, for example—the unconscious may activate defense mechanisms, as well as powers from a dimension other than that of our ordinary space–time. From this point of view, it seems to me that the phenomenon of bilocation requires a different explanation. It is not clear what the unconscious would have to do with it.

EEV: *Psychoanalysis does not concern the unconscious alone; it also deals with the ego, among other things. Experiencers often speak about the death of the ego. Do you have any comments on this subject?*

ML: In my opinion, this is a very important question. I think that if we could resolve it, we would have the key to many of the problems encountered in our discussion. We cannot help it, the ego is something quite bad, as it is described rather mystically by the doctrine of original sin. For example, we easily become jealous of others. Pascal wrote that the self, the ego, was detestable; this seems to derive essentially from the finite nature of our being. The need for the absolute, which exists at the depths of our spiritual being, is tied down, so to speak, by our psycho-physiological self, our ego. I am referring to the self that has qualities, such as being tall or short, good-looking or ugly, strong or weak, with such and such an IQ, and so on. But our most profound being is not this psychophysiological self, this ego. Beyond the brain and the ties that bind us to our physical and social environment, there is, upon death, a return to the source of all spontaneity. In other words, as a thinking being with free will, we are born in the flesh and with the flesh at the moment of our conception, *but not of the flesh*. There is another source, and it is to this other source that we most likely return at death. Our individuality is then transformed. It ceases to be a prisoner constrained by time and space and by the brain that provides it access to the world. What is absolute in it is no longer lost in the pretension of the psychophysiological self; it opens itself up and expands to the fullness of a new dimension—its true dimension—for it was in this dimension that it received its being, its spontaneity in being born in the flesh. Death and birth are two sides of the same mystery, since at birth the spirit mysteriously incarnates in the flesh and at death disincarnates just as mysteriously. Incorporation and decorporation are equally difficult to imagine—incorporation nevertheless did occur. And it is the near-death experience that offers us a perspective on decorporation.

Notes

Foreword

1. Herman Melville, *Moby Dick*. New York: Barnes and Noble Books, 1994. (Originally published in 1851.)

Chapter One

1. Bruce Greyson, as quoted in Barbara Harris and Lionel C. Bascom, *Full circle*. New York: Pocket Books, 1990, p. 253.
2. Raymond A. Moody, *Life after life: The investigation of a phenomenon—survival of bodily death*. New York: Bantam Books, 1976.
3. Out-of-body experience: The psychological sensation of perceiving oneself from an external perspective, as though the mind or soul has left the physical body and is acting of its own volition. *American Heritage Dictionary. Microsoft Bookshelf.* 1996–97 ed. CD-ROM. Redmond, WA: Microsoft Corporation.
4. Moody, *Life after life*, p. 78.

5. Ibid, p. 79.

Chapter Two

1. Melvin Morse and Paul Perry, *Transformed by the light: The powerful effect of near-death experiences on people's lives*. London: BCA, 1992, p. 49.
2. Raymond A. Moody, *Life after life: The investigation of a phenomenon—survival of bodily death*. New York: Bantam Books, 1976, p. 35.
3. Ibid, pp. 35–36.
4. Ibid, p. 39.
5. Morse and Perry, p. 18.
6. Moody, p. 32.
7. Kenneth Ring, *Heading toward Omega: In search of the meaning of the near-death experience*. New York: William Morrow, 1984, p. 54.
8. Moody, p. 58.
9. Morse and Perry, p. 166.
10. Ring, pp. 53–54.
11. Ibid, p. 88.
12. Ibid, p. 71.
13. Ibid, p. 62.
14. Morse and Perry, p. 139.
15. Ring, pp. 64–65.
16. Ibid, pp. 75–76.
17. Morse and Perry, pp. 51–53.
18. Ring, pp. 72–73.
19. Morse and Perry, p. 12.
20. Ring, pp. 62–63.
21. Ibid, pp. 58–59.
22. Ibid, p. 72.
23. Ibid, p. 116.
24. Ibid, p. 119.
25. Ibid, p. 137.
26. Ibid, p. 75.
27. Morse and Perry, p. vii.
28. Moody, p. 50.
29. Ibid, pp. 41–42.

30. Ring, p. 88.
31. Ibid, p. 66.
32. Morse and Perry, p. x.
33. Moody, p. 48.
34. Morse and Perry, p. 75.
35. Ring, p. 39.
36. Ibid, p. 57.
37. Moody, p. 53.
38. Ibid, p. 49.
39. Morse and Perry, p. 149.
40. Moody, pp. 55–56.
41. Ibid, p. 56.
42. Morse and Perry, pp. 115–116.
43. Ibid, pp. 114–115.
44. Ring, pp. 68–69.
45. Moody, pp. 65–68.
46. Ring, p. 70.
47. Ibid, p. 108.
48. Moody, p. 37.
49. Ibid, p. 51.
50. Ibid, p. 51.
51. Ibid, pp. 51–52.
52. Ring, p. 42.
53. Moody, p. 27.
54. Ring, p. 60.
55. Moody, p. 44.
56. Ibid, p. 45.
57. Ibid, pp. 73–74.
58. Ibid, pp. 75–76.
59. Morse and Perry, p. 73.
60. Ibid, p. 57.
61. Ring, p. 40.
62. Morse and Perry, p. 155.
63. Ring, p. 60.
64. Morse and Perry, pp. 69–70.
65. Ibid, pp. 4–5.
66. Ibid, p. 78.
67. Ring, p. 92.
68. Morse and Perry, p. 33.
69. Moody, p. 26.

70. Ibid, pp. 53–54.
71. Ring, p. 68.
72. Ibid, pp. 186–187.
73. Morse and Perry, p. 115.
74. Ring, p. 176.
75. Morse and Perry, p. 91.
76. Ring, p. 179.
77. Morse and Perry, p. 79.
78. Ring, pp. 81–82.

Chapter Five

1. Maurice S. Rawlings, *Beyond death's door*. Nashville, TN: Thomas Nelson, 1978.
2. Herman Melville, *Moby Dick*. New York: Barnes & Noble Books, 1994. (Originally published in 1851.)
3. William James, *The varieties of religious experience*. New York: Macmillan, 1961, p. 305. (Originally published in 1902.)
4. Melvin Morse and Paul Perry, *Closer to the light*. London: Souvenir Press, 1991, p. 160.

Chapter Six

1. François Villon, *La ballade des pendus*. Paris: On les vend à Paris en la Rue de Beaune à l'enseigne du pot cassé, 1463, p. 66.
2. Louis-Marie Vincent, *Peut-on croire à la résurrection?* Paris: Dervy, 1988.
3. Cytoplasm: The protoplasm outside the nucleus of a cell. *American Heritage Dictionary. Microsoft Bookshelf.* 1996–97 ed. CD-ROM. Redmond, WA: Microsoft Corporation.
4. Pierre le Comte du Nouy, *Le temps et la vie*. Paris: Gallimard, 1942.
5. Lévy, *Le temps psychologique*. Paris: Dunod, 1969.
6. Louis-Marie Vincent, "L'énergie et la pensée," *3e millénaire* (1989).
7. Daniel Durand, *La systémique*. Paris: Presses universitaires de France, 1979.
8. Kenneth Ring, *Heading toward Omega: In search of the meaning of the near-death experience*. New York: William Morrow, 1984, p. 39.

9. Ibid, p. 39.
10. Moody, *Life after life: The investigation of a phenomenon—survival of bodily death*. New York: Bantam Books, 1976, p. 38.
11. Ring, *Heading toward Omega*, pp. 42–43.
12. Ibid, pp. 53–54.
13. Ibid, p. 88.
14. Ibid, p. 88.

Chapter Seven

1. Some passages of this discussion were taken from Régis Dutheil and Brigitte Dutheil, *La médecine superlumineuse*, Paris: Sand, 1992.
2. The Oxford English Dictionary, 2nd edition. Oxford University Press, 1989.

Chapter Eight

1. Paul Chauchard, *Le cerveau et la conscience*. Paris: Ed. du Seuil, 1960, p. 20.
2. Melvin Morse and Paul Perry, *Closer to the light*. London: Souvenir Press, 1991, p. 99–102.
3. Chauchard, *op. cit.* pp. 81–82.
4. Guy de Maupassant, *Le Horla*. Paris: P. Ollendorff, 1894. Originally published in 1887.
5. Melvin Morse and Paul Perry, *Closer to the light*, p. 111.
6. Chauchard, *op. cit.*
7. Friedrich Engels, *Dialectics of nature* (trans. German by C. Dutt). Moscow: Progress Publisher, 1972. (Originally published in 1925.)
8. Chauchard, *op. cit.*, p. 135.
9. Paul Chauchard and Taisen Deshimaru Roshi, *Zen et cerveau*. Paris: Courrier du livre, 1976.
10. Jean-Paul Sartre, *Les mots*. Paris: Gallimard, 1963.
11. Sheila Ostrander and Lynn Schroeder, Les étonnants pouvoirs de la mémoire. Paris: Robert Laffont, 1991, p. 114.
12. Paul Chauchard, *La mort*. Paris: Presses universitaires de France, 1947, pp. 63–64.
13. Kenneth Ring, *Heading toward Omega*, pp. 61–62.

Chapter Nine

1. Patrice van Eersel, *La source noire*. Paris: Grasset, 1986.
2. Jean Vernette, *Jésus dans la nouvelle religiosité*. Paris: Desclée, 1994.

Chapter Ten

1. Michel Lefeuvre, *Nature et cerveau*. Paris: Klincksieck, 1991, p. 19.
2. Ibid, p. 76.

Bibliography

Abanes, R. *Embraced by the light and the Bible*. Camp Hill, PA: Horizon Books, 1994.

Adam György. *Perception, consciousness, memory: Reflections of a biologist*. New York: Plenum Press, 1980.

Allison, R. *Mind in many pieces*. New York: Rawson and Wade, 1980.

Anderson, George. *We don't die*. New York: Berkeley Books, 1988.

Anderson, Ray S. *Theology, death and dying*. Oxford, UK: Blackwell, 1986.

Aries, Philippe. *Western attitudes towards death: From the Middle Ages to present*. Baltimore, MD: Johns Hopkins University Press, 1974.

Aries, Philippe. *The hour of our death*. New York: Knopf, 1981.

Aries, Philippe. *Images of man and death*. Cambridge, MA: Harvard University Press, 1985.

Armstrong, David M., and Malcolm, Norman. *Consciousness and causality: A debate on the nature of mind*. Oxford, UK: Blackwell, 1985. (Originally published in 1984)

Arnold, Magda B. *Memory and the brain*. Hillsdale, NJ: Erlbaum, 1984.

Atwater, P. M. H. *I died three times in 1977*. Dayton, VA: s.n., 1980.

Atwater, P. M. H. *Coming back to life: The after-effects of the near-death experience*. New York: Dodd and Mead, 1988.

Atwater, P. M. H. *Beyond the light: What isn't being said about the near-death experience*. New York: Birch Lane Press, 1994.

Atwater, P. M. H. *Future memory: How those who "see the future" shed new light on the workings of the human mind*. New York: Birch Lane Press, 1996.

Badham, Paul. *Christian beliefs about life and death*. London: Macmillan, 1976.

Badham, Paul, and Badham, Linda. *Immortality or extinction?* Totowa, NJ: Barnes and Noble, 1982.

Badham, Paul, and Badham, Linda. *Death and immortality in the religions of the world*. New York: Paragon House, 1987.

Bailey, Alice. *Death: The great adventure*. London: Lucis, 1985.

Barrett, William. *Deathbed visions: The psychical experiences of the dying*. London: Methuen, 1926.

Barrett, William. *Death of the soul*. Oxford, UK: Oxford University Press, 1986.

Basford, Terry. *Near-death experiences: An annotated bibliography*. New York: Garland, 1990.

Bateson, Gregory. *Mind and nature: A necessary unity*. New York: E. P. Dutton, 1979.

Beard, Paul. *Living on*. London: Allen and Unwin, 1980.

Beard, Paul. *Hidden man*. Norwich, UK: Pilgrim Books, 1986.

Becker, C. *Paranormal experience and survival of death*. Albany, NY: State University of New York Press, 1993.

Becker, E. *The denial of death*. New York: Free Press, 1974.

Benton, R. G. *Death and dying*. New York: Van Nostrand Reinhold, 1978.

Bentov, I. *Stalking the wild pendulum*. New York: E. P. Dutton, 1977.

Bermudez, Jose L., Marcel, Anthony, and Eilan, Naomi (Eds.). *The body and the self*. Cambridge, MA: MIT Press, 1995.

Blackburn, Simon. *Essays in quasi-realism*. Oxford, UK: Oxford University Press, 1993.

Blackmore, Susan J. *Parapsychology and out-of-the-body experiences*. East Sussex, UK: Transpersonal Books, 1978.

Blackmore, Susan J. *Beyond the body: An investigation of out-of-the-body experiences*. London: Heinemann, 1982.

Blackmore, Susan J. *Out of the body*. London: Granada, 1983.

Blackmore, Susan J. *Dying to live: Science and the near-death experience*. Buffalo, NY: Prometheus, 1993.

Bloch, M., and Parry, J. (Eds.). *Death and the regeneration of life*. New York: Cambridge University Press, 1982.

Bluebond-Langer, Myra. *The private worlds of dying children*. Princeton, NJ: Princeton University Press, 1978.

Bohm, David. *Quantum theory*. London: Constable, 1954.

Bohm, David. *The special theory of relativity*. New York: Benjamin, 1965.

Bohm, David. *Causality and chance in modern physics*. London: Routledge and Kegan Paul, 1967.

Bohm, David. *Wholeness and the implicate order*. London: Ark, 1983.

Bohm, David. *Unfolding meaning*. London: Ark, 1987.

Bohm, David. *The undivided universe: An ontological interpretation of quantum theory*. London: Routledge and Kegan Paul, 1993.

Bohm, David, and Factor, Donald (Eds.). *Unfolding meaning: A week-end of dialogue with David Bohm*. London: Ark, 1994.

Bohm, David, and Krishnamurti, J. *The ending of time*. London: Gollancz, 1985.

Bohm, David, and Peat, F. David. *Science, order, and creativity*. London: Routledge and Kegan Paul, 1989.

Bornstein, R. F., and Pittman, T. S. (Eds.). *Perception without awareness*. New York: Guilford, 1992.

Borst, C. V. (ed.). *The mind–brain identity theory*. Basingstoke, UK: Macmillan, 1984. (Originally published in 1970)

Borstner, B., and Shawe-Taylor, J. (Eds.). *Consciousness at the crossroads of philosophy and cognitive science: Selected proceedings of the final meeting of the Tempus Project "Phenomenology and cognitive science," Maribor, Slovenia, August 23–27, 1994*. Thorverton: Imprint Academic, 1995.

Bragdon, Emma. *The call of spiritual emergency*. New York: Harper and Row, 1990.

Bramblett, John. *When good-bye is forever: Learning to live again after the loss of a child*. New York: Ballantine Books, 1991.

Brennan, Andrew. *Conditions of identity: A study of identity and survival*. Oxford, UK: Clarendon Press, 1988.

Brim, Orville G. *et al*. *The dying patient*. New York: Russell Sage Foundation, 1970.

Brooke, Tal. *The other side of death: Does death seal your destiny?* Wheaton, IL: Tyndale House, 1979.

Brookesmith, P. *Life after death*. London: Orbis, 1984.

Brown, Hanbury. *The wisdom of science*. Cambridge, UK: Cambridge University Press, 1986.

Brown, J. A. *Relationships between phenomena of consciousness and interhemispheric brainwave patterns during nonordinary states of consciousness*. Ph.D. dissertation, Saybrook Institute, San Francisco, CA, 1986.

Brown, Jason W. *Mind, brain and consciousness: The neuropsychology of cognition*. New York: Academic Press, 1977.

Brown, L. R. *Vital signs: The trends that are shaping our future*. New York: Norton, 1994.

Brzezinski, Jerzy (Ed.). *Consciousness: Methodological and psychological approaches*. Amsterdam: Rodopi, 1985.

Bubulka, G. *Beyond reality: A personal account of the near-death experience*. Fresno, CA: Author, 1992.

Buckingham, Robert W. *Care of the dying child*. New York: Continuum, 1989.

Budge, E. A. W. *The Egyptian book of the dead*. New York: Dover, 1967.

Bunge, M. *The mind–body problem: A psychobiological approach*. Oxford, UK: Pergamon, 1980.

Burnham, S. *A book of angels: Reflection on angels past and present and true stories of how they touch our lives*. New York: Ballantine Books, 1990.

Burnham, S. *Angel letters: What you wrote to me*. New York: Ballantine Books, 1991.

Burr, H. S. *Blueprint for immortality: The electric patterns of life*. London: Neville Spearman, 1972.

Callanan, Maggie, and Kelley, Patricia. *Final gifts: Understanding the special awareness, needs, and communications of the dying*. New York: Poseidon Press, 1992.

Calvin, William H. *The cerebral symphony: Seashore reflections on the structure of consciousness*. New York: Bantam, 1990.

Campbell, John. *Past, space, and self*. Cambridge, MA: MIT Press, 1994.

Capra, Fritjof. *The turning point*. New York: Bantam, 1982.

Capra, Fritjof. *Uncommon wisdom*. London: Century, 1987.

Capra, Fritjof. *The Tao of physics* (3rd ed.). Berkeley, CA: Shambhala, 1991.

Carrier, Martin, and Mittelstrass, Jurgen. *Mind, brain, behavior: The mind–body problem and the philosophy of psychology*. (Trans.). Berlin: Walter de Gruyter, 1991.

Castle, K., and Bechtel, S. *Katherine—it's time*. New York: Harper and Row, 1989.

Changeux, Jean-Pierre. *Neuronal man: The biology of mind*. New York: Oxford University Press, 1985.

Christianson, S. (Ed.). *The handbook of emotion and memory: Research and theory*. Hillsdale, NJ: Erlbaum, 1992.

Churchland, P. S. *Neurophilosophy: Toward a unified science of the mind–brain*. Cambridge, MA: MIT Press, 1989.

Coan, R. W. *Human consciousness and its evolution: A multidimensional view*. Westport, CT: Greenwood, 1987.

Cohen, Neal J. *Memory, amnesia, and the hippocampal system.* Cambridge, MA: MIT Press, 1993.

Cole, David J., Fetzer, James H., and Rankin, Terry L. (Eds.). *Philosophy, mind, and cognitive inquiry: Resources for understanding mental processes.* Boston: Kluwer Academic, 1990.

Combs, A., and Holland, M. *Synchronicity: Science, myth, and the trickster.* New York: Paragon House, 1990.

Cook, Sarah S. *Children and dying: An exploration and selective bibliographies.* New York: Health Sciences, 1974.

Cornwell, John. *The hiding places of God.* New York: Warner Books, 1991.

Couliano, I. P. *Out of this world: Otherworld journeys from Gilgamesh to Albert Einstein.* Boston: Shambhala, 1991.

Crick, F. H. C. *The astonishing hypothesis: The scientific search for the soul.* London: Simon and Schuster, 1994.

Crookall, Robert. *Events on the threshold of the afterlife.* Moradabad, India: Darshana International, 1967.

Crookall, Robert. *Ecstasy: The release of the soul from the body.* Morabadad, India: Darshana International, 1973.

Crookall, Robert. *What happens when you die.* London: Colin Smythe, 1978.

Davies, Martin, and Humphreys, Glyn W. (Eds.). *Consciousness: Psychological and philosophical essays.* Oxford, UK: Blackwell, 1993.

Davies, P. C. W. *Other worlds.* New York: Simon and Schuster, 1980.

Davies, P. C. W. *The mind of God: Science and the search for ultimate meaning.* New York: Simon and Schuster, 1992.

Davis, J. *Hurry home, Dad: Today I'm going to die.* Salt Lake City, UT: Hawker, 1982.

Dennett, Daniel C. *Consciousness explained.* Boston: Little, Brown, 1991.

Donaldson, Margaret. *Human minds: An exploration.* London: Penguin, 1993.

Doore, Gary. *What survives? Contemporary explorations of life after death.* Los Angeles: Tarcher, 1990.

Dossey, L. *Recovering the soul: A scientific and spiritual search.* New York: Bantam, 1989.

Dudai, Yadin. *The neurobiology of memory: Concepts, findings, trends.* Oxford, UK: Oxford University Press, 1989.

Eadie, Betty J., and Taylor, C. *Embraced by the light.* Placerville, CA: Gold Leaf Press, 1992.

Eby, Richard F. *Caught up into paradise.* Tarrytown, NJ: Fleming H. Revell, 1978.

Eby, Richard E. *Tell them I am coming*. Tarrytown, NJ: Fleming H. Revell, 1980.

Eccles, John C. *Facing reality: Philosophical adventures by a brain scientist*. New York: Springer, 1970.

Eccles, John C. *The understanding of the brain* (2nd ed.). New York: McGraw-Hill, 1977.

Eccles, John C. *The human psyche*. Berlin: Springer International, 1980.

Eccles, John C. *Evolution of the brain: Creation of the self*. London: Routledge and Kegan Paul, 1991.

Eccles, John C. *How the self controls its brain*. New York: Springer, 1994.

Eccles, John C., and Karczmar, A. G. (Eds.). *Brain and human behavior*. New York: Springer, 1972.

Eccles, John C., and Popper, Karl R. *The self and its brain*. London: Routledge and Kegan Paul, 1990. (Originally published in 1977)

Eccles John C., and Robinson, Daniel N. *The wonder of being human: Our brain and our mind*. New York: Collier Macmillan, 1984.

Einstein, Albert. *Relativity*. New York: Crown, 1961.

Einstein, Albert. *The world as I see it*. New York: Philosophical Library, 1979.

Enright, D. J. *The Oxford book of death*. Oxford, UK: Oxford University Press, 1983.

Evans, H. *Alternate states of consciousness*. Wellingborough, UK: Aquarian Press, 1989.

Evans-Wentz, W. Y. (Ed.). *The Tibetan book of the dead*. New York: Oxford University Press, 1960.

Farr, S. S. *What Tom Sawyer learned from dying*. Norfolk, VA: Hampton Roads, 1993.

Farthing, G. W. *The psychology of consciousness*. Englewood Cliffs, NJ: Prentice-Hall, 1992.

Feifel, Herman. *The meaning of death*. New York: McGraw-Hill, 1959.

Feifel, Herman. *New meanings of death*. New York : McGraw-Hill, 1977.

Ferguson, M. *The Aquarian conspiracy: Personal and social transformation in the 1980s*. Los Angeles: Tarcher, 1980.

Fiore, Edith. *We have been here before*. London: Sphere, 1980.

Fiore, Edith. *The unquiet death*. Garden City, NY: Dolphin/Doubleday, 1987.

Fiore, Edith and Landsburg, A. *Death encounters*. New York: Bantam, 1976.

Flanagan, O. *Consciousness reconsidered*. Cambridge, MA: MIT Press, 1992.

Flynn, Charles P. *After the beyond: Human transformation and the near-death experience.* Englewood Cliffs, NJ: Prentice-Hall, 1986.

Forti, Kathleen. *The door to the secret city.* Walpole, NH: Stillpoint Press, 1984.

Frankl, Viktor. *Man's search for meaning.* London: Hodder and Stoughton, 1964.

Frankl, Viktor. *The unconscious God.* London: Hodder and Stoughton, 1975.

Friedman, W. J. *About time: Inventing the fourth dimension.* Cambridge, MA: MIT Press, 1990.

Gabbard, Glen O., and Twemlow, Stuart W. *With the eyes of the mind: An empirical analysis of out-of-body states.* New York: Praeger, 1984.

Gallup, G. *Adventures in immortality: A look beyond the threshold of death.* New York: McGraw-Hill, 1982.

Gardner, Howard. *The mind's new science: A history of the cognitive revolution.* New York: Basic Books, 1985.

Gardner, Howard. *Creating minds.* New York: Basic Books, 1993.

Gennaro, Rocco J. *Consciousness and self-consciousness.* Amsterdam: John Benjamins, 1995.

Gibson, Arvin S. *Glimpses of eternity: New near-death experiences examined.* Bountiful, UT: Horizon, 1992.

Gibson, Arvin S. *Echoes from eternity: New near-death experiences examined.* Bountiful, UT: Horizon, 1993.

Gleick, J. *Chaos: Making a new science.* New York: Penguin Books, 1987.

Globus, Gordon G., Maxwell, Grover, and Savodnik, Irwin (Eds.). *Consciousness and the brain: A scientific and philosophical inquiry.* New York: Plenum Press, 1977.

Gomez, Elaine Ann. *The aftereffects of near-death experience.* Columbus, OH: Ohio State University Press, 1986.

Graf, Peter, and Masson, M. E. J. (Eds.). *Implicit memory: New directions in cognition, development, and neuropsychology.* Hillsdale, NJ: Erlbaum, 1993.

Graham, George. *Philosophy of mind: An introduction.* Cambridge, MA: Blackwell, 1993.

Gregory, Richard L. *Mind in science: A history of explanation in psychology and physics.* London: Weidenfeld and Nicolson, 1981.

Grey, Margot. *Beyond death: The near-death experience.* Master's thesis, Keene, UK: Antioch University, 1983.

Grey, Margot. *The near-death experience: Its place in humanistic psychology.* Keene, UK: Antioch University, 1983.

Grey, Margot. *Return from death: An exploration of the near-death experience*. London: Arkana, 1985.

Greyson, Bruce, and Flynn, Charles P. (Eds.). *The near-death experience: Problems, prospects, perspectives*. Springfield, IL: Charles C. Thomas, 1984.

Grof, Stanislav. *Realms of the human unconscious: Observations from LSD research*. New York: Viking, 1975.

Grof, Stanislav, and Halifax, Joan. *The human encounter with death*. New York: E. P. Dutton, 1977.

Grof, Stanislav. *Beyond the brain: Birth, death, and transcendence in psychotherapy*. Ithaca, NY: State University of New York Press, 1985.

Grof, Stanislav, and Bennet, H. Z. *The holotropic mind: The three levels of human consciousness and how they shape our lives*. San Francisco: Harper, 1990.

Grof, Stanislav, and Grof, Christina. *Beyond death: The gates of consciousness*. New York: Thames and Hudson, 1980.

Grof, Stanislav, and Grof, Christina (Eds.). *Spiritual emergency: When personal transformation becomes a crisis*. Los Angeles: Tarcher, 1989.

Grosso, Michael. *The final choice: Playing the survival game*. Walpole, NH: Stillpoint Press, 1985.

Gutzwiller, Martin C. *Chaos in classical and quantum mechanics*. New York: Springer, 1990.

Haake, Fritz. *Quantum signatures of chaos*. New York: Springer, 1992.

Hampe, Johann C. *To die is gain: The experience of one's own death* (trans. Margaret Kohl). Atlanta, GA: John Knox, 1979.

Harding, D. E. *The hierarchy of heaven and earth: A new diagram of man in the universe*. Gainesville, FL: University Press of Florida, 1979.

Harding, D. E. *The little book of life and death*. New York: Viking Penguin, 1989.

Harding, D. E. *The trial of the man who said he was God*. London: Arkana, 1992.

Hardt, Dale V. *Death: The final frontier*. Englewood Cliffs, NJ: Prentice-Hall, 1979.

Harlow, Ralph. *Life at death*. New York: McFadden Bartell Books, 1968.

Harpur, T. *Life after death*. Toronto: McClelland and Stewart, 1991.

Harris, Barbara. *Spiritual awakenings: A guidebook for experiencers and those who care about them*. Baltimore, MD: Stage Three Books, 1993.

Harris, Barbara, and Bascom, L. C. L. *Full circle: The near-death experience and beyond*. New York: Pocket Books, 1990.

Hartocollis, P. *Time and timelessness: The varieties of temporal experience (a psychoanalytic inquiry)*. New York: International Universities Press, 1983.

Hauck, R. (Ed.). *Angels: The mysterious messengers*. New York: Ballantine Books.

Hawking, S. *A brief history of time: From the big bang to black holes*. New York: Bantam, 1988.

Hedin, D. *Death as a fact of life*. New York: Norton, 1973.

Heinberg, R. *Memories and visions of paradise*. Los Angeles: Tarcher, 1989.

Helene, Nina. *An exploratory study of the near-death encounters of Christians*. Boston: Boston University, 1984.

Herbert, N. *Quantum reality: Beyond the new physics*. Garden City, NY: Anchor Press/Doubleday, 1985.

Herndon, Ileen. *The near-death experience*. Northridge, CA: California State University, 1986.

Herrmann, N. *The creative brain*. Lake Lure, NC: Author, 1990.

Hick, J. H. *Death and eternal life*. San Francisco: Harper and Row, 1976.

Hobson, Douglas P. *A comparative study of near-death experiences and Christian eschatology*. Master's thesis, Waco, TX: Baylor University, 1983.

Hobson, John A. *The chemistry of conscious states: How the brain changes its mind*. Boston: Little, Brown, 1994.

Hodgson, David H. *The mind matters: Consciousness and choice in a quantum world*. Oxford, UK: Clarendon Press, 1991.

Hoffman, R. *Disclosure decisions and patterns after a near-death experience*. Unpublished doctoral dissertation, Louisiana State University, Baton Rouge, LA, 1993.

Hofstadter, Douglas R., and Dennett, Daniel C. (Eds.). *The mind's I: Fantasies and reflections on self and soul*. Hammondsworth, UK: Penguin Books, 1985. (Originally published by Basic Books in 1981)

Holden, Janice M. *Visual perception during the naturalistic near-death out-of-body experience*. Dekalb, IL: Northern Illinois University Press, 1988.

Hooper, Judith, and Teresi, Dick. *The three pound universe: The brain, from the chemistry of the mind to the frontiers of the soul*. New York: Dell Books, 1986.

Humphrey, Nicholas. *Consciousness regained: Chapters in the development of mind*. Oxford, UK: Oxford University Press, 1984.

Humphrey, Nicholas. *A history of mind: Evolution and the birth of consciousness*. New York: Harper Perennial, 1993.

Irwin, H. J. *Flight of the mind: A psychological study of the out-of-body experience.* Metuchen, NJ: Scarecrow Press, 1985.

Iverson, Jeffrey. *In search of the dead: A scientific investigation of evidence for life after death.* San Francisco: Harper-Collins, 1992.

Izard, C. E. *The face of emotion.* New York: Appleton-Century-Crofts, 1971.

Izard, C. E. *Human emotions.* New York: Plenum Press, 1977.

J'Auregui, Jose A. *The emotional computer.* Oxford, UK: Blackwell, 1995.

Jackendoff, Ray S. *Consciousness and the computational mind.* Cambridge, MA: MIT Press, 1987.

James, William. *The principles of psychology.* New York: Henry Holt, 1890.

James, William. *Human immortality.* London: Constable, 1899.

James, William. *Pragmatism.* London: Longman, 1921.

James, William. *The varieties of mystical experience.* New York: Random House, 1929.

James, William. *Psychology: Briefer course.* Cambridge, MA: Harvard University Press, 1984. (Originally published in 1892)

James, William. *The varieties of religious experience.* New York: Macmillan, 1961. (Originally published in 1902)

Jantsch, E., and Waddington, C. H. (Eds.). *Evolution and consciousness: Human systems in transition.* Reading, MA: Addison-Wesley, 1976.

Jaynes, J. *The origin of consciousness in the breakdown of the bicameral mind* (rev. ed.). Boston: Houghton Mifflin, 1990.

Jibu, Mari, and Yasue, Kunio. *Quantum brain dynamics and consciousness: An introduction.* Amsterdam: J. Benjamins, 1995.

Johansson, Lars-Göran. *Understanding quantum mechanics: A realist interpretation without hidden variables.* Stockholm: Almqvist and Wiskell International, 1993.

John, Dafree. *Easy death.* Clearlake, CA: Dawn Horse Press, 1983.

John, E. R., and Harmony, Thalia (Eds.). *Machinery of the mind: Data, theory and speculations about higher brain function.* Boston: Birkhauser, 1990.

Johnson, George. *In the palaces of memory: How we build the worlds in our heads.* New York: Knopf, 1991.

Johnson, K. *The living aura: Radiation field photography and the Kirlian effect.* New York: Hawthorne, 1975.

Joseph, Rhawn. *The right brain and the unconscious: Discovering the stranger within.* New York: Plenum Press, 1992.

Josephson, B. D., and Ramachandran, V. S. (Eds.). *Consciousness and the physical world: Edited proceedings of an interdisciplinary symposium on consciousness held at the University of Cambridge in January 1978.* Oxford, UK: Pergamon Press, 1980.

Joy, W. *Joy's way.* Los Angeles: Tarcher, 1979.

Jung, Carl G. *Symbols of transformation.* Princeton, NJ: Princeton University Press, 1956.

Jung, Carl G. *Memories, dreams, reflections.* New York: Vintage Books, 1961.

Jung, Carl G. *The archetypes and the collective unconscious.* Princeton, NJ: Princeton University Press, 1971.

Jung, Carl G. *Modern man in search of a soul.* London: Ark, 1984.

Kalish, Richard A. *Death, dying and transcendence.* Farmingdale, NY: Baywood, 1980.

Kalish, Richard A. (Ed.). *The final transition.* Farmingdale, NY: Baywood, 1985.

Kappraff, Jay. *Connections.* New York: McGraw-Hill, 1991.

Kastenbaum, Robert J. (Ed.). *Between life and death.* New York: Springer, 1979.

Kastenbaum, Robert J. *Death, society, and human experience* (2nd ed.). St. Louis: Mosby, 1981.

Kastenbaum, Robert J. *Is there life after death ?* New York: Prentice-Hall, 1984.

Kastenbaum, Robert J., and Aisenberg, I. *The psychology of death* (2nd ed.). New York: Springer, 1992.

Kelly, W. *Psychology of the unconscious.* Buffalo, NY: Prometheus, 1991.

Kelso, J. A. S. *Dynamic patterns: The self-organization of brain and behavior.* Cambridge, MA: MIT Press, 1995.

Kirk, Robert. *Raw feeling: A philosophical account of the essence of consciousness.* Oxford, UK: Clarendon Press, 1994.

Komp, Diane. *A window to heaven.* Grand Rapids, MI: Zondervan, 1992.

Kosslyn, S., and Koenig, O. *Wet mind: The new cognitive neuroscience.* New York: Free Press, 1992.

Kübler-Ross, Elisabeth. *On death and dying.* New York: Macmillan, 1969.

Kübler-Ross, Elisabeth. *Questions and answers on death and dying.* New York: Collier Books, 1974.

Kübler-Ross, Elisabeth. *Personal communication.* New York: Macmillan, 1976.

Kübler-Ross, Elisabeth. *On children and death.* New York: Macmillan, 1983.

Kübler-Ross, Elisabeth. *Death: The final stages of growth.* Englewood Cliffs, NJ: Prentice-Hall, 1985.

Kübler-Ross, Elisabeth. *Death is of vital importance: On life, death and life after death.* Tarrytown, NY: Station Hill Press, 1995.

Kübler-Ross, Elisabeth, and Preston, Heather. *Remember the secret.* Berkeley, CA: Celestial Arts, 1982.

Kübler-Ross, Elisabeth, and Warshaw, M. *To live until we say goodbye.* Englewood Cliffs, NJ: Prentice-Hall, 1978.

Laberge, S., and Rheingold, H. *Exploring the world of lucid dreaming.* New York: Ballantine Books, 1990.

Lazarus, R. S. *Emotion and adaptation.* New York: Oxford University Press, 1991.

Ledoux, Joseph E., and Hirst, William (Eds.). *Mind and brain: Dialogues in cognitive neuroscience.* Cambridge, UK: Cambridge University Press, 1987.

Lee, Jung Y. *Death and beyond in the Eastern perspective.* New York: Gordon and Breach, 1974.

Leming, Michael R., and Dickson, George E. *Understanding dying, death and bereavement.* Fort Worth, TX: Holt, Rinehart and Winston, 1990.

Leshan, L. *Alternate realities: The search for the full human being.* New York: M. Evans, 1976.

Leshan, L., and Margenau, H. *Einstein's space and van Gogh's sky: Physical reality and beyond.* New York: Macmillan, 1982.

Levine, Stephen. *Meetings at the edge: Dialogues with the grieving and the dying, the healing and the healed.* New York: Doubleday, 1984.

Levine Stephen. *Healing into life and death.* New York: Anchor Press, 1987.

Levine, Stephen. *Who dies?* Oakland, CA: Gateway Books, 1988.

Lewis, H. D. *Persons and life after death.* New York: Harper and Row, 1978.

Loar, Brian. *Mind and meaning.* Cambridge, UK: Cambridge University Press, 1986.

Lockwood, Michael. *Mind, brain and the quantum: The compound "I".* Oxford, UK: Blackwell, 1989.

Lonetto, R. *Children's conceptions of death.* New York: Springer, 1980.

Lorimer, David. *Survival? Body, mind and death in the light of psychic experience.* London: Routledge and Kegan Paul, 1984.

Lorimer, David. *Whole in one: The near-death experience and the ethic of interconnectedness.* London: Arkana, 1990.

Lumsden, C. J., and Wilson, E. O. *Promethean fire: Reflections on the origin of mind.* Cambridge, MA: Harvard University Press, 1983.

Lundahl, Craig R. (Ed.). *A collection of near-death research readings: Scientific inquiries into the experiences of persons near physical death.* Chicago: Nelson-Hall, 1982.

Luria, A. R. *The working brain: Introduction to neuropsychology* (trans. Basil Haigh). London: Penguin Books, 1973.

Luria, A. R. *Higher cortical functions in man* (2nd ed.). New York: Basic Books, 1980.

Lycan, William G. *Consciousness.* Cambridge, MA: MIT Press, 1987.

Lycan, William G. (Ed.). *Mind and cognition: A reader.* Cambridge, MA: Blackwell, 1990.

MacDonald, Cynthia. *Mind–body identity theories.* London: Routledge and Kegan Paul, 1989.

Malerstein, Abraham J. *The conscious mind: A developmental theory.* New York: Human Sciences Press, 1986.

Malz, Betty. *Angels watching me.* New York: Chosen Books, 1986.

Malz, Betty. *My glimpse of eternity.* Old Tappan, NJ: Spire Books, 1977.

Malz, Betty. *Touching the unseen world.* New York: Chosen Books, 1991.

Mandler, G. *Mind and emotion.* New York: Wiley, 1975.

Marcel, A. J., and Bisiach, E. (Eds.). *Consciousness in contemporary science.* Oxford, UK: Clarendon Press, 1993. (Originally published in 1988)

Martindale, C. *Cognition and consciousness.* Homewood, IL: Dorsey, 1981.

Maslow, A. H. *The farther reaches of human nature.* New York: Penguin Books, 1971.

Maslow, A. H. *Toward a psychology of being* (2nd ed.). New York: Van Nostrand Reinhold, 1982.

Matson, Archie. *The waiting world: What happens at death.* New York: Harper and Row, 1975. (Originally published as *The Waiting World*)

Maturana, H. R., and Varela, F. J. *The tree of knowledge: The biological roots of human understanding.* Boston: Shambhala, 1992.

Mayer, R. S. *Satan's children: Case studies in multiple personality.* New York: G. P. Putnam, 1991.

McCall, Storrs. *A model of the universe: Space–time, probability, and decision.* Oxford, UK: Clarendon Press, 1996.

McCarthy, James B. *Death anxiety: The loss of the self.* New York: Gardner Press, 1980.

McDowell, John. *Mind and world.* Cambridge, MA: Harvard University Press, 1994.

McEvoy, Mary Dee. *The relationships among the experiences of dying: The evidence of paranormal events and creativity in adults.* New York: New York University, 1987.

McMahan, Forrest R. *Near death.* Parkesburg, VA: Synergetics Press, 1985.

Medawar, Peter. *The limits of science*. Oxford, UK: Oxford University Press, 1986.

Meek, George. W. *After we die, what then?* Franklin, NC: Metascience Corporation Publications, 1980.

Mickel, H. *The near-death experience: A basic introduction*. Wichita, KS: Theta Project, 1985.

Mishlove, Jeffrey. *The roots of consciousness*. New York: Random House, 1975.

Monod, Jacques. *Chance and necessity*. London: Collins, 1974.

Moody, Raymond A. *Life after life: The investigation of a phenomenon—survival of bodily death*. Covington, GA: Mockingbird Books, 1975.

Moody, Raymond A. *Reflections on "Life after life."* Atlanta, GA: Bantam, 1977.

Moody, Raymond A. *Elvis after life: Unusual psychic experiences surrounding the death of a superstar*. Atlanta, GA: Peachtree, 1987.

Moody, Raymond A. *Coming back: A psychiatrist explores past-life journeys*. New York: Bantam, 1990.

Moody, Raymond A., and Perry, Paul. *The light beyond*. New York: Bantam, 1988.

Moody, Raymond A., and Perry, Paul. *Reunions: Visionary encounters with departed loved ones*. New York: Villard, 1993.

Moore, Brooke N. *The philosophical possibilities beyond death*. Springfield, IL: Charles C Thomas, 1981.

Morse, Melvin, and Perry, Paul. *Closer to the light: Learning from children's near-death experiences*. New York: Villard, 1990.

Morse, Melvin, and Perry, Paul. *Transformed by the light: The powerful effect of near-death experiences on people's lives*. New York: Villard, 1992.

Motoyama, H. *Science and the evolution of consciousness*. Brookline, MA: Autumn Press, 1978.

Moulyn, Adrian C. *Mind–body: A pluralistic interpretation of mind–body interaction under the guidelines of time, space, and movement*. New York: Greenwood Press, 1991.

Nelson, L. *Beyond the veil* (3 vols.). Orem, UT: Cedar Fort, 1988–1990.

Nerlich, Graham. *The shape of space* (2nd ed.). Cambridge, UK: Cambridge University Press, 1994.

Nerlich, Graham. *What space–time explains: Metaphysical essays on space and time*. Cambridge, UK: Cambridge University Press, 1994.

Neumann, E. *The origins and history of consciousness*. Princeton, NJ: Princeton University Press, 1973.

Ornstein, Jack H. *The mind and the brain: A multi-aspect interpretation.* The Hague: M. Nijhoff, 1972.

Ornstein, Robert E. *The psychology of consciousness.* New York: Penguin Books, 1972.

Ornstein, Robert E. *Multimind.* London: Macmillan, 1988.

Ornstein, Robert E. *The evolution of consciousness: Of Darwin, Freud and cranial fire: The origins of the way we think.* New York: Prentice-Hall, 1991.

Osis, Karlis. *Deathbed observations by physicians and nurses.* New York: s.n., 1961.

Osis, Karlis, and Haraldsson, Erlendur. *At the hour of death* (rev. ed.). New York: Hastings House, 1990.

Oyler, Chris, Becklund, Laurie, and Polson, Beth, with Oyler, Chris. *Go toward the light.* New York: Harper and Row, 1988.

Parkins, E. J. *Equilibration, mind, and brain: Toward an integrated psychology.* New York: Praeger, 1990.

Pearce, J. C. *The crack in the cosmic egg: Challenging constructs of mind and reality.* New York: Crown, 1988.

Pearce, J. C. *Evolution's end: Claiming the potential of our consciousness.* San Francisco: Harper, 1992.

Peat, F. David. *Synchronicity: The bridge between matter and mind.* New York: Bantam, 1987.

Penfield, Wilder. *The mystery of the mind: A critical study of consciousness and the human brain.* Princeton, NJ: Princeton University Press, 1975.

Penfield, Wilder, and Jasper, H. H. *Epilepsy and the functional anatomy of the human brain.* Boston: Little, Brown, 1954.

Penfield, Wilder, and Rasmussen, T. *The cerebral cortex of man: A clinical study of localization of function.* New York: Macmillan, 1950.

Pennebaker, J. W. *Opening up: The healing power of confiding in others.* New York: Morrow, 1990.

Plato. *The republic.* (Francis Cornford, trans.). New York: Oxford University Press, 1941.

Plato. *The last days of Socrates* (Hugh Tredennick, trans.). Baltimore, MD: Penguin Books, 1959.

Platthy, Jeno. *Near-death experiences in antiquity.* Santa Claus, IN: Federation of International Poetry Association of UNESCO, 1992.

Pope, John E. *Near-death experiences and attitudes towards life, death and suicide.* Master's thesis, Armidale, Australia: New England University, 1991.

Preston, Betty. *Fear not.* Seattle, WA: Ibbybooks, 1991.

Pribram, Karl H. (Ed.). *Brain and behavior*. Hammondsworth, UK: Penguin Books, 1969.

Pribram, Karl H. *Language of the brain: Experimental paradoxes and principles in neuropsychology*. New York: Brandon House, 1981.

Pribram, Karl H. *Brain and perception: Holonomy and structure and figural processing*. Hillsdale, NJ: Erlbaum, 1991.

Pribram, Karl H., and Broadbent, Donald E. (Eds.). *Biology of memory*. New York: Academic Press, 1970.

Pribram, Karl H., and Eccles, John (Eds.). *Rethinking neural networks: Quantum fields and biological data*. Hillsdale, NJ: Erlbaum/Inns Press, 1993.

Pribram, Karl H., and Gill, Merton M., *Freud's "project" reassessed: Preface to contemporary cognitive theory and neuropsychology*. New York: Basic Books, 1976.

Pribram, Karl H., and Lurija, A. R. (Eds.) *Psychophysiology of the frontal lobes*. New York: Academic Press, 1973.

Prigogine, I., and Stengers, I. *Order out of chaos: Man's new dialogue with nature*. New York: Bantam, 1984.

Provonsha, Jack. *Is death for real? An examination of reported near-death experiences in the light of the resurrection*. Boise, ID: Pacific Press, 1981.

Rawlings, Maurice S. *Beyond death's door*. Nashville, TN: Thomas Nelson, 1978.

Rawlings, Maurice S. *Before death comes*. Nashville, TN: Thomas Nelson, 1980.

Rawlings, Maurice S. *Life wish*. Nashville, TN: Thomas Nelson, 1981.

Rawlings, Maurice S. *To hell and back: Life after death—startling new evidence*. Nashville, TN: Thomas Nelson, 1993.

Ray, Christopher. *Time, space and philosophy*. New York: Routledge and Kegan Paul, 1991.

Reanney, D. *The still point: Beyond the edges of consciousness*. Melbourne: Hill of Content, 1996.

Reiser, Morton F. *Mind, brain, body: Toward a convergence of psychoanalysis and neurobiology*. New York: Basic Books, 1984.

Restak, R. M. *The brain: The last frontier*. New York: Bantam, 1984.

Restak, R. M. *The mind*. New York: Bantam, 1988.

Revonsuo, Antti, and Kamppinen, Matti (Eds.). *Consciousness in philosophy and cognitive neuroscience*. Hillsdale, NJ: Erlbaum, 1994.

Reyes, Benito F. *Conscious dying*. Ojai, CA: World University of America, 1986.

Richards, H. J. *Death and after*. London: Fount, 1980.

Ring, Kenneth. *Life at death: A scientific investigation of the near-death experience.* New York: Coward, McCann and Geoghegan, 1980.

Ring, Kenneth. *Heading toward Omega: In search of the meaning of the near-death experience.* New York: Morrow, 1984.

Ring, Kenneth. *The Omega project: Near-death experiences, UFO encounters, and mind at large.* New York: Morrow, 1992.

Rinpoche, Sogyal. *The Tibetan book of living and dying.* San Francisco: HarperCollins, 1992.

Ritchie, Georges. *My life after dying.* Hampton Roads, VA: Hampton Roads, 1991.

Ritchie, Georges, and Sherrill, E. *Return from tomorrow.* Waco, TX: Chosen Books, 1978.

Rivard, P. *A comparison of near-death experience and religious experience.* Storrs, CT: University of Connecticut.

Roberts, B. *What is self? A study of the spiritual journey in terms of consciousness.* Austin, TX: Mary Goens, 1989.

Roberts, B. *The path to no-self: Life at the center.* Albany, NY: State University of New York Press, 1991.

Roberts, B. *The experience of no-self: A contemplative journey* (rev. ed.). Albany, NY: State University of New York Press, 1993.

Rogo, D. Scott. *NAD: A study of some unusual "other world" experiences.* New York: University Books, 1970.

Rogo, D. Scott. *NAD: A psychic study of the "music of the spheres."* New York: University Books, 1972.

Rogo, D. Scott (Ed.). *Mind beyond the body.* New York: Penguin Books, 1978.

Rogo, D. Scott. *Miracles.* New York: Dial, 1982.

Rogo, D. Scott. *The search for yesterday: A critical examination of the evidence for reincarnation.* Englewood Cliffs, NJ: Prentice-Hall, 1985.

Rogo, D. Scott. *Life after death: The case for survival of bodily death.* Wellingborough, UK: Aquarian Press, 1986.

Rogo, D. Scott. *The return from silence: A study of near-death experiences.* New York: Harper and Row, 1990.

Rose, Seraphim. *The soul after death: Contemporary "after-death" experiences in the light of orthodox teaching on the afterlife.* Platina, CA: Saint Herman of Alaska Brotherhood, 1980.

Rosenfield, Israel. *The strange, familiar, and forgotten: An anatomy of consciousness.* New York: Knopf, 1992.

Rossman, Neil. *Consciousness: Separation and integration.* Albany, NY: State University of New York Press, 1991.

Rucker, R. *The fourth dimension: Toward a geometry of higher reality.* Boston: Houghton Mifflin, 1984.

Rudolph, E., and Stamatescu, I.-O. (Eds.). *Philosophy, mathematics and modern physics: A dialogue.* New York: Springer, 1994.

Ruelle, D. *Chance and chaos.* Princeton, NJ: Princeton University Press, 1991.

Russell, P. *The global brain.* Los Angeles: Tarcher, 1983.

Ryall, E. W. *Born twice: Total recall of a seventeenth-century life.* New York: Harper and Row, 1974.

Sabom, Michael B. *Recollections of death: A medical investigation.* New York: Harper and Row, 1982.

Schatzman, Morton. *The story of Ruth.* New York: Putnam, 1980.

Schroedinger, Erwin. *What is life? The physical aspect of the living cell, and mind and matter.* Cambridge, UK: Cambridge University Press, 1992.

Schwarz, Hans. *Beyond the gates of death.* Minneapolis, MN: Augsburg, 1981.

Scott, Alwyn. *Stairway to the mind: The controversial new science of consciousness.* New York: Copernicus, 1995.

Searle, John Rogers. *The rediscovery of the mind.* Cambridge, MA: MIT Press, 1992.

Selzer, Richard. *Raising the dead: A doctor's encounter with his own mortality.* New York: Viking Penguin, 1994.

Sheldrake, Rupert. *A new science of life: The hypothesis of formative causation.* Los Angeles: Tarcher, 1981.

Sheldrake, Rupert. *The presence of the past: Morphic resonance and the habits of nature.* London: Collins, 1988.

Sheldrake, Rupert. *The rebirth of nature: The greening of science and God.* London: Century, 1990.

Simonov, Pavel V. *The emotional brain: Physiology, neuroanatomy, psychology, and emotion* (trans. Marie J. Hall). New York: Plenum Press, 1986.

Smith, A. *The mind.* New York: Viking, 1984.

Smith, M., and Pazder, L. *Michelle remembers.* New York: Pocket Books, 1980.

Smythies, John Raymond. *The walls of Plato's cave: The science and philosophy of brain, consciousness and perception.* Aldershot, UK: Avebury, 1994.

Sorenson, M. R., and Willmore, D. R. *The journey beyond life.* Orem, UT: Family Affair Books, 1988.

Springer, Rebecca. *Within the gates.* Dallas, TX: *s.n.*, 1971.

Squire, Larry R. *Memory and brain.* New York: Oxford University Press, 1987.

Stack-O'Sullivan, Deborah Jean. *Personality correlates of near-death experiences.* Storrs, CT: University of Connecticut, 1981.

Stannard, David E. (Ed.). *Death in America.* Philadelphia: University of Pennsylvania Press, 1975.

Stapp, Henry P. *Mind, matter, and quantum mechanics.* Berlin: Springer, 1993.

Steiger, B., and Steiger, S. H. *Angels over their shoulders: Children's encounters with heavenly beings.* New York: Columbine, 1995.

Stevenson, Ian. *Twenty cases suggestive of reincarnation* (2nd ed.). Charlottesville, VA: University Press of Virginia, 1974.

Stevenson, Ian. *Xenoglossy: A review and report of a case.* Charlottesville, VA: University Press of Virginia, 1974.

Stevenson, Ian. *Cases of the reincarnation type* (3 vols.). Charlottesville, VA: University Press of Virginia, 1975–1977.

Stevenson, Ian. *Children who remember previous lives.* Charlottesville, VA: University Press of Virginia, 1987.

Strongman, K. T. *The psychology of emotion.* New York: Wiley, 1978.

Sutherland, Cherie. *A very different way: A sociological investigation of life after a near-death experience.* Unpublished doctoral dissertation, University of New South Wales, Kensington, Australia, 1991.

Sutherland, Cherie. *Transformed by the light: Life after near-death experiences.* Sydney: Bantam, 1992.

Sutherland, Cherie. *Within the light.* Sydney: Bantam, 1993.

Sutherland, Cherie. *Reborn in the light.* New York: Bantam, 1995.

Swihart, Phillip J. *The edge of death.* Downers Grove, IL: Inter-Varsity Press, 1978.

Talbot, M. *The holographic universe.* New York: HarperCollins, 1991.

Taliaferro, Charles. *Consciousness and the mind of God.* Cambridge, UK: Cambridge University Press, 1994.

Tanous, A. *Beyond coincidence.* New York: Doubleday, 1976.

Tart, C. T. *States of consciousness.* New York: E. P. Dutton, 1975.

Tart, C. T. (Ed.). *Altered states of consciousness* (rev. and updated ed.). San Francisco: Harper, 1990.

Taylor, Gordon. *The natural history of the mind.* New York: Penguin Books, 1986.

Teichman, Jenny. *The mind and the soul: An introduction to the philosophy of mind.* London: Routledge and Kegan Paul, 1981. (Originally published in 1974)

Teilhard de Chardin, P. *The phenomenon of man* (trans.) New York: Harper and Row, 1959.

Teilhard de Chardin, P. *The future of man* (trans.) New York: Harper and Row, 1964.

Teilhard de Chardin, P. *Let me explain* (trans.) London: Fontana, 1974.

Terr, Lenore. *Unchained memories: True stories of traumatic memories, lost and found*. New York: Basic Books, 1994.

Top, B., and Top, W. *Beyond death's door*. Salt Lake City, UT: Bookcraft, 1993.

Toynbee, Arnold. *Man's concern with death*. London: Weidenfeld and Nicolson, 1968.

Toynbee, Arnold (Ed.). *Life after death*. London: Weidenfeld and Nicolson, 1976.

Umilta, Carlo, and Moscovitch, Morris (Eds.). *Conscious and nonconscious information processing*. Cambridge, MA: MIT Press, 1994.

Urfer, Billy O. *Beyond tomorrow*. Heber Springs, AR: Urfer, 1981.

Valle, R. S., and Von Eckartsberg, R. (Eds.). *The metaphors of consciousness*. New York: Plenum Press, 1981.

Van Fraassen, Bastiaan C. *Quantum mechanics: An empiricist view*. Oxford, UK: Clarendon Press, 1991.

Van Wees, B. R. M., and Van Lummel, W. *Progress report on the research into near-death experiences*. Loosdrecht, The Netherlands: Stichting Merkawah, 1990.

Vernon, G. M. *The sociology of death*. New York: Ronald Press, 1970.

Villanueva, Enrique (Ed.). *Consciousness*. Atascadero, CA: Ridgeview, 1991.

Wade, Jenny. *Changes of mind: A holonomic theory of the evolution of consciousness*. New York: State University of New York Press, 1996.

Walker, Barbara Ann. *Assessing knowledge and attitudes of selected Illinois registered psychologists on near-death phenomena: Implications for health education*. Carbondale, IL: Southern Illinois University, 1987.

Wambach, Helen. *Life before life*. London: Bantam, 1979.

Wambach, Helen. *Reliving past lives*. London: Hutchinson, 1979.

Warner, Richard, and Szubka, Tadeusz (Eds.). *The mind–body problem: A guide to the current debate*. Cambridge, MA: Blackwell, 1994.

Weeler, Davide R. *Journey to the other side*. New York: Grosset and Dunlap, 1976.

Weiss, Brian L. *Many lives, many masters*. New York: Simon and Schuster, 1988.

Weiss, Jess. E. (Ed.). *The vestibule*. New York: s.n., 1974.

Weldon, John, and Levitt, Zola. *Is there life after death?* Irvine, CA: *s.n.*, 1977.

White, J. (Ed.). *The highest state of consciousness.* Garden City, NY: Anchor Doubleday, 1972.

White, J. (Ed.). *Frontiers of consciousness: The meeting ground between inner and outer reality.* New York: Julian, 1974.

White, J. *The meeting of science and spirit.* New York: Paragon, 1990.

Whitfield, Charles. *Healing the child within.* Deerfield Beach, FL: Health Communications, 1987.

Whitfield, Charles. *A gift to myself.* Deerfield Beach, FL: Health Communications, 1990.

Whitton, Joel L., and Fisher, Joe. *Life between life.* New York: Warner Books, 1986.

Wilber, Ken. *Eye to eye: The quest for the new paradigm.* Boston: Shambhala, 1990.

Wilber, Ken, Engler, Jack, and Brown, Daniel P. (Eds.). *Transformations of consciousness.* New York: Shambahla, 1986.

Wilkerson, Ralph. *Beyond and back: Those who died and lived to tell it.* Anaheim, CA: Melody Land, 1977.

Wilson, Colin. *Afterlife: An investigation of the evidence for life after death.* London: Grafton Books, 1988.

Wilson, I. *All in the mind: Reincarnation, hypnotic regression, stigmata, multiple personality, and other little understood powers of the mind.* Garden City, NY: Doubleday, 1982.

Wilson, I. *The after death experience.* London: Corgi Books, 1990.

Winson, J. *Brain and psyche: The biology of the unconscious.* Garden City, NY: Anchor/Doubleday, 1985.

Wisdom, John. *Problems of mind and matter.* Cambridge, UK: Cambridge University Press, 1970.

Wollheim, Richard. *The mind and its depths.* Cambridge, MA: Harvard University Press, 1994.

Wolman, B. B., and Ullman, M. (Eds.). *Handbooks of states of consciousness.* New York: Van Nostrand Reinhold, 1986.

Woolger, R. K. *Other lives, other selves: A Jungian psychotherapist discovers past lives.* New York: Doubleday, 1987.

Young, J. Z. *Philosophy and the brain.* New York: Oxford University Press, 1988.

Zaleski, Carol. *Otherworld journeys: A comparative study of medieval Christian and contemporary accounts of near-death experience.* Cambridge, MA: Harvard University Press, 1984.

Zaleski, Carol. *Otherworld journeys: Accounts of near-death experience in medieval and modern times.* New York: Oxford University Press, 1987.

Zimberg, N. E. (Ed.). *Alternate states of consciousness.* New York: Free Press, 1977.

Zohar, D. *Through the time barrier.* London: Heinemann, 1982.

Index

This index uses synonyms like "dimension, different," "reality, another scale of," "surreality," "universe, superluminal," "life, next," "domain, imaginal," and so on to respect the terminology employed by the interviewed persons.